STAN LEE

STAN LEE

THE MAN BEHIND MARVEL

YOUNG ADULT EDITION

BOB BATCHELOR

ROWMAN & LITTLEFIELD
Lanham • Boulder • New York • London

Published by Rowman & Littlefield
An imprint of The Rowman & Littlefield Publishing Group, Inc.
4501 Forbes Boulevard, Suite 200, Lanham, Maryland 20706
www.rowman.com

86-90 Paul Street, London EC2A 4NE

Distributed by NATIONAL BOOK NETWORK

British Library Cataloguing in Publication Information Available

Library of Congress Cataloging-in-Publication Data Available

ISBN 978-1-5381-6205-7 (pbk. : alk. paper) | ISBN 978-1-5381-6206-4 (ebook)

♾️™ The paper used in this publication meets the minimum requirements of American National Standard for Information Sciences—Permanence of Paper for Printed Library Materials, ANSI/NISO Z39.48-1992.

To Kassie and Sophia,
my wonderful daughters
who continue to inspire me every day!

CONTENTS

FOREWORD

Walking through downtown San Diego on a warm summer evening, I saw countless children dressed as goblins, aliens, wizards, and robots. Across the street were space-fighters, zombies, and vampires—legions of creatures. But the odd thing—holding their hands were their parents.

The fathers and mothers of these supernatural specimens were dressed just the same. There were flags, banners, and toys being handed out. Lines of teenagers were waiting in the hot sun to get a $200 ticket to enter. Buses were wrapped in an infinite array of color, text, and good ol' sci-fi wholesomeness. Yes . . . I was at Comic-Con. My own son was even dressed as a Transformer—Optimus Prime. I watched him become overwhelmed with the immersion. He stood there drowning in complete sensory overload. This was seriously the FIRST time I'd ever seen a celebration of *imagination* of this magnitude—where a parent could be a kid—*with their kid.*

When I was young, I cut my teeth playing with Legos. I built my sci-fi chops by filling my backyard with spaceships, secret spaceports, and flying astronauts. I envisioned a multidimensional environment. My space-faring soldiers explored every object. Over time, we started to imagine that they were heroes or had special powers. I remember that moment specifically, because Batman and Spider-Man cartoons were seeping into my head.

Later, in creating Blink-182, Angels & Airwaves, and the entertainment company To the Stars*, I realized that I could create a whole new multimedia world across music, books, video, and film—a kind of transmedia art project that would project my hopes, dreams, and aspirations for the world the way I saw it with superheroes as a kid. For example, my character Poet Anderson is an antihero (like Spider-Man!) who grapples with dreams and nightmares as a Dream Walker, a guardian of the Dreamscape charged with protecting sleeping innocents from the nightmares that threaten both worlds. Poet led to an award-winning short film, a chart-topping album, acclaimed comic book series, a graphic novel, and a YA science fiction novel. Who says you can't bring dreams to life?

When I look back now, I realize that Stan Lee and his contemporaries had started playing with ideas and contracts that would honestly lead me to wonder what started this flow of consciousness in the first place. I thought about the clones from outer space in *Star Wars* with a rebel band of heroes that have special Jedi powers. Or the clones that come from the ground in *Lord of the Rings*, while advanced elves and wizards with extraordinary (natural) powers fight them off. And, again, the Avengers—who battle insects from another dimension that, like the other replicas, are missing that empathy component that seems exclusive to our human souls.

With the current UFO phenomenon, there is a ton of evidence suggesting that ETs are interdimensional, don't share our consciousness, and may have insectile or cloning origins. So does consciousness beam a signal to humanity directly into our minds that we need to hear, like a radio receiver? Do people like Stan Lee bring it out in a way that gets us to think and ponder? This is complicated stuff! Maybe our great sci-fi writers and creators are having a grand time preparing us for what's next. Perhaps they have no clue of the enormity and weight behind their (seemingly common) ideas.

After I went to Comic-Con and experienced the Marvel, *Star Wars*, and Disney overload, I wanted to follow in their footsteps—constructing amazing new narratives that would change the world. At To the Stars*, we're utilizing our deep connections to bring to light an amazing story (and possibly) . . . *the story of the millennia*. I often wondered the best way to tell an important story like this, especially one that most people might not be ready for. I wanted to give people a newfound appreciation of the profound yet unresolved mysteries involving science and the universe through entertainment directly informed by science.

Each time I thought about it, I remembered what Stan did to prepare the way for all of us. He made the supernatural world blend seamlessly into our physical world. Stan's vision is similar to what I expect will be the next great scientific leap for humanity—a collision of physics and metaphysics. The result will be a unified theory of everything, only possible with the discovery of *consciousness*. And Stan gave us a glimpse of *what could be*. For me, someone who sits in a chair next to former high-ranking CIA, DOD, and military officials, Stan may be right about a few things . . . although possibly minus the supersuits.

No one could have imagined how important these comic stories would be to so many people or the gravitational impact that those first superhero films would have when they hit our culture. Just like the Spider-Man animated TV series that was so important to me, the Marvel Universe has become a game changer. Countless people across all age groups now have a north star. Stan paved a path for artists like me to be creative *and* make a living from our creative energy. What a wonderful idea: legions of young people creating and imagining a better world, but one that might actually be a bit more on the nose than anyone would suspect . . . but minus the supersuits. Or not?

—Tom DeLonge, Blink-182 and To the Stars*

CHAPTER 1

A HERO IS BORN!

"A professional writer!"

The eighteen-year-old looked at the title again—"Captain America Foils the Traitor's Revenge." He quickly leafed through the rest of the comic book and then flipped back to the cover. It seemed like yesterday he had been sitting in his high school English class dreaming of this day. Now he was a real writer! It had all happened so fast.

He inspected the cover. How thrilling to turn it over in his fingers and feel the pages for the first time. The 3-D "Captain America" title seemed to spring out from the page, enclosed in a shockingly bright yellow border. The teen took a closer look, inspecting the hit series that had taken the nation by storm.

The action leapt from the page! In it, Captain America knocked out a bad guy clad in a militaristic green uniform with a fierce swing of his red, white, and blue shield, simultaneously deflecting a bullet meant to murder him. In the opposite corner of the page, the evil supervillain Red Skull tied the superhero's teen sidekick, Bucky, to a bomb, while heartthrob Betty Ross was encased in a glass capsule about to be shot into the war zone. Red Skull had a black Nazi swastika stamped on his chest, in direct opposition to Cap's white star, representing hope, humanity, and democracy. Though outnumbered and in peril, the hero stood ready, his right fist clenched for battle.

CAPTAIN AMERICA
FOILS the
TRAITOR'S
REVENGE
By
Stan Lee

"I'm sorry, Haines, but there is no place in this army camp for the likes of you. You have lied, cheated, spied, and stolen. Your conduct is no longer tolerable and I'm giving you a dishonorable discharge. Now get out!"

Private Steve Rogers, doing sentry duty nearby, was watching the scene interestedly. He had never seen Colonel Stevens so angry; and Lou Haines, too, was threateningly mad. The muscular giant shook his enormous fist at the Colonel.

"O.K. Colonel," snarled Lou, "I'll get out. But let me warn you now, you ain't seen the last of me! I'll get even somehow. Mark my words, you'll pay for this!" Haines walked toward the camp gates, muttering insults under his breath.

Suddenly Haines felt a strong hand grasp his arm. He looked around into the flashing eyes of Steve Rogers! "I wouldn't act like that if I were you," murmured Steve, softly, "you were insulting a man in the uniform of the United States Army! Here are the camp gates; now beat it!"

Haines left, but there was a look of hate in his eyes which Steve could not help but notice!

* * * * *

Later that evening, Steve Rogers was sitting in his tent playing checkers with his young side-kick, Bucky, the camp mascot. Bucky looked disappointed.

"Gosh, Steve," wailed Bucky, "don't you EVER lose a game? I've forgotten what it feels like to win."

Steve smiled cheerfully. "I'll tell you what, kid: suppose you borrow a book on 'how to play checkers' and read it. That'll give me a chance to get some shut-eye. You don't know how tired it makes me to beat you all the time!"

Steve ducked just in time to dodge the pillow that Bucky threw at him. "Why, you little squirt," he grinned, "I ought to put you over my knee!"

"Oh yeah, you big palooka? You and what other army?" Bucky picked up another pillow and was holding it ready.

Suddenly Steve's smile left his face and he put his fingers

The expectations for *Captain America #3* were enormous. The first two issues had sold millions of copies, turning the artistic team of Joe Simon and Jack Kirby into bona fide comic book superstars. As a result, they were always busy—planning, drawing, writing, and revising the art and scripts, while at the same time chomping away on cigars that filled their cramped office with thick, acrid smoke. Page after page of drawings, scripts, and doodles littered every square inch of the space. Joe and Jack pinned ideas for new superheroes to the walls, along with character sketches and action scenes. Yet they constantly fought to keep up with the production schedule. The demand never stopped.

Tall and rail thin, Simon shuffled through illustrations dropped off by a freelancer. An arm's reach away, Kirby hunched over his drawing board, his fingers a blur as the pencil whizzed across the page. They ignored the teen as he mooned over his first publication. The typewriter on the desk gleamed.

"I had become a published author," young Stanley Lieber exclaimed. "I was a pro."[1]

The teen thought back on receiving that first assignment. Joe needed copy, and he needed it right away. The first two issues had put the small publisher on the map. However, the success led to several snags, like all the other comic book publishers attempting to imitate the red, white, and blue hero. Creatively, Joe and Jack had to work even harder to stay ahead of the pack. Simon hired a bunch of freelancers just to meet production timetables.

In the midst of that initial hiring burst, Joe also gave a job to Lieber, the skinny teenager who seemed so eager and enthusiastic. The kid was essentially a low-level assistant. He did odd jobs around the office—including picking up lunch orders and even sweeping up the place at the end of the day. Stanley did all the odd jobs that Joe and Jack didn't have time to worry about. They had important work—Captain America was the country's star superhero and an inspiration as the war waged on in Europe.

The public worried about whether President Roosevelt would keep the US out of the melee. People found encouragement in the red, white, and blue superhero. Joe and Jack even had him battling the Nazis and punching out Hitler on the cover of the first issue.

"We had Stan erasing the pencils off the inked artwork, and going out for coffee....
We let Stan hang around with us when we went bowling or played billiards. I thought
he was a cute kid." —Joe Simon, Timely Comics editor and cocreator of Captain
America (Joe Simon, *My Life in Comics*)

Yet selling comic books wasn't just about colorful antics and supervillains. Joe had real-world concerns in running the business side of Timely Comics, like ensuring that the publisher qualified for the less expensive second-class shipping charges. This meant that each comic book series had to have a certain number of text-based prose stories included with all the outrageous artwork and illustrations. Joe decided to make good use of this requirement by tossing several of these odd copy-filler stories to his young apprentice as a kind of test run to see if the kid had any actual talent.

Stanley definitely had chutzpah, that's for sure. After his first week on the job, the kid informed Simon that he felt he deserved a raise since he had already learned everything about comic books in his short time there. At first, Joe kept Stanley busy with menial tasks. "I'd fill the ink wells. I'd run down and get them sandwiches at the drug store, and I'd proofread the pages," the youngster recalled. "Sometimes in proofreading I'd say, 'You know, this sentence doesn't sound right. It ought to be written like this.' 'Well, go ahead and change it!' They didn't care!"[2]

Then Stanley took it on himself to become the office entertainment, playing a small flute-like instrument called an ocarina. The teen yearned to be the center of attention. The ensuing cacophony nearly got the boy brained by Kirby, who seemed to get increasingly irritated with every missed note that emanated from the instrument. Simon laughed as the two bickered, and Jack's threats grew progressively more colorful. Kirby, the quintessential artist, had a manic—almost obsessive—need to draw and draw fast. He didn't appreciate the kid distracting him.

But office hijinks aside, Joe needed copy. Stanley had been asking to write ever since he started at Timely (more like begging and pleading). Although Simon and Kirby seemed like grizzled industry veterans, the entire comic book industry was young in the early decades of the twentieth century: Joe was just twenty-seven years old, and Jack was twenty-three. Giving the kid a shot was based on necessity and great timing. If he could nail the two-pager, maybe they could use him for more important work. The initial two-page short story would serve as Stanley's on-the-job audition.

Getting the opportunity to fulfill his dream in becoming a published writer, young Stanley sat down at the typewriter and thought about Captain America's many heroic traits. What had made the character so popular? Certainly, patriotic fervor was at a high point across the nation. Yet there was a great deal of outright fear about the future. Many people were scared of the power a superhero like Captain America symbolized. Millions of people were against America's entry into the war, so they viewed feeding the masses with pro-US propaganda as dangerous. Others loved the comic book's stance against Germany. Hitler was Captain America's enemy, not only on the first issue cover but in the second issue too. Kirby and Simon drew the German leader and his henchman Herman Goering attacking the heroes and then being knocked unconscious when hit with Bucky's vicious kick. Sticking closely to these themes, Stanley used the idea of Cap and Bucky's zealous defense of liberty and justice as the primary motif of his short story.

"Captain America Foils the Traitor's Revenge" appeared in *Captain America Comics #3* (May 1941). Comic books were dated about three months later than when they appeared on the newsstands, so the teen probably wrote the story sometime at the end of 1940 or in the first couple of months of 1941.

Opening the copy to his story, he glanced at the name below the story title and smiled. "By Stan Lee," he read to himself. "Yup, used a pen name," he thought, one that had been on his mind since high school. "I simply cut my first name in half and slyly changed the *y* to a second *e*," he said. A simple case of pulling "Stanley" apart and making it "Stan Lee."[3] At the time, he believed he was saving his real name for the Great American Novel he someday hoped to write.

Simon was amused when the teenager presented himself as "Stan Lee" on the copy, but he knew the kid had talent to go along with his natural enthusiasm. It was a small assignment but important in the young man's development. Later, despite his pride, Stanley acknowledged that the two-page piece was just filler, admitting: "Nobody ever took the time to read them, but I didn't care. I had become a published author. I was a pro!"[4]

Every origin story has some attention-grabbing beginning. Under Simon's tutelage, young Lieber used that first short story to gain a new pen name and launch his career as a writer. He seemed a long way from fetching sandwiches and pushing a broom. "It gave me a feeling of grandeur," Lee recalled.[5]

Even though it was a text-based story, an action-filled drawing of Captain America knocking a man silly accompanied Lee's piece. As it turned out, not only was it Stan's first publication, it was also his initial collaboration with Jack Kirby, who drew the ferocious right uppercut and explosive connection that sent the bad guy reeling.

In Stan's short story, the villain was "traitor" Lou Haines. Although this was two decades before the world would become familiar with Lee's writing voice, the evildoer showed signs of that developing style. Haines snarled at

Stan writing his first story: "Captain America Foils the Traitor's Revenge."
Illustration by Jason Piperberg.

base commander Colonel Stevens: "But let me warn you now, you ain't seen the last of me! I'll get even somehow. Mark my words, you'll pay for this!" Later, in hand-to-hand combat, Captain America landed a crippling blow, just when the reader thought the hero was doomed. "No human being could have stood that blow," Lee wrote. "Haines instantly relaxed his grip and sank to the floor—unconscious!" The next day when the officer asked Steve Rogers (Captain America's secret identity) if he heard anything the night before, Rogers claimed he slept through the hullabaloo. Stevens, Rogers, and sidekick Bucky all shared a laugh at the thought.

> "The American Avenger saw Lou Haines about to plunge his knife into the sleeping Colonel's heart! . . . With the speed of thought, he sent his shield spinning through the air to the other end of the tent where it smacked the knife out of Haines' hand!"
> —Stan Lee, "Captain America Foils the Traitor's Revenge"

While Stan's "Traitor" short story did not exude the confidence fans would later associate with his writing (or the knowing wink at the reader), the piece exhibited his blossoming understanding of audience, pace, and style. Simon gave the teenager more assignments and even let him introduce characters that he had created.

Captain America #5 (August 1941) contained Stan's first paneled story: "Headline Hunter, Foreign Correspondent." Jerry Hunter, the titular character, was a newspaper reporter serving in war-torn London. Not actually a superhero, Hunter did have super strength and cunning. He even had a kind of superhero costume, a snazzy blue suit and red tie, obviously homage to Captain America.

In the story, Hunter foiled a Nazi plan to steal Navy cargo route maps and later blew up a German munitions plant. "Oh, gosh, it wasn't anything! And besides, boy! Look at the swell scoop I got," Hunter told the American ambassador as the story ended. The teen language and "golly-gee" tone flashed Stan's budding comic book style. In the way Hunter spoke and acted, the character might have been an early incarnation of Peter Parker. Lee's ear for dialogue was already taking shape and would be further honed in a series of writing credits.

Timely continued to grow under Simon's watch, particularly as the company introduced new characters. Stan moved from office boy to writer and editor based on Timely's limited resources. The small crew necessitated that Lee, even though new to publishing, produce content *and* new characters.

Stan's first original superhero—Jack Frost—appeared in *U.S.A. Comics #1* (August 1941). He filled the story with evocative dialogue and a sense of motion. Giving the new hero an origin story, Stan wrote that "the king of the cold" found a dying man in his "eternal deathly quiet" kingdom and vowed to bring the murderer to justice. Jack Frost exclaimed: "Dead! I have heard that crime flourishes throughout the world, but it has now reached my land. . . . I will avenge this deed and prevent more like it!"

Jack Frost (like many of Stan's later superheroes) was actually a kind of antihero. When he ventured to New York City, he was initially misunderstood by the police chief and mocked by the chief of detectives. Eventually, though, Frost rescued the damsel in distress and wiped out a gang of "puny evil-doers." However, when the police attempted to arrest him, the story ended with Frost exclaiming: "After this sort of reception I've changed my mind—if I can't work with you, I'll work against you—the next time we meet beware!"

The idea that a comic book superhero could not be perfect would several decades later make Stan and Marvel famous across the globe. Even in his earliest writing, though, one could see that Lee's ideas about heroism and its responsibilities were different than other writers. His heroes and villains were not wholly good or totally evil. Shockingly, this idea appeared in Stan's writing some two decades before that code would change comic books forever.

Given Captain America's popularity, it was no surprise that Lee used a similar origin story for a successful character he cocreated (with artist Jack Binder) called Destroyer. Appearing on the cover of *Mystic Comics #6* (October 1941), the superhero was reporter Kevin Marlow, accused of being a spy in Nazi Germany and thrown in a concentration camp (before that phrase was associated with the Holocaust). The tie to Captain America occurred when Marlow was given a superserum that gave him otherworldly strength and turned him into Destroyer (his emblem is a skull). Like Joe and Jack's Captain America, the superhero battled Nazis, wreaking havoc on Hitler's inhuman forces.

The Destroyer never became a household name like Captain America, but sales increased as the character was portrayed battling across ravaged Europe against Nazi forces that were diabolical, gruesome, and drawn to appear animalistic. To mask his identity, Destroyer donned a costume of blood-red-striped pants and long crimson gloves, making him appear as inhuman as the villains.

The US entry into World War II would dominate headlines and change the course of human history. On December 28, 1941, just three weeks after the Japanese attacked Pearl Harbor, Stan Lee turned nineteen years old.

For the teenager, the year had been one of adventure, hard work, and new beginnings. He had found his calling in publishing, authoring a series of heroic stories that shaped his thinking about superheroes and comic books. With Joe and Jack as mentors, the teen began developing a cadence and style that was a rough version of the bravado, high-spirited language, and witty wordplay that marked his subsequent work.

In less than a year, Stanley Lieber had created a new identity. Even someone with Stan Lee's imagination could not have conceived such a spectacular rise or what lay ahead. And it all started on a blustery winter night in the early years of the Jazz Age. This is where Stan's origin story begins . . .

CHAPTER 2

ORIGIN STORY

Window shoppers cautiously ventured out onto Times Square on Thursday, December 28, 1922, flipping up their collars against the icy wind. A sudden gust might knock a woman off the sidewalk or send a man scurrying to retrieve his errant hat. The storm dumped rain and snow across the East Coast.

In a tiny Manhattan apartment on Ninety-Eighth Street and West End Avenue, Jack and Celia Lieber barely noticed the dreary weather. They were about to welcome their first child, naming the tyke Stanley Martin.

The newborn entered the world at a chaotic time. The nation was still recovering from World War I. The American economy had slipped and sputtered, but manufacturing picked up in 1922 as consumer goods companies produced everything from sleek automobiles to new clothing and electric kitchen gadgets.

Newfound wealth fueled the "Roaring Twenties," an era filled with jazz, dance crazes, illegal alcohol, and glamour. Yet, for people on the lower end of the economic spectrum, it was a more difficult journey. The 1929 Wall Street crash swept the Lieber family to near destitution. Despite their woes, Celia and Jack raised Stanley to believe in a bright future. He emerged an optimist, bedeviling the clouds filling the sky on his birthday and the dark years of the Great Depression.

This is how superheroes are born.

Stanley's parents were among the millions of immigrants to enter America in the early twentieth century. Born in Romania in 1886, Hyman Lieber docked in the New York City Harbor in 1905. Hyman (who later went by Jacob or the Americanized "Jack") was just nineteen years old. He traveled with fourteen-year-old Abraham (a relative and possibly his brother). The teens joined the wave of Jewish immigrants fleeing Eastern Europe. After decades of anti-Jewish pogroms (anti-Semitic terror campaigns) across Europe and Russia that left countless thousands of Jews murdered, immigration to the United States skyrocketed from 5,000 in 1880 to 258,000 in 1907. In total, some 2.7 million from all over Europe migrated to America between 1875 and 1924.

Jacob left behind life in gritty Romania, a country then sandwiched between Austria-Hungary, Serbia, Bulgaria, and Russia, under the rule of monarch Carol I (1881–1914). The tickets cost the boys about 179 rubles each (roughly $90)—an enormous sum. They needed 50 rubles to show the Ellis Island immigration staff that they had enough on which to subsist.[1]

Carol I forbade Jewish citizens from studying law or medicine and outlawed rabbinical seminaries. Romania considered Jewish people "aliens" or "foreigners," leading to discrimination. One writer explained: "Romanians used veiled anti-Jewish legislation while avoiding outward use of barbarous acts and brutality that would draw the attention and disapproval of the civilized world."[2] The decree led to countless anti-Jewish riots and increased violence.

In America, Romanian immigrants found jobs as laborers. However, factory life proved dangerous, resulting in extensive injuries and deaths among all immigrant workers. Despite these struggles, America still offered a chance at a better life, including religious freedom and safety from violence.

Teenaged Jacob scraped out a meager existence. He lived with other young men in boardinghouses or rented rooms from Romanian families. Jewish immigrants faced anti-Semitism in America, so assembling with fellow countrymen provided some protection. Relatively few could speak or read English, another reason for kinship as they entered the English-speaking culture. Novelist Maurice Samuel recalled gatherings at a Romanian Jewish restaurant on the Lower East Side "to eat karnatzlech, beigalech, mammaligge, and kachkeval, to drink . . . and to play six-six and tablanette," all while speaking in Yiddish. The stories were filled with nostalgia but also tinged with regret because of the violent pogroms.[3]

Jacob and Abraham entered the clothing industry when the garment district clamored for workers, and they lived with fellow immigrants. In 1910, they boarded in the home of Gershen Moshkowitz, a fifty-two-year-old Russian, and his Romanian wife, Meintz, along with their two children, Rosie and Joseph, on Avenue A in Manhattan. Census takers reported that they attended school and could read and write English, but they almost certainly spoke Romanian Yiddish in the neighborhood.

Ten years later, thirty-four-year-old Jacob still lived as a boarder. However, just two years later, he was married to Celia Solomon. Stanley arrived just after Christmas in 1922.

The Solomon family had a more typical immigrant experience, arriving in 1901. Nine years later, the family lived in an apartment building on Fourth Street in a Romanian neighborhood. Celia's parents (Sanfir and Sophia) had eight children. Her younger brother Robbie was the first born in America (1903).

In 1910, Celia worked as a salesperson in a five-and-dime store. She and older brother Louis did not attend school, unlike her four younger siblings (Frieda, Isidor, Minnie, and Robbie). In many immigrant families, older children provided financial support, enabling younger siblings to go to school. The children were fluent in English. Later, they moved to West 152nd Street.

A bone-chilling wind whipped down Twenty-Ninth Street in Manhattan as two thousand men braced against the frigid air. Breadlines snaked up Fifth Avenue. When food ran out, a quarter of them would be turned away hungry. The sight of destitute men at wit's end unnerved New Yorkers. They were humiliated and reluctant to accept charity, even to survive. Most had no choice.

The economic collapse left the nation despondent. Money had been at the core of American culture in the 1920s. Investment bankers were society's new celebrities—like the tycoons in F. Scott Fitzgerald's *The Great Gatsby*. The overheated economy put the kindling in place; greed provided the spark.

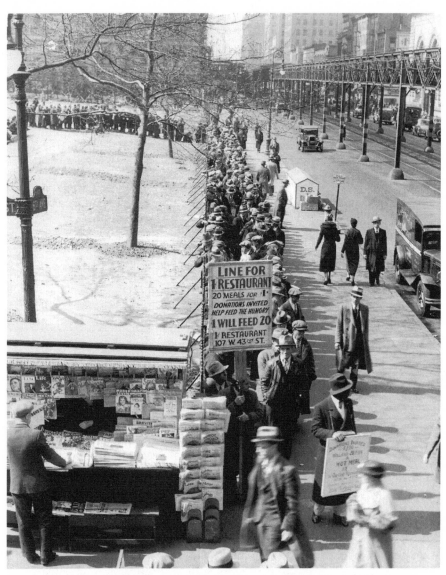

Breadlines in New York City during the Great Depression. Courtesy of National Archives, Franklin D. Roosevelt Library Public Domain Photographs, 1882–1962.

Soup lines created a riveting picture of national despair, defeat, and financial collapse.

Jacob, Celia, and Stanley moved from West Ninety-Eighth and West End Avenue to Washington Heights around the time Stanley's younger brother, Larry, was born (October 26, 1931). The move signaled a downsizing in the family's fortunes. Like so many others, the Great Depression cut the heart out of the Lieber family, halting their path toward the American Dream. "My earliest recollections were of my parents talking about what they would do if they didn't have the rent money," Stanley remembered. "Luckily we were never evicted."[4] The lack of work forced many families into perpetual crisis.

Garment district employment simply vanished. According to Stanley's autobiography *Excelsior!*, his father also attempted to run a diner but failed, draining his life's savings. Chronic unemployment wrecked Jacob and Celia's marriage. Stanley, not yet seven, witnessed his parents "arguing, quarreling incessantly." The arguments were always the same: "over money, or the lack of it."[5] Stanley watched his father venture out after scouring the job ads, but each evening he returned downcast and desperate. According to his son, the older man sat at the kitchen table staring out listlessly as the family teetered near ruin. Sometimes, Jacob would try to goad his wife into going for a walk in the park. She "hated it," Lee recalled in *Excelsior!*. "They never got along."

> "He just wasn't working. He couldn't find a job. He would be sitting home reading the want ads. I felt so sorry for him." —Stan Lee on his father's unemployment (Danny Fingeroth, *A Marvelous Life: The Amazing Story of Stan Lee*)

Celia turned to her sisters for money, but they were forced to move into a smaller apartment in the Bronx. Stanley slept on the couch in the living room, situated—like in so many low-rent apartments—in the back of the building. Stan remembered: "All we could see was the brick wall of the building across the alley. I could never look and see if the other kids were out in the street playing stickball or doing anything that I might join in."[6] The cramped confines and Larry's birth (another mouth to feed) sadly amplified their despair. The bickering only paused on Sunday nights when the family gathered around the radio. Stanley loved ventriloquist Edgar Bergen and his wooden sidekick, Charlie McCarthy, on NBC's *The Chase and Sanborn Hour*.

Too young to fully understand his family's plight, Stanley bounced along, relying on his mother's love to overcome his father's anxiety. Aunt Jean recalled Jack as "exacting with his boys," demanding adherence to daily routines: "brush your teeth a certain way, wash your tongue, and so on."[7] Celia took a different route, filling Stanley with her hopes and dreams. "She often asked me to read aloud to her," he remembered. "I enjoyed doing that, imagining I was on some Broadway stage reading for a vast, entranced audience." She instilled a sense of greatness in her son despite their bleak conditions. Reading helped Stanley cope: "It was my escape from the dreariness and sadness of my home life."[8] More importantly, reading empowered a sense of adventure and creativity. "Used to scribble my own comics, as far back as I can remember," Lee said. "Used to draw horizon line and add stick-figure people, telling myself little stories all the while."[9]

Celia pushed him to excel at school. As a result, he claimed: "I was always something of an outsider. My mother wanted me to finish school as soon as possible so I could get a job and help support the family."[10] Eager to please her, Stanley skipped grades, despite the teasing from older students. He eventually developed a precocious intellect, but his youth and brightness did not help him socially.

The youngster did find a mentor in a young Jewish teacher—Leon B. Ginsberg, who began class with a thrilling baseball story featuring imaginary slugger Swat Mulligan. The stories were "funny and exciting," Lee remembered. He drew life lessons from Ginsberg's daily tale: "Whenever I want to communicate to others, I always try to do it in a lighter-hearted way and make it as entertaining as possible."[11]

Stanley's other passion was movies. He imagined a larger-than-life future personified by film icon Errol Flynn, who burst onto the screen in *Captain Blood* (1935). With good looks, charisma, and athletic grace, Flynn became a star. His movies had fight scenes and swordplay, like his first color film, *The Adventures of Robin Hood* (1938). "There on the screen were worlds that dazzled my mind, worlds of magic and wonder, worlds which I longed to inhabit, if only in imagination," Lee later recalled.[12]

Stanley went to the movies at Loew's 175th Street Theatre, one of New York's "Wonder Theatres," featuring an enormous seven-story-high Robert Morton Wonder organ. He also loved Marx Brothers and Laurel and Hardy comedies. Within a three-block radius of 181st Street, the youngster could choose from five movie theaters. He eagerly anticipated *Tarzan* and his other favorite, *The Jungle Mystery*, the adventures of a man-ape. After the films, he met with his cousin Morty Feldman on Seventy-Second Street, where the boys ate pancakes and talked about the movies.[13]

Stanley grew into a self-described "voracious reader." In later years, he often cited Shakespeare as his most important influence, shaping his ideas about storytelling, particularly the "rhythm of words," explaining, "I've always been in love with the way words sound."[14] Stanley took a book or magazine with him everywhere—even the breakfast table—using a little wooden contraption his mother found that held the pages open.

Although he loved reading, the boy had no illusions about comic books. In the 1920s, black-and-white strips were popular, particularly the slapstick humor of Bud Fisher's *Mutt & Jeff*. "Creating comic books was never part of my childhood dream," Stanley explained.[15] He did, however, read *Famous Funnies*, widely considered the first modern American comic book, distributed at Woolworth department stores. He specifically remembered enjoying *Hairbreadth Harry*, a strip created by C. W. Kahles, featuring the hero in various melodramatic adventures to keep his rival, Rudolph Ruddigore Rassendale, from the heroine, Belinda Blinks.[16]

Jack's unemployment meant Stanley had to work; any extra income would help the family stave off poverty. In his midteen years, the boy (along with millions of other teens) either worked or continuously searched for jobs. The mix of Celia's fawning support and grade jumping eventually paid off though. The enterprising teen—smart and already a budding storyteller and wordsmith—found odd jobs: usher at a movie theater, factory office boy, and even writing obituaries of celebrities filed away for when they died.

Lieber attended DeWitt Clinton High School, a twenty-one-acre campus in the Bronx, described as the "castle on the parkway." One of the world's largest high schools, Clinton enrolled ten thousand to twelve thousand students (male only but of diverse ethnicities, heavily tilted toward immigrants and their children). The teen's high school years were filled with clubs and opportunities to exhibit his budding leadership and showmanship traits. The pensive boy who holed up with a book grew into a handsome, tall young man (though rail thin). He joined the public-speaking club and the law society, contemplating a future as a famous courtroom attorney.

Nicknamed "Gabby" because of his charming personality and incessant chitchat, Lieber envisaged a dazzling future. His classmates had similar opinions. High school friend Bob Wendlinger remembered thinking Stanley was headed to greatness. "You always knew that he was going to be successful," Wendlinger said. "It was a given."[17]

Lieber experimented with a variety of personas, first gravitating toward publicity with a job on the business staff of the Clinton literary magazine, the *Magpie*. Despite his budding writing skills, he confined himself to "publicity director." Part of the Lieber youthful lore is that before a meeting in the tower, the high-ceilinged part of the school where the *Magpie* staff worked, he found a ladder left there by a worker. Showing off, he scurried up, then wrote, "Stan Lee is God," on the ceiling. Perhaps unwilling to risk getting in trouble with the maintenance crew or administrators for defacing the building using his real name—or just playing around with a stage name—this was the first recorded use of the moniker that would later travel the globe.[18]

"Stan Lee is God." —Lee's autobiography, *Excelsior!*

While Lieber imagined a number of careers—including acting—advertising seemed his true calling. Several jobs centered on words or selling, including writing publicity materials for a Jewish hospital in Denver, the obituary job, and hawking newspaper subscriptions. In high school, he also adopted a magician's persona—the great "Thimbilini"—performing sleight-of-hand tricks with small thimbles that drew crowds of curious classmates. Stan recognized his dramatic flair and public-speaking talents.

As a fifteen-year-old, Lieber entered an essay competition sponsored by the *New York Herald Tribune* called "The Biggest News of the Week Contest." Ogden Reid and his wife, Helen, owned the paper. Although politically conservative, it focused on the Big Apple's gritty realism. Lieber claimed to have won the prize three straight weeks, allegedly goading an editor to ask him to let someone else win. According to Stanley, the newspaperman suggested he look into becoming a writer, which, the boy claimed, "probably changed my life."[19]

Like many tall tales from Lee's life, the story is apocryphal. Young Lieber actually won a seventh-place prize of $2.50 and two honorable mentions—hardly the rags-to-riches path to future greatness. "After all," comic book historians Jordan Rapheal and Tom Spurgeon said, "Lee is a storyteller, and his account of the *Herald Tribune* essay contest certainly made for a good story, even if it's untrue."[20] While the story veers from truth, the prize money made an impression on a poor Jewish kid. A year later, in 1939, he worked a total of twelve weeks, pulling in $150 via part-time jobs and whatever work he could muster.

Leaving Clinton's hallowed halls in 1939, Stanley entered a skittish job market. His high school years coincided with some of the worst days of the Depression. College was out. He needed to help support his family.

President Franklin D. Roosevelt attempted to alleviate the turmoil, but gross national product actually fell 4.5 percent in 1938 and unemployment climbed to 19 percent. Ironically, Hitler's invasion of Poland several months after Stan's graduation led to increased war planning and a boost to the economy. Prior to Pearl Harbor, the United States shipped much-needed armaments to desperate Allied nations while also prepping for its seemingly inevitable entry into the conflict. The economic rebound, however, did not happen soon enough to aid Lieber.

Stanley's perspective was forever shaped by his father's unemployment. "The most important thing for a man is to have work to do," he explained. "To be busy, to be needed."[21] The idea molded him. "Even when I made a good living, my dad didn't think of me as a success," Stanley remembered. "He was pretty wrapped up in himself. . . . Some of that rubbed off on me. I was always looking at people who were doing better than I was and wishing I could do what they were doing." Sadly, he explained: "Part of me always felt I hadn't quite made it yet."[22]

Fear caused him to honor work and a paycheck. Lee shared this feeling with comic book contemporaries and first-generation Jewish immigrants (like future cocreator Jack Kirby). They knew each other's neighborhoods and had parallel experiences navigating Depression-era New York. They had seen the breadlines! One writer described these consequences—producing a young man "agonizingly sensitive, desperate for approval and easily influenced by others." Highly intelligent, Stanley yearned for a marvelous life that would fulfill his mother's prediction about future fame and fortune.[23]

CHAPTER 3

MR. TIMELY COMICS

Joe Simon, head writer and editorial director at Timely Comics, rose from his seat, towering over a messy desktop covered with drawings and letters. He reached out his hand to welcome his new assistant.

Stanley Lieber vigorously pumped the older man's hand. A steady salary—eight dollars a week!

Just out of high school, the money meant he could help his parents. More importantly, the position gave him financial security and a shot at writing. Stanley dreamed of writing the Great American Novel.

But, with no training, the youngster had to start at the bottom, serving as office boy for Simon and the one other full-time employee—artist and writer Jack Kirby. Little more than an assistant, some days he refilled Kirby and Simon's inkwells or picked up their lunch. No matter the task—sweeping floors or erasing stray pencil marks from comic book pages—Lieber worked with enthusiasm. He watched and learned from two of the industry's budding stars.

More importantly, Stanley had a job! His father's fate would not befall him. He set off on a career.

Similar to other episodes in Stanley's early life, this one is shrouded in uncertainty. How the teen bounded from Clinton High School to Simon and Kirby's side involves a bit of mystery and a touch of mythmaking.

There are several versions of his Timely Comics origin story. One begins with Celia telling Stanley about a job opening at a publishing company where her brother Robbie worked. Without delay, the young high school grad shows up at the McGraw-Hill Building on West Forty-Second Street but knows little about comic books. However, with Robbie's prodding, Simon explains the business and how comic books are made, ultimately offering the teen a job. Basically, he and Kirby are so overworked, particularly with their new hit *Captain America*, that they just need someone (anyone, really) to provide extra hands.

Robbie Solomon is also at the center of another account but as a conduit between Simon and owner Martin Goodman. In addition to being Celia Lieber's brother, Robbie married the publisher's sister Sylvia. Goodman surrounded himself with family, despite the imperious role he played, lording over his employees. "His entire publishing empire was a family business," explain Blake Bell and Michael J. Vassallo.[1] Robbie's stamp of approval (and the familial tie) made the boy's hire fait accompli. Simon basically had to take Lieber on.

While the family connection tale plays into Goodman's nepotism, Lee offered a third viewpoint: "I was fresh out of high school. I wanted to get into the publishing business, if I could." Coincidentally, he explained, "There was an ad in the paper that said, 'Assistant Wanted in a Publishing House.'"[2] This version places his start date in 1940, which is usually listed as the year of his hiring, or 1939, as he later implied.

Lieber recognized publishing as a viable option. He knew that he could write but had no way of gauging his creative talents. Although Goodman was related by marriage, he did not have much interaction with his younger relative, so it wasn't as if Goodman purposely brought Lieber into the firm. No one will ever really know how much of a wink and nod Solomon gave Simon or if Goodman even knew about the hiring, though the kid remembered the publisher being surprised the first time he saw him in the building.

The teen's early tenure at Timely Comics served as a kind of extended apprenticeship at comic book university—the break he needed during the Depression. Lieber was earnest in learning from Simon and Kirby as they scrambled to create content. Since they were known for working fast, the teen witnessed firsthand how two of the industry's greatest talents operated. The lessons he learned set the foundation for his own career as a writer and editor, as well as a manager of talented individuals.

Martin Goodman had formed a publishing company in 1933 to sell taw-
dry men's magazines, not great art or literature. Dollar signs drove him. He
wanted to make a pile of money in the least taxing manner possible. Goodman's single demand was that cover art be provocative (frequently featuring
seminude women). Some of the magazines Goodman and his competitors
sold were salacious—basically semipornographic and sold only behind
closed doors. The backdoor mentality opened the industry to gangsters
and the mafia underworld. They saw pulp magazines as easy money and a
method for laundering funds.

From his expansive office perch in the McGraw-Hill Building on West
Forty-Second Street between Eighth and Ninth Avenues, Goodman excelled
following the lead of larger publishers. When a trend hit, he threw the weight
of his company into the craze. Like the other men who ran pulp publishers,
Goodman came of age in a rough-and-tumble industry, filled with stories of
horrific bankruptcies and wholesale corruption. His goals: spend little, make
a lot, and afford himself a comfortable living.

Many publishers grew rich during the men's pulp craze in the 1920s.
They fed an eager public (with more leisure time to devote to things like
reading and the extra money to purchase magazines) via advanced print
technology that enabled higher-quality photos and better distribution. Despite their successes, they faced criticism based on coarse content and lurid
photography.

In response, many publishers set up false-front companies to play fast
and loose with the accounting books. One big company might set up dozens
of smaller ones. If any single entity went under, it would not topple the entire
empire. Debts could then be loaded onto one, which would go bankrupt and
have its assets bought by a secret sister firm at pennies (or less) on the dollar. With little oversight or regulation, the publishers jumped from one fad
to the next—from highly sexual adventure stories to true-crime dramas with
scantily clad damsels in distress or science fiction. Titles like *Real Confessions*
and *Mystery Tales* played to base desires.

The pulps catered to male fantasies, but eventually New York City at-
torneys were determined to clean up the industry. The hubbub enabled a
new medium to emerge—comic books. They had originally been reprints
bound together and sold at newsstands and aimed at children, like Richard
F. Outcault's *Yellow Kid* or Bud Fisher's *Mutt & Jeff*. Later, pulp magazines
featured more heroic characters designed to titillate the magazine-hungry

masses. Tarzan, Doc Savage, and the Shadow had superhero powers, secret origins, and extraordinary abilities. Millions of readers responded, creating a kind of intermediary publication between lurid magazines and early kid-friendly comic books.

In 1929, Dell published *The Funnies*, the first comic book comprised of original work, not reprints. The publication lasted only a year but gave rise to others. M. C. Gaines, a salesman at Eastern Color (the company printing color Sunday comics for many large northeastern newspapers), experimented with smaller-sized comic books in the early to mid-1930s for ten cents. *Famous Funnies No. 1* sold out, and other comics were a hit as give-away promotions for major corporations like Proctor & Gamble and retailers like Kinney Shoes. Soon sales eclipsed one hundred thousand monthly, while promotional comics reached the millions. A craze took shape.

The comic book industry in the mid-1930s grew out of the strange convergence of two wild, nearly mythical characters: Major Malcolm Wheeler-Nicholson and Harry Donenfeld. Wheeler-Nicholson had a murky past that he filled with swashbuckling tales of serving in World War I and fighting the Bolsheviks in Russia. Venturing to New York City, his fame grew as a magazine writer who gave readers a realistic portrayal of the hardships and adventures of warfare.

Donenfeld was a Romanian Jewish immigrant from the Lower East Side. As he rose through the publishing ranks, Donenfeld formed ties with mobsters (rumors circulated that he used his publishing network to help the mafia run liquor during Prohibition). Catering to a base audience, Donenfeld published smutty pulp magazines that bordered on pornography, most frequently called "girlie magazines," long before Hugh Hefner created *Playboy*.

The two men's paths intersected when Wheeler-Nicholson agreed to a distribution deal for his *Detective Comics* line with Donenfeld's Independent News Company. In 1937 and 1938, Wheeler-Nicholson fought to remain solvent. Always strapped for cash and facing a large debt to his distributor, he agreed to form Detective Comics, Inc., with Donenfeld publishing the first issue (soon known simply as DC). Later, Independent News bought Wheeler-Nicholson's National Allied Publications at auction and forced him out.[3]

The comic book revolution required one more spark. That catalyst ignited in Cleveland, Ohio, when struggling writer Jerry Siegel and artist Joe Shuster created Superman. After a long march toward publication, the superhero appeared on the cover of the first issue of *Action Comics* hoisting a car over his head and smashing the front end, pieces flying off as onlookers fled.

The sales figures that came in months later backed up what newsstand owners reported to Donenfeld. The independent Superman comic book launched in early 1939 sold nine hundred thousand copies. Eventually, *Action Comics* sold more than a million copies each month. Sadly, Siegel and Shuster, like many early comic book creators, sold their ownership rights (making $10 a page, thus earning a combined $130 for the first Superman story).

The Superman craze led to super marketing: a newspaper strip, radio show, and series of animated cartoons. According to one writer, "The comic strip sold to nearly three hundred newspapers by 1941." The publicist hired to promote Superman claimed "35 million people were following Super-man in at least one medium."[4] Beyond the media avenues, other licensing included trading cards, buttons, and metal action figures. The merch made Donenfeld rich.

Carousing with friends (and his mistress) at posh bars and restaurants around the Big Apple, people pointed at Donenfeld in awe as the publisher of Superman. Never one for discretion, Donenfeld got in on the act, wearing the Superman logo under his suit. He would wait for some minor accident to happen, leap up, and rip open his white tux shirt to reveal the hero's logo underneath.[5]

Not one to let a craze go by, Goodman jumped on the superhero band-wagon. Frank Torpey, a Funnies, Inc., sales manager who had worked with Goodman at Eastern Distributing, urged him to launch a comic book divi-sion. They shook hands on a deal for Timely to publish the work of Bill Ev-erett and Carl Burgos, two virtually unknown writers who also did their own artwork. Their superheroes, a term used loosely to describe the angst-ridden Namor the Sub-Mariner and troubled android the Human Torch, served as the centerpieces of *Marvel Comics #1* (August 1939). Supremely cautious, the publisher took a wait-and-see attitude toward comic books, outsourcing production entirely to Funnies, Inc.[6]

The first issue was a hit, selling eighty thousand copies its first month. Ultimately, the series sold ten times that amount, eventually rivaling *Super-man* sales. Marvel Comics was renamed Marvel Mystery Comics, focusing on its two superheroes. Namor and Human Torch grew more powerful in subsequent issues—in other words, more Superman-like. A familiar demand rang out from New York City publishers—"Find me the next Superman!"

Goodman decided to bring the comic book in-house rather than pay Funnies, Inc. He lured away veteran freelancer Joe Simon, paying him $12 a page, much more than the writer/artist had made with Funnies. Simon brought along a young artist named Jacob Kurtzberg, a tough Jewish kid from the Lower East Side who had been in gangs but grew obsessed with writing and drawing. His experience included working at the famous Fleischer Brothers animation house on *Popeye* and *Betty Boop* cartoons.

Simon and the artist (employing the pseudonym "Jack Kirby") formed a partnership, initially working on Blue Bolt, a character Simon created. Simon and Kirby excelled together since each could do every part of the job, from writing and penciling to drawing covers. When people asked who did what, Simon shrugged: "We both did everything."[7] Goodman recognized the duo's talents, offering them a percentage of royalties in addition to page rates. In late 1939, he named Joe Simon as Timely's first editor. Simon then convinced Goodman to hire Kirby at a higher page rate, explaining that he worked so fast that it was like getting two artists for the price of one. Goodman purposely kept the comic book division small, but Joe and Jack began creating new superheroes. Although there were early misfires, including the Red Raven and the Vision, Simon and Kirby hit their stride when they cocreated Captain America.

Steve Rogers obtained superpowers (near invincibility) from an Army experimental superserum, becoming Captain America. Realizing they needed a perfect villain, the creative team featured Hitler on the first issue cover. As evil Nazi soldiers shoot at Cap in vain, he knocks the German leader off balance with a strong right.

Simon and Kirby's *Captain America #1* appeared on newsstands on December 20, 1940 (the cover date for comic books usually ran three months ahead, so the official date is March 1941). The comic book "sold a near-Superman number of one million copies."[8] Simon and Kirby shot to fame with Captain America, one of the first successful superheroes not published by DC Comics, which put out the two hottest commodities, Superman and Batman.

Captain America Comics #1 (March 1941) created by Joe Simon and Jack Kirby, with the hero punching Adolf Hitler. © 1939–2022 Marvel Characters, Inc.

Early comic book history came to life in the war for talent. DC had deeper pockets and lured Joe and Jack with huge raises, which eased Jack's mind, since he was perpetually nervous about money. But they had to keep the moonlighting secret. They took on freelance projects at a hotel room near Timely. The entire industry seemed contingent on these backdoor deals.

According to Simon, Stan followed along one day when they snuck off to their hotel studio. He realized they were working for DC, but Simon said he "swore him to secrecy," despite "my theory that in comics, everybody knew everything. . . . There were no secrets there."[9] Given industry jealousy and publisher collusion, it probably wasn't a surprise when Simon and Kirby were inevitably discovered. In his memoir, Simon remembered working on *Captain America #10* when several of the Goodman clan who worked for Martin—Abe, Dave, and Robbie—crammed into the Timely office to confront Simon and Kirby.

"You guys are working for DC," Abe accused the duo. "You haven't been true to us. You haven't been loyal. . . . You should be ashamed of yourselves." Abe delivered the knockout punch—when they finished the current issue of *Captain America*, Joe and Jack were fired. Yet one quasi-member of the Goodman clan was not present, according to Simon: "Stan was nowhere to be seen."[10]

Joe called the scene "very humiliating," but it enraged Kirby, known for his short temper. He pinned the firing on Stan, deducing that the timing seemed too coincidental. "Jack always thought Stan had told his uncle that we were working for DC," Simon explained. "He never gave up on that idea, and hated him for the rest of his life—to the day he died." Decades later in his memoir, Joe cast doubt on Kirby's allegation.[11]

The suggestion that Kirby held Stan responsible and held a grudge adds a new twist to the creative duo's relationship. Later, they would have to get past (or bury) this episode. The animosity that spilled out as they tangled over credit for cocreating the Marvel universe must have brought Kirby's "hatred" back to the surface with newfound ferocity.

Lee's recollection of the incident was that Goodman personally fired Jack and Joe after discovering their work for DC. Lee explained: "Unexpectedly, Joe and Jack left Timely Comics! Supposedly it was because they were working on the side for National Periodicals." He then added: "Truth is, I never knew exactly *why* they left. I only knew this: it was suddenly *my* job to be in charge of the comics."[12] When describing how "Joe and Jack left Timely in

1941," Stan called their ouster "a surprisingly unexpected development." He also chalked it up to the "luck" that "seems to deal most of the cards in the game of life."[13]

> "It was suddenly my job to be in charge of the comics! I guess Martin had no choice[;] there was no one else around." —Stan Lee (Stan Lee, Peter David, and Colleen Doran, *Amazing Fantastic Incredible: A Marvelous Memoir*)

Simon and Kirby's abrupt dismissal is yet another enigmatic episode in Lee's career. Although it would have been underhanded to rat out his mentors, the memories of financial struggle just a few years earlier may have fueled a betrayal. Or it could be as Simon suggests, an open secret that Martin Goodman had to confront. The publisher did not abide disloyalty.

Speculation is one thing, but evidence suggests considerable dishonesty on all sides. First, Goodman ripped off Kirby and Simon, knowingly reporting lower sales figures to reduce their share of profits. On the other hand, Simon and Kirby were secretly working for DC. Joe covertly negotiated a $500-a-week combined salary, but they still drew Timely paychecks as they attempted to figure out the transition, ultimately making money from both companies.

Even a teenager with Lee's advanced imagination could never have dreamed that he would take over the comic book division. In addition to his youth, he was hindered by an utter lack of experience managing anything. Luckily, the comics were produced by a small number of creatives who all needed the work. Artists Al Avison and Syd Shores continued to draw the red, white, and blue hero, while Lee shouldered the writing.[14]

The success of Captain America, though, did exert extra pressure on Lee. He had little time to contemplate what it all meant—the publication calendar slowed for no one. Kirby and Simon worked on #10 before they left (dated January 1942), meaning that they probably left Timely in late fall 1941.

Thrust into a leadership role, Lee made a wise decision—he mimicked Kirby and Simon, working assiduously across numerous projects. "I was responsible for all the stories," Lee recalled, "either writing them myself or buying them from other people." The range of work expanded: "Always when I was there—being the editor meant being the art director too, because you can't just edit the stories without making sure the artwork is done the right way so it enhances the stories . . . and the stories have to enhance the artwork. They have to go hand in hand."[15] Stan became head writer, editor-in-chief, and art director.

Lee utilized thinly veiled pseudonyms to make it seem that Timely had a large team, including "Stan Martin," "Neel Nats," and other variations. According to Stan Goldberg, who managed Timely's coloring department, Lee served as "the only editor." He also had an assistant named Al Sulman, whom Goldberg remembers not doing much work, and two female administrative aides.[16] Lee worked with freelancers to fill the issues in Kirby's absence. Luckily, the youngster had talented artists and writers to draw from, including artist Alex Schomburg, as well as Burgos and Everett.

Under intense pressure to fill pages, Lee worked fast—perhaps the writing version of Kirby (known for prodigious productivity). Unlike Jack, though, the quality was debatable. "Lee's early comic book work was hardly ground-breaking," explains comic book writer and historian Arie Kaplan. "His 1940s-era superhero comics were written just as well as anyone else's, but there was little room for innovation or complex characterization under the watchful eye of Martin Goodman."[17] Yet artist Dave Gantz held a different opinion: "I thought he was the Orson Welles of the comic book business."[18]

> "I thought he was the Orson Welles of the comic book business. He had energy and was young, tall, and good-looking." —Artist David Gantz on Stan Lee (Stan Lee, Peter David, and Colleen Doran, *Amazing Fantastic Incredible: A Marvelous Memoir*)

Goodman may have just wanted the kid to keep the seat warm until he could find a different editor, but Lee proved that he could handle the job. "I assume he wanted to find someone who wasn't just out of his teens," Stan recalled. "But apparently he had a short interest span and eventually stopped looking." The teenager gave himself a new moniker: "Mr. Timely Comics."[19] As he honed his craft as primary writer, editor, and art director, he grew up and into the role.

CHAPTER 4

THROUGH WAR AND COLD WAR

Pearl Harbor brought the war to America. Winning hinged on creating an interlocked infrastructure to support the troops. Businesses of all sizes rallied to the cause. Democracy hung in the balance!

Although still a teenager, Stan enlisted on November 9, 1942, just as the US faced its first skirmish on the coast of North Africa. He took the Army General Classification Test and scored high, qualifying for the Signal Corps.[1]

The war was good for comic books. In 1943, more than 140 were on newsstands, reportedly "read by over fifty million people each month." In 1944, Fawcett's *Captain Marvel Adventures* sold fourteen million copies (up 21 percent). Superhero titles drove sales, but publishers also expanded into humor, funny animals, and teen romance. *Captain America* remained Timely's most popular series.[2]

"How would you like my job?" Lee asked his friend Vince Fago.[3]

Veteran animator Fago had worked on Superman and Popeye for Fleischer Studios. Battling with Disney, Max Fleischer's shop differed by focusing on human characters, such as Betty Boop and Koko the Clown, rather than talking mice, ducks, and other anthropomorphic figures. Goodman paid Fago $250 a week.

The fighting overseas was heavy stuff; readers yearned for lighter comedic fare. Fago specialized in funny animals, so Timely used Disney as a model, essentially transforming into Disney-lite. They published amusing animal tales, such as *Comedy Comics* and *Joker Comics*. Lee had concocted some of these characters, like Ziggy Pig and Silly Seal (cocreated with artist Al Jaffee, the future *Mad* magazine illustrator). Fago estimated that each comic had a print run of about five hundred thousand. "Sometimes we'd put out five books a week or more," Fago remembered. "You'd see the numbers come back and could tell that Goodman was a millionaire."[4]

Goodman also wanted to gain female readers. Miss America, a teenage heiress who gained superhuman strength and the ability to fly after being struck by lightning, first appeared in *Marvel Mystery Comics #49* (November 1943), with Human Torch and Toro thwarting a Japanese battleship on the cover. In January 1944, Miss America became a title character. However, when sales dropped, the next issue was delayed until November, publishing as *Miss America Magazine #2*. A real-life model portrayed the character in her superhero outfit. For the relaunch, Fago and his team gradually eliminated superhero material in favor of topics deemed more appropriate for teen girls.

Lee went through basic training at Fort Monmouth, an enormous base in New Jersey that housed the Signal Corps. It also served as a research center—radar was developed there and the handheld walkie-talkie. In subsequent years, they would learn to bounce radio waves off the moon.

Stan learned how to string and repair communications lines—a path to combat duty (like his former boss Jack Kirby). Army strategists knew wars were often won by infrastructure—the Signal Corps kept communications flowing, but they could barely keep up with demand. Other training centers opened at Camp Crowder, Missouri, and Camp Kohler, near Sacramento. By mid-1943, the Corps consisted of 27,000 officers and 287,000 enlisted men, backed by another 50,000 civilians.

Pearl Harbor heightened concern that German subs or planes might mount a surprise attack during the cold New Jersey winter. Lee patrolled the base perimeter, claiming the frigid wind whipping off the Atlantic nearly froze him to death.

Lee freezing while on guard during his army years, guarding the water-ways near Fort Monmouth. Illustration by Jason Piperberg.

The beachfront burden ended when Lee's superior officers discovered his work in publishing. They placed him in a special outfit producing instructional films and other wartime materials. Lee wrote fast and in a breezy style that recruits and trainees could comprehend. The Army liked these traits too. At the Training Film Division, based in Astoria, Queens, he joined eight other artists, filmmakers, and writers to create public relations pieces, propaganda materials, and information-sharing documents. Education was critical for the war effort.

The Army purchased a large building flanked by rows of tall, narrow windows at Thirty-Fifth Avenue and Thirty-Fifth Street. Colonel Melvin E. Gillette commanded the efforts. Inside the Army built the largest soundstage on the East Coast, enabling filmmakers to create a variety of military settings and scenes. The old movie studio (built in 1919) soon rivaled the major Hollywood production companies.

"I wrote training films, I wrote film scripts, I did posters, I wrote instructional manuals," Lee said. "I was one of the great teachers of our time!"[5] The Signal Corps group included many famous or soon-to-be-famous individuals, including three-time Academy Award–winning director Frank Capra, *New Yorker* cartoonist Charles Addams, and children's book writer and illustrator Theodor Geisel, whom the world already knew as "Dr. Seuss." The stories that must have floated around during staff meetings!

Lee took up a desk in the scriptwriter bullpen, to the right of eminent author William Saroyan—at least when the pacifist author visited the office. Saroyan, who had won a Pulitzer Prize (but rejected it) for his play *The Time of Your Life* (1939), usually worked from a Manhattan hotel. Lee and the others, including screenwriter Ivan Goff and producer Hunt Stromberg Jr., earned the official Army military occupation specialty designation "playwright."[6]

As home-front efforts intensified, Lee traveled to other bases, essentially crisscrossing the Southeast and Midwest. Each base had a critical need for easy-to-understand manuals, films, and public relations documents. Stan wrote about using combat cameras, caring for weapons, and other topics he knew little about. In these situations, he utilized a familiar motto—simplify the information. "I often wrote entire training manuals in the form of comic books. It was an excellent way of educating and communicating."[7]

One post took Lee to Fort Benjamin Harrison in Indiana, just northeast of Indianapolis—a jarring locale for a New York City native who had not ventured outside the city. He worked with the Army Finance Department, which struggled to keep up with payrolls. Watching the wannabe accountants march, Lee noticed they lacked vigor. He penned a song for them, inserting new lyrics over the famous "Air Force Song." The peppy tune included memorable lines, like "We write, compute, sit tight, don't shoot," but it improved morale.

Stan used humor to help the men absorb the complex procedures. "I rewrote dull army payroll manuals to make them simpler," Lee remembered. "I established a character called Fiscal Freddy who was trying to get paid. I made a game out of it. I had a few little gags. We were able to shorten the training period of payroll officers by more than 50 percent." He joked: "I think I won the war single-handedly."[8]

Lee moved to another project, calling it "my all-time strangest assignment," creating anti–venereal disease posters aimed at troops in Europe.[9] Sexually transmitted diseases have plagued armies throughout history. American leaders considered the effort deadly serious. Despite implementing extensive education campaigns, the military still lost men to syphilis and gonorrhea. The British—less willing to confront the taboo epidemic—had forty thousand men a month being treated for VD during the Italian campaign.

Military leaders went to extreme measures to thwart STDs, including the creation of propaganda posters showing Hitler, Mussolini, and Tojo deliberately plotting to disable Allied troops via disease. Many of these images, such as the ones famously created by artist Arthur Szyk, depicted the Axis leaders as subhuman animals with rat-like features or as ugly buffoons.

Unsure how to combat the scourge, Lee promoted the prophylactic stations set up by the armed forces. Men visited the huts when they thought they were infected, which involved a series of rough and painful treatments. "Those little pro stations dotted the landscape," Stan said, "with small green lights above the entrance to make them easily recognizable." He wrestled

Lee during World War II, a copy of *Terry-Toons Comics #25* (Oct. 1944) on his desk and a sketch of his famous "VD Not Me" poster over his left shoulder. Courtesy of Stan Lee Papers, American Heritage Center, University of Wyoming.

with different taglines, ultimately hitting upon the simplest: "VD? Not me!"[10] Lee illustrated the poster with a cartoon image of a happy serviceman walking into the station, the green light clearly visible. Army leaders liked its simplicity and flooded bases with the posters. Ironically, the print may have ranked among Lee's most-seen, yet also the most roundly ignored.

According to lore, the other "playwrights" couldn't keep up with Stan, forcing the commanding officer to order him to slow down. While it is difficult to quantify the importance of the films, posters, photos, and training aids the Signal Corps produced, analysts determined they cut training time by 30 percent. Signal Corps efforts also provided from 30 percent to 50 percent of newsreel footage for movie theaters, which kept the public informed. Lee, Capra, Geisel, and the other Army "playwrights" did vital work.

Lee used downtime to keep his fingers dipped in Timely ink and his pockets filled with Goodman's money as a freelance writer. With the extra money, Stan purchased his first automobile for $20—a 1936 Plymouth with a fold-up windshield. While Lee was stationed near Duke University in Durham, North Carolina, the unique windshield allowed the warm southern air to blow in his face as he cruised the back roads of tobacco country.

No matter where the Army sent him, Lee received letters outlining stories from Fago every Friday. Stan then typed up the scripts, sending them back on Monday. In addition to working on comics, Lee also helped out with the pulps. He wrote cartoon captions for *Read!* magazine, including this short ditty in January 1943: "A buzz-saw can cut you in two / A machinegun can drill you right thru / But these things are tame, compared— / To what a woman can do!" The accompanying drawing shows a plump woman feeding her bald husband—chained to a doghouse.[11] The ribald humor fit within Goodman's magazines, filled with sexist overtones and racy photographs.

Stan also wrote mystery-with-a-twist-ending short stories, similar to the ones in *Captain America*. In "Only the Blind Can See" (*Joker*, 1943–1944), the gag is on the reader, who eventually realizes a supposedly blind panhandler (assumed a phony) was telling the truth. Written in second person so Lee can speak directly to the reader (addressed as "Buddy"), one learns that the down-on-his-luck beggar had been too prideful. The truth comes to light when a speeding car hits the blind man.[12] These short stories served as training for the science fiction and monster comic books that Lee would write after the war.

Stan's after-hours writing for Timely went largely unnoticed by his superiors but once got him arrested (in typical Lee madcap fashion). One Friday a bored mail clerk overlooked Stan's letter, reporting an empty mailbox. Lee swung by the closed mailroom on Saturday and spied a letter in his cubby—with the Timely return address.

Fearful of missing a deadline, Lee asked the officer in charge for the letter. The harried officer told Lee to worry about the mail on Monday. Angry, Stan used a screwdriver to gently loosen the hinges and freed the missive. When he realized what Lee did, the mailroom supervisor went berserk, reporting him to the base captain. They charged Lee with mail tampering and threatened to throw him in Leavenworth prison. Luckily, the colonel in charge of the finance department intervened. In this instance, Fiscal Freddy really did save the day![13]

Stan's signature and a quick roll of his ink-stained thumb across the Army discharge papers made it official—in late September 1945, Sergeant Lee returned to civilian life. Practically before the ink dried, the twenty-three-year-old roared off base. His new black Buick convertible had hot red leather seats, flashy whitewall tires, and shiny hubcaps—a noticeable upgrade from the battered $20 Plymouth.

Lee received a $200 bonus (called "muster out pay"), given to soldiers so they could jumpstart their postmilitary lives. Half went into a savings account, and Lee pocketed the rest. The Army had allotted him $42.12 to get back to New York City from Camp Atterbury in central Indiana, about fifty miles south of Fort Harrison.

Excited to get back to the Big Apple, Stan joked that he "burned my uniform, hopped into my car, and made it non-stop back to New York in possibly the same speed as the Concorde!"[14] The editor desk awaited in the new headquarters on the fourteenth floor of the Empire State Building. Lee zoomed off on the seven-hundred-mile trip to the Big Apple.

Arriving in New York, Stan was filled with optimism. He dashed along the two-and-a-half-mile trek south from his new two-room abode at the Alamac Hotel to the majestic Empire State Building. Like an animated character—all gangly arms and legs—he proved a frenetic blur, weaving through ambling pedestrians window-shopping along Broadway. Lee's feet scratched across the sidewalk, creating a wild beat matched only by the thoughts bursting in his head and the scripts playing like film scenes in his mind.

The postwar years brimmed with opportunity. New York shimmered with confidence. Comic book sales skyrocketed during the war as readers yearned for distractions from death tolls and fierce battles. After the war, industry insiders estimated that 90 percent of children and teens from ages eight to fifteen read comic books on a regular basis. From comic books to Madison Avenue advertising campaigns, popular culture burst with vivid new colors, sounds, and images in stark contrast to wartime rationing and sacrifice.

Lee lived at the Alamac Hotel (Broadway and Seventy-First Street), a stately nineteen-story dark-brown brick edifice built in 1925. Jazz bands and baseball teams stayed there when visiting New York. It featured six hundred guest rooms, as well as shops and a restaurant on the ground level. In the early 1950s, the CIA used the Alamac as a safe house for German scientists working for American national defense during the Cold War.

Stan embraced the sights and sounds on his daily commute: the thrills of Times Square, towering skyscrapers, and masses of humanity coursing through the streets. He had a new lease on life: superb apartment, steady (and growing) income, and many dates in the heady, joyous postwar era. Yet there were aggravations, too. "One thing that both irritated and frustrated me," Lee explained, "was the fact that nobody, outside of our own little circle, had a good word to say about comic books."[15]

The negativity triggered bouts of self-consciousness, yet Stan felt predestined for success—something larger than comic books. Although he bristled at reactions he received from people who asked him what he did for a living, he really loved the focus on writing and creating. During the war, he witnessed the value of animation, film, and entertainment as a means to educate. He had served with some of the nation's great creative minds; now in his mid-twenties, he was back to being *just* a comic book writer. Lee had to reconcile his joy with the sideways glances he received when people found he worked in comics.

The popularity of Archie and friends in *Archie Comics* (first published in 1942) influenced the whole industry. Reacting to the trend, Lee published comics featuring young female heroines and teen humor. Ruth Atkinson, a renowned artist/writer, created *Millie the Model*, launched in late 1945. As one of the first women in comic books, Atkinson paved the way for others, also creating *Patsy Walker*, a spin-off from *Miss America Magazine.* Lee jumped on the bandwagon, creating *Nellie the Nurse*, another teen humor/ romance title.

Wartime paper restrictions ended in 1945, enabling publishers to go full tilt. The next year, forty million copies sold monthly. Fawcett's *Captain Marvel* and DC's *Superman* and *Batman* sold well, but readers looked to other genres: crime stories, teen romps, and science fiction. Late in 1946, Lee tried to capitalize on the popularity of female heroine stories by cocreating Blonde Phantom.[16] As secretary to private eye Mark Mason, Louise Grant kept her Blonde Phantom identity a secret. At night she donned a bright-red evening gown and mask, fighting criminals with a mix of martial arts skills and a trusty .45-caliber pistol. Similar to Wonder Woman and Timely's Miss America, Blonde Phantom lasted about two years.

In an effort to revive superhero titles, Lee combined several into a super team, similar to DC's Justice Society of America, which had debuted in *All Star Comics #3* (Winter 1940–1941). *All Winners Comics #19* (Fall 1946) featured Captain America, Human Torch, Sub-Mariner, Whizzer, Miss America, and their teen sidekicks. Lee's cover promised "a complete SIZZLING, ACTION THRILLER!" He hired *Batman* cocreator Bill Finger to script the book. Finger's initial story focused on a villain's attempt to steal a nuclear weapon, but fans were not impressed—*All Winners* proved a shipwreck of All Losers! Goodman cancelled it and *Young Allies Comics #20*, a Simon and Kirby series that had launched in 1941.

Stan received his first dose of national publicity in November 1947 when *Writer's Digest* magazine asked him to pen its cover article. Not yet twenty five years old, the boyish Lee chomped on a pipe for the cover photo, attempting to look older and wiser. Although he still doubted his long-term future, Lee played up his role as a seasoned editor. "There's Money in Comics!" offered would-be writers advice—emphasizing realistic dialogue and character development. Lee divulged ideas about writing and creativity (foreshadowing Marvel's 1960s style).

"He was referred to as 'the boy wonder' when I met him. He was a nice-looking, tall, thin man . . . always a workaholic." —Artist Ken Bald on Stan Lee in 1946 (Danny Fingeroth, *A Marvelous Life: The Amazing Story of Stan Lee*)

Publishers continued to test different genres. Simon and Kirby created the teen romance genre with *Young Romance* in September 1947 for Crestwood/Prize. A narrative of "true" stories, *Young Romance* sold millions of copies, perhaps upward of five million copies a month for the rest of the decade.[17] The series ran through June 1963, when Crestwood sold it to DC (continuing through 1975).

Genres habitually shifted: superheroes gave way to teen comedy, which then morphed into romance titles and next mutated into cowboy comics and true-crime books. With Stan at the helm, Goodman's company stayed among the leaders in sales but never pushed originality. For example, in 1947 *Sub-Mariner Comics* morphed into *Official True Crime Cases Comics #24*, with the latter taking over the sequential order of the superhero title.

Television and film had a pervasive influence. Cowboy movie stars—first Gene Autry, then Roy Rogers—sparked interest in Western comics. Rogers, along with his trusty horse, Trigger, and wife, Dale Evans, appeared in popular films like *King of the Cowboys* (1943) and *Home in Oklahoma* (1947). Rogers's groundbreaking licensing agreement put his image on numerous products, second only to Disney characters. He was the first star to conquer the entire media landscape, from hit recordings to starring in a long-running radio show that later moved to television.

Stan responded with *Wild Western* (1948–1957), starring Kid Colt and a rotating group of heroes, from Apache Kid to Arizona Annie. In March 1948, Lee launched *Two-Gun Kid #1*, a singing hero like Rogers and Autry. Five months later, *Kid Colt, Hero of The West #1* hit newsstands, giving a stand-alone book to the popular character—a fast-draw sharpshooter who hunts for and kills the villain who murdered his father, then searches for redemption by becoming a hero. Kid Colt—a hero that was neither fully good nor fully bad—served as a precursor to the superheroes Lee and his cocreators would birth a little more than a decade later.

Lee's personal favorite was Black Rider, a doctor who battled outlaws. For a *Black Rider* issue, Lee even donned the ominous black outfit and mask, appearing on the cover holding two six-shooters.

In 1948, trouble began with true-crime comics. Many were tame, but others featured lurid stories and explicit violence. For example, the cover of Fox's *Murder Incorporated* (January 1948) showed a buxom female firing a bullet into a man who cheated at cards, depicting his reaction as the bullet entered his chest. Although the cover blurb announced "For Adults Only," it seemed aimed at younger readers.

The skyrocketing popularity of crime titles jumped circulation by 20 percent and 50 percent over two years earlier, but adults loathed the violence. In 1948, *Time* magazine implied that some juveniles committed copycat crimes after reading comic books. Influential author and psychiatrist Frederic Wertham fueled the propaganda, organizing a symposium that concluded comic books glorified crime, violence, and sexuality. The comic book industry faced a bona fide crisis.

Stan remained conflicted about his work but focused on production and his team, which he enjoyed. Goodman's directives to mimic the competition bothered him: "We'd be right there, faithfully following each one. . . . I felt that we were a company of copycats."[18]

Instead, Stan tried to build his personal brand. In 1947, he self-published *Secrets Behind the Comics*, selling it for one dollar (comics were ten cents). Using comic book fonts and illustrations, it featured "by Stan Lee" in prominent script. He dedicated the book to his younger brother, Larry, and Goodman's children, Iden, Judy, and Chip.

Ironically, "Secret No. 1" was Stan himself and outlined his career and rationale for the book. Using an illustrated headshot—pencil behind the ear and dotted bowtie—Lee listed his many publications as Timely's "Managing Editor and Art Director." The familiar voice leaps from the page: "NOW, for the first time ever in the world, Stan Lee will show you exactly how comic strips are WRITTEN!!!" In addition to his "secrets," the book contained blank illustration areas where readers could draw the Blonde Phantom.[19]

Occasionally, Lee also edited magazines aimed at adults. Ironically, the pulps were actually more respectable (a *real* career), even the tripe Goodman published. Stan edited the 1950 celebrity pinup *Focus*, dubbed a "photo bedsheet" because it measured 10 x 14 inches. *Focus* aimed at male readers with bikini-clad cover models (including future screen icon Marilyn Monroe) and vivid headlines. Stan also took on additional freelance work, much of it anonymously since he did not want to get fired like Joe and Jack had early in his career. "I ghosted them under other people's names," including television shows, radio programs, and advertising copy. However, Lee did sign his name to the popular Sunday *Howdy Doody* newspaper strip (1950 to 1953), another shot at respectability.[20]

Stan's personal life hummed along with the revitalized spirit of postwar New York. In 1947, however, his world spun into a different orbit when by happenstance he met English model and actress Joan Clayton Boocock. On a fluke blind date, Joan answered his knock at the door. Love at first sight! Stan blurted out that he loved her, claiming he had been drawing her face since he was a boy. Rather than run in horror, she laughed at the offhanded exultation. Soon they were an item.

Joan had come to the United States as a war bride (marrying an American officer in Great Britain). The hasty marriage didn't last, so she planned a trip to Reno, Nevada, to get a divorce. (New York state laws made female-initiated divorce nearly impossible.) In the Wild West of Nevada, she only needed six weeks' residency.

Lee with wife, Joan Boocock Lee, late 1940s. Courtesy Stan Lee Papers, American Heritage Center, University of Wyoming.

Stan waited nervously, but she had many suitors. After he received a letter from her addressed, "Dear Jack," Lee threw caution to the wind, embarking on a convoluted, twenty-eight-hour plane trip. They rekindled their relationship. On December 5, 1947, the couple pulled a Reno special: a judge nullified her marriage in one room; then they walked next door, where the same judge married them. In a matter of minutes, Joan Boocock became Mrs. Stan Lee.[21]

They took the train back, arriving during the holiday season. The couple moved into a tiny apartment in Manhattan on Ninety-Sixth Street, between Lexington Avenue and Fifth Avenue. They also got two dogs: cocker spaniels Hamlet and Hecuba.

Stan had always been reserved when discussing his parents. He rarely mentioned Celia's death (December 16, 1947), just eleven days after his marriage. Larry, then fifteen years old, moved in, so they bought a small house in Hewlett Harbor, a Long Island hamlet. Stan picked up a green Buick convertible that had been owned by a Blue Angel pilot with "a huge flying female as a radiator ornament."[22]

The couple enjoyed his success (like many men back then he did not want Joan working). In 1951, they and their young daughter, Joan Celia (born a year earlier in 1950, then called "Little Joan," but later "J. C."), moved into a house at 226 Richards Lane in Hewlett Harbor. The street may have influenced Lee's decision to later name the leader of the Fantastic Four Reed Richards.[23]

"Stan and Joan were very charismatic. They were a perfect pair." —Pauline Goldberg, wife of artist Stan Goldberg (Danny Fingeroth, *A Marvelous Life: The Amazing Story of Stan Lee*)

After moving to Long Island, Stan commuted to Manhattan to meet with artists and pick up pages but worked from home a couple days per week. During warm months, he set up his typewriter atop a bridge table outside, creating a makeshift standing desk. Joan bought the family a little twelve-foot round plastic pool. Lee said that he could "swim" it in a stroke and a half, joking at the office: "Well, I did 100 laps today."[24]

Martin Goodman and his family lived a few miles away. His son Iden learned to drive in Stan's driveway. Publicly, then and later, Lee distanced himself from Goodman, portraying their relationship as detached. However, substantial evidence reveals how intertwined they actually were. The Lees needed family support in 1953 when their second child (a little girl named Jan) died just three days after birth. Unlike many couples facing tragedy, Stan and Joan managed to overcome their grief, building a stable family for themselves and J. C.

Stan poured his energy into writing, editing, and art direction. Although prone to wild behavior, like jumping on desks to act out scenes as onlookers sat dumbfounded, Lee was an energetic, encouraging, and savvy editorial director. People liked working with him. His own writing was fast—perfect for the quick pace and relentless publication deadlines. Yet Stan still faced bouts of depression and anxiety, calling this era his "limbo years." He had slipped into a rut: "Go to the office—come home and write—weekends and evenings. Between stories, go out to dinner with Joanie, play with little Joanie, look at cars."[25]

As America moved from postwar euphoria to Cold War fear, Stan had achieved what many would call the American Dream. Still, he felt unfulfilled. While he enjoyed working with creative people, the relentless production cycle created a pressure-filled workplace. More importantly, he bristled at the perception that writing for comic books didn't count as *real* writing. Lee yearned for opportunities that might enable him to leap out of the business.

Stan wasn't quite sure what he should do next.

Comic books burned!

Across America makeshift bonfires blazed in town squares, church parking lots, and schools. As smoke lifted skyward, parents and youngsters sent a message to New York publishers, political leaders, and others: we will no longer stand for this!

"Criminal or sexually abnormal ideas . . . an atmosphere of deceit, trickery and cruelty"—these are the ideas comic books ensconced in readers' minds, according to Frederic Wertham, author of the polemic *Seduction of the Innocent*.[26] Since the late 1940s, Wertham had railed against comics, labeling them a form of evil that surpassed even the wanton cruelty, murder, and destruction propagated by Adolf Hitler. He saw a correlation between juvenile delinquency and the violence, gore, and lurid sexuality in some comic books.

For Wertham, the nation's morality stood in the balance!

In 1938, the National Organization for Decent Literature (NODL) rallied against "indecent literature." Several Catholic bishops denounced comics as "printed obscenity" and "an evil of such magnitude as seriously to threaten the moral, social and national life of our country . . . and thereby destroy religion and subvert the social order."[27] The criticism mirrored censoring James Joyce's *Ulysses* and the implementation of the Hays Code, forcing filmmakers to adhere to morality standards. Many media outlets ran anti-comic book material, including ABC radio, *New Republic*, and *Collier's*. Some local jurisdictions attempted to ban comics.

The self-appointed culture police did not specifically target Goodman or Lee. While Stan claims to have participated in debates with Wertham or one of his minions in the early 1950s, there is little evidence supporting the claim. However, he did satirize Wertham in *Suspense #29* (April 1953), a story illustrated by Joe Maneely, one of Lee's closest friends.

Displaying his bombastic style—and lack of subtlety—Lee titled the story "The Raving Maniac" and wrote himself in an argument with a Wertham-like figure. The editor in the story (who is a stand-in for Lee) delivers a blistering soliloquy: "In a dictatorship, people try to change your mind by **force**! You should be grateful you're in a land where only **words** are used!!" The twist ending—one of Lee's specialties—is that the intruder is an insane asylum escapee. In the final frames, Joan and J. C. greet Lee. He rocks his daughter to sleep, telling a bedtime story about the "excited little man." We don't know if this fictional account ever reached Wertham's desk, but publishing it was risky. "To me," he explained, "Wertham was a fanatic, pure and simple. I never cease to be amazed at the gullibility of human beings."[28]

In 1953, as a result of the publicity, the Senate created the Subcommittee on Juvenile Delinquency to investigate. They utilized the power of televised hearings after a similar subcommittee on organized crime led by Estes Kefauver produced huge ratings. Robert Hendrickson (R-NJ) led the investigation with proceedings taking place at different locations (including Denver, Boston, and Philadelphia).

In April 1954, hearings opened in room 110 of the New York Federal Courthouse. A parade of educators, sociologists, and child welfare officials criticized publishers, but most found the evidence underwhelming.

Wertham kept up the bombast, exclaiming: "I think Hitler was a beginner compared to the comic book industry. They get the children much younger. They teach them race hatred at the age of four, before they can read."[29] The senators never questioned Wertham's authority.

The proceedings took a dramatic turn when Kefauver questioned EC publisher William Gaines, who had stayed up all night popping Dexedrine diet pills (a kind of middle-class wonder drug at the time, prescribed to overcome fatigue). Gaines thought he could bring people to their senses. Kefauver had different ideas.

Gaines felt sick and had difficulty with the barrage of questions after the pills wore off. As if on cue, Kefauver pulled out *Crime SuspenStories #22*, a gruesome drawing of a man holding a bloody ax in one hand and a blond woman's severed head in the other. Her mouth dripped blood, as did the ax.

Gaines foolishly insisted the image was appropriate. The exchange was featured on the front page of the *New York Times*, as well as in *Time* and *Newsweek*. The resulting uproar forced many publishers into bankruptcy. Goodman's sales plummeted from 15 million monthly in 1953 to 4.6 million in 1955.[30] "Parents everywhere were forbidding their children to read anything that even hinted at action or adventure or any sort of gripping conflict," Lee remembered.[31]

The industry responded by creating an editorial code administered by the Comics Magazine Association of America (CMAA). The "Comics Code" obliged publishers to submit pre-publication materials to a review board that determined decency standards. Issues that passed could print the "Approved By" stamp on the cover.

"The market for comic books disintegrated with artists and writers being fired by the barrelful," Stan recalled. "I was amazed that Martin kept me on, but then, he had to have somebody to fire all those other people for him." After the carnage, Lee struggled with the emotional baggage. "I was the hackiest hack who ever lived," he lamented.[32] "Goodman left it all up to Stan," remembered colorist Stan Goldberg. "I don't think Martin ever came into Stan's office, and I never saw him in the bullpen."[33]

Quantity categorically trumped quality. "I felt I was a better writer. . . . I shouldn't be wasting my life on this," Stan lamented. The only positive was that he enjoyed working alongside other creative talents, convincing himself: "I'll stay just a little bit longer because this is fun."[34]

Goodman vacated the Empire State Building for smaller offices at 655 Madison Avenue, the heart of the advertising industry. Lee settled into a small office and attempted to resurrect comic books. The other editors and writers basically ignored Stan, finding his work appalling at best and at worst utterly depraved.

Compounding the turmoil, Goodman made several regrettable business decisions. In 1956, he closed his distribution operations, turning to industry leader American News Company (ANC). Few realized ANC had been waging a four-year battle with antitrust regulators amid rumors of mob connections. Goodman's bet turned sour.

Timely was renamed Atlas Comics in the early 1950s, just as the distributor situation worsened. Two of ANC's most successful magazines folded (*Collier's* and *Woman's Home Companion*), and Dell left, which had been its largest client. ANC lost $8 million and fired eight thousand employees, folding two months later.

"It was like we had been the last ones to book passage on the *Titanic!*" Stan declared.[35] ANC's collapse threatened Goodman's whole business, including magazines. Desperate, he begged Independent News (owned by National Periodical/DC Comics) to distribute Atlas's catalog. Independent News executives signed an agreement but with stringent stipulations, allowing Atlas to publish only eight comic books per month.

In one fell swoop, Independent News neutered its (now dependent) competitor. Martin and Stan resolved to publish sixteen bimonthly comic books, including stalwarts *Millie the Model*, *Patsy Walker*, *Strange Tales*, *Wyatt Earp*, and *Two-Gun Kid*. Freelancers were out of luck. Despite his reputation for toughness, Goodman left on a Florida vacation, giving Lee the onerous task of (again) firing staff, including venerable artists like John Romita and Joe Sinnott. "Toughest thing I ever did in my life," Stan recalled.[36] Many creators left the business, opting for stability in advertising or a corporate job.

Lee feared Goodman might ax him next. "I couldn't shake that gnawing feeling of depression," Stan explained. "It was like I was chasing my tail all the time. I could never shake that feeling of vague dissatisfaction."[37] Yet Stan had several points in his favor: he worked fast and was family, and Martin did not want to miss out on the next comic book wave.

Goodman's publishing machine ultimately rebounded. The magazines were a mix of conventional titles about Hollywood and its stars (like Jackie Gleason) and romance magazines. Spicier titles, such as *Stag*, *For Men Only*, and *Man's World*, were filled with explicit photographs and content. Nonetheless, many first-rate writers published in Goodman's magazines, including Ogden Nash, Graham Greene, and William Saroyan (Lee's old Army office mate). Stan shifted between the two. People viewed a brassy pinup magazine like *Focus* as more prestigious than comic books, even if the former featured risqué photographs, provocative drawings, and stories heavy on sexuality (such as "I Kidnapped the King's Harem Girl" and "Divorcees Are Dynamite").

In June 1958, Stan made a decision that would later change comic book history when he brought in artists Jack Kirby and Steve Ditko as freelancers. Ditko's fluid style and gripping sense of shapes and sizes worked perfectly for the science fiction and fantasy titles. Having burned bridges with the editorial team at DC and seeing his partnership with Joe Simon evaporate (Simon settled into advertising), Kirby was in difficult straits.

With few assignments and reduced page rates, Kirby had few options. There is no record of how Goodman felt or if there was resentment between them about what had happened in the past with Captain America. From a similar background as Lee, yet more hardscrabble and even poorer as a kid, Kirby developed a manic drive to support his family. Stan assigned Jack monster books to keep him active. These weren't difficult assignments for an artist of Kirby's abilities but did provide a steady paycheck.

At the time, Stan and Jack both had reservations about comic books but shared an overriding concern with earning a living. They were united by work ethic and apprehension. Neither was truly happy in the comic book business, yet here they were together. Jack said he felt "shipwrecked." Stan remembered Martin walking past him without saying a word. The chill spoke volumes: "It's like a ship sinking, and we're the rats. And we've got to get off."[38]

Little did Lee, Kirby, and Ditko realize that they would soon revolutionize the comic book industry and global popular culture forever.

CHAPTER 5

NEW HEROES FOR A NEW AGE— THE FANTASTIC FOUR

Barely glancing at the road, Stan Lee barreled toward Long Island in a souped-up Buick convertible. Jack Kirby, chewing on a cigar, sat to Lee's right. John Romita, one of Lee's favorite artists, gripped the back of Kirby's seat. With one eye on the duo in the front and one on traffic, Romita was a captive audience—and fearing for his life.

Lee didn't stop talking. Over the booming sounds of the city, he barked out soliloquies about the intergalactic adventures of a superhero quartet. Shot through with gamma rays after crashing a spaceship returning to Earth, each member developed a superpower. With their newfound powers, they vowed to battle evil.

Kirby punctuated his ideas with a jab of his stogie. Even in the swirl of wind, he shifted the cigar from one side of his mouth to the other, waiting for Lee to pause. The arguments over plots and scenarios began as soon as Lee's foot stomped on the gas.

Nonchalant, Lee swerved and juked between passing vehicles. Kirby focused on the plot, seemingly unfazed by Lee's daredevil driving. As they bickered over details, Romita realized that neither was actually listening to the other. "They would both come in with their ideas," he recalled. "They would both ignore each other. . . . I never really knew which way they would go because both of them had a different aspect on the story."[1]

High-speed *Fantastic Four* story conference as Stan drives with artists Jack Kirby and John Romita. Illustration by Jason Piperberg.

The bickering didn't end until Lee dropped Kirby off at his house in East Williston on Long Island, a bucolic little village of less than three thousand. The tiny hamlet was a world away from Jack's youth on the crime-ridden streets of the Lower East Side.

Such story conferences, whether they took place in a whizzing convertible shooting toward Long Island, over the phone, or in Lee's cramped office on Madison Avenue, defined the way Stan and Jack created stories in the 1960s. Neither the writer nor the artist realized it at the time, but these arguments actually reinvented the way comics would be created. Ultimately, this was their greatest contribution to Marvel's successes and, sadly, the final nail in the coffin of their disintegrating partnership.

The new writing style mixed storytelling, plot, and visual representation (later dubbed the "Marvel Method"). Both the writer and artist had a say in how the final product unfolded, rather than the artist merely following a script, as done in the past.

When readers went nuts for a new superhero team they cocreated, Lee and Kirby realized that they were at the dawn of a new era. It all began with those gamma rays and the Fantastic Four!

From the planet-smashing opening burst, pistol shot, and train churning headlong around a bend and seemingly directly at the viewer, *The Adventures of Superman* gave television audiences chills. The orchestra blared, while the announcer proclaimed that the hero fought for "truth, justice, and the American way." Tall, with dark slicked-back hair and a broad chest, actor George Reeves brought Jerry Siegel and Joe Shuster's character to life. *The Adventures of Superman* blazed across the 1950s.

Julius "Julie" Schwartz, the editorial director of DC Comics, Goodman's chief competitor, realized *The Adventures of Superman*'s success gave DC an opportunity to rekindle interest in superhero comic books. He had been editing Wonder Woman, Flash, and Green Lantern since 1944. Despite the ongoing challenges with Wertham's crusades and television's lure, Schwartz figured that if the company focused on superheroes, their fortunes might be reversed.

Beginning in 1956, Schwartz gingerly pushed DC back into superheroes, bringing out updated versions of the Flash, Green Lantern, Hawkman, and the Atom. The early success of Flash led him to introduce a superhero team modeled after the Justice Society of America, which had ended in 1951. The new group, with a modified name, was called the Justice League of America, first appearing in *The Brave and the Bold #28* (March 1960). Although Superman did not appear on the cover, both he and Batman were members. The combination of the Superman television show and his inclusion in the new lineup helped National Comics stay atop the industry.[2]

Schwartz wasn't the only comic book insider to understand Superman's consequences. As usual, Goodman smelled a trend in the making. He pursued a simple directive: move mountains of paper as fast as possible. Although he had a lifelong affinity for cowboys and some interest in science fiction, magazines and comic books were simply products to be exploited. Martin's business acumen wasn't dynamic: watch the competitors, then brazenly copy them. Goodman wasn't the only one doing this; many others followed the same course. Many publishers knew each other well, playing cards and drinking, dining at the same high-end restaurants, golfing, and even vacationing near each other in Miami Beach. They shared the commonality of comic books and publishing, which made them a kind of odd tribe—kings of a notorious industry.[3]

From the mid-1940s through the early 1960s, Goodman cut every corner to make money. Often, he dipped into rather seedy and unscrupulous tactics. Titles like *For Men Only* and *Stag* appealed to sordid interests. He dabbled in soft-core pornography, horrific crime-scene photos, and pirated movie stills of famous Hollywood stars. He even persuaded employees and freelancers to pose as cover models, which saved him money versus hiring real models or actors (even the publicity-shy Kirby did so).[4] The bonus was that *Stag* and other lascivious magazines were sold for twenty-five cents versus the comic books at just ten cents.

Goodman believed that comic book buyers were mainly children, preteen and teenage boys (interested in rock 'em, sock 'em stories with excessive fight scenes and action-filled pictures), and dim-witted adults. According to Goodman, they did not give a hoot about quality. He famously exclaimed: "If you get a title that catches on, then add a few more, you're in for a nice profit."[5]

Stan had dreamed of writing a novel or screenwriting, but years of work for Goodman knocked those ideas on their ear. He knew the reality—publishing was a moneymaking venture. His number one priority centered on creating products that would sell. Yet Stan also understood that comics could play a more significant role—helping young people learn to read or building creativity. These impulses warred inside Lee. Am I wasting my life in comic books? he wondered. "I felt we were merely doing the same type of thing, over and over again with no hope of either greater financial rewards or creative satisfaction."[6] In 1960, approaching two decades in the business, Lee grew despondent. Depressed and desperate, he thought he should try some other career path—anything to get away from comics.

Almost forty years old, Stan considered other options with his usual optimistic outlook but certainly prudently. Watching his father battle internal demons brought on by the Depression caused him to hesitate. Jacob Lieber had been just a little older than Stan when he lost his job. The resulting fallout left his family in tatters. Stan had to make a decision, balancing two conflicting notions: a regular paycheck and a stable, happy life for his family on one hand versus his personal despondency on the other.

Lee believed the comic books might be headed for doom. Sales figures that had taken off in the years after the Senate investigations plummeted at the end of the decade. "There we were blithely grinding out our merry little monster yarns," Stan explained. "We were turning out comics by the carload, but nothing much was happening."[7] He spent long days scripting and editing teen romance and humor comics, like *Teen-Age Romance* and *Life with Millie*, as well as Westerns, such as *Rawhide Kid*, *Wyatt Earp*, and *Two-Gun Kid*. *Strange Tales* and *Journey into Mystery* (monster and sci-fi comics) also took up much of his time. No matter which way he turned, Lee felt pressure: staying in comics meant trading malaise for a regular paycheck and churning out derivative characters to satiate Goodman's demands. The only option might be to leave behind the only career he had ever known.

In the summer of 1961, Lee found a new path, creating a superhero team with Jack Kirby that would put the second-rate publishing house on the map. Contrary to the Justice Society and the Justice League, which were formed by disparate individuals, Lee saw the team as a family. Like a traditional family, they would confront real-world challenges and also be forced to negotiate the superpowers they never asked for. Lee wondered: how would people who lived next door or down the street react to living through a rocket crash only to find they had abilities that could empower or destroy the world?

Stan's goal was new at the time—"make the unreal real." The stories involved extraordinary people, placing them in extraordinary circumstances, and then having them behave like ordinary people. Lee thought about the ideas that had attracted him to books, movies, and radio programs as a youth. He would mirror that kind of storytelling: "Plop an earthly superhero into a familiar setting, and you've got some classic pulp fiction."[8]

Like a compelling dramatic film (and just like the heart of most families), Lee began with the love story between central characters Reed Richards and Susan Storm. Then he upped the drama and family dynamic by adding her hot-tempered younger brother, Johnny. Lee rounded out the new team with tough-guy everyman Ben Grimm. When Grimm later became the Thing, the group gained both comedic relief and a sense of humanity. The monster's exterior concealed a sensitive soul. The team's interactions—both as superheroes and individuals coping with a new world and one another—served as jet fuel to send the comic racing. Lee saw that action as the central facet: "I like to have characters to work with as though it's a movie or a soap opera, where the characters' own personal lives would help write the dialogue and come up with situations."[9] The quartet would be a loving yet dysfunctional family, held together by affection but dealing with challenges brought on by their newfound powers.

Lee and Kirby pulled from current events to give the origin story context. The team risked spaceflight "to the stars" in an attempt to beat the Soviet Union into space. The Russians—referred to as "commies" in the parlance of the day—had actually beaten the US into space, initially with the launch of Sputnik (the first satellite), then in 1960, sending the dogs Belka and Strelka into orbit, so the Fantastic Four plot served as a kind of revisionist history.

When the group battled Mole Man, its first supervillain, they were on red alert because the evildoer struck an "atomic plant behind the iron curtain" and a French facility in Africa. These references to reality—even keeping the team unmasked in a nod to the burgeoning celebrity culture—made the team more interesting. The familiar territory and use of common lingo helped readers relate to the plight.

Jack Kirby had been dutifully crafting covers and stories for Lee for years, essentially creating the company's house style. He excelled at space epics and drawing action scenes that made readers feel the force of a roundhouse punch or the ground shake as an enormous intergalactic monster shambled through a cityscape. "I didn't discuss it with Jack first," Lee explained. "I wrote it first, after telling Jack it was for him because I knew he was the best guy to draw it."[10] Kirby, according to his cocreator, "has the uncanny ability to visualize unforgettable scenes so clearly in his mind's eye that all he has to do is put down on paper what already exists in his incredible imagination."[11] The explosive imagery and snappy dialogue came together in a way that excited comic book readers.

A horrifying green monster pushes up through the city pavement, clutching a half-invisible blond woman as a human flame circles in flight. Onlookers react in horror. The reader sees another character from behind, a kind of monster, while the fourth seems to have limbs that stretch, loosening ropes that entangle him. A callout box tells us their names and announces that they are "Together for the first time in one mighty magazine!"

The Fantastic Four have arrived!

The Marvel universe begins with *The Fantastic Four #1* (November 1961), cocreated by Lee and artist Jack Kirby. © 1939–2022 Marvel Characters, Inc.

The scene is dramatic and intense. What really draws the reader's eye is the bold-red fanciful script used to title the comic book. It leaps from the page, a representation of the atomic age in the early Cold War. Next to the title is a tiny box with a capital "M" atop a smaller "c." Already, Lee and Kirby were thinking "Marvel Comics."

Inside, *The Fantastic Four* comic is a four-part story that they tell in a nonlinear narrative. Although we know from the cover that the heroes will battle a monster, the story doesn't reach this point until the third act. The first two sections introduce the team and its origin.

Initially, when Richards uses a "4" smoke signal to assemble his teammates, citizens and the police react with terror. Thing is viewed as a monster, and the police wonder if he is part of "an alien invasion." They attempt to shoot him before he uses the city's sewer system to evade further confrontation. Later, the government launches jetfighters against Torch, shooting at him with nuclear missiles. Mister Fantastic saves Johnny—and the city—as he "hurls the mighty missile far from shore where it explodes harmlessly over the sea."

The next section begins with an argument between Reed and Ben over the safety of the experimental rocket and the possible consequences of flying through "cosmic rays." Although he doesn't want to pilot an unsafe ship, Susan manipulates him, invoking the dreaded "Commies" as rationale for the dangerous mission. Then she implies that Ben is a "coward." Soon after, decked out in dark plum-colored spacesuits and blue helmets, the team sneaks past a guard and into the rocket. In what might be Kirby's strongest panels in the entire book, the rays pulse through the ship, causing Ben to collapse and Johnny to combust. You can almost smell the teen's flight suit go up in flames.

After the ship crashes to safety, the team emerges from the wreckage dazed and angry. Susan is the first to be impacted, slowly turning invisible. The others look on in horror. "Wha—What if she never gets visible again?" her brother asks. Next, as Ben and Reed start to get angry, the former turns into the Thing, an orange-skinned monster, like a giant rock pile gone amuck. He reveals his secret longing for Susan, exclaiming: "I'll prove to you that you love the wrong man, Susan," and swings a tree trunk at Richards. The latter eludes the violence by stretching his body and neck. Then, using his newfound ability, he wraps Ben up using his arms as ropes. Finally, Johnny bursts into flames, which starts a brush fire. They collectively think:

"We've changed! All of us! We're more than just human." Speaking for the group, Ben declares that they "gotta use that power to help mankind." They band together under the "Fantastic Four" moniker.

The final two sections of *The Fantastic Four* #1 find the team—back in their purple jumpsuits—tracking a mysterious threat to "Monster Isle." They battle a flying three-headed monster, a giant rock monster, and various gargoyles, including the green giant from the cover. Using Torch's immense heat, they thwart Mole Man, ultimately entombing the villain and monsters underneath Monster Isle. The team flies away in a private jet, grimly facing the future.

The Kirby-Lee partnership brought the Fantastic Four to life, but neither had grand expectations for its success. "Okay, that's it," Lee figured. "I'm going to get fired. I got that out of my system."[12]

Lee took pride in the comic, but neither he nor Kirby could wait to see if *The Fantastic Four* was successful. Comic books were released about three months prior to the month printed on the cover, and it took another handful of months for the sales figures to trickle in. Plus, the writer and artist couldn't really stop working, given the ten to twelve issues that had to be produced within the stipulations of Goodman's punitive agreement with the DC Comics distributor.

As Lee and his team pushed to meet the tight deadlines, they experienced something new—fan mail piled up in the office. Readers loved the new superhero team. According to Lee, receiving mail from fans was virtually unprecedented. Jack and Stan had struck gold. "We were swamped with it," Lee recalls, "and it just kept growing with each new issue."[13] The sales figures that came in months later reiterated the comic book's popularity. The success took Lee by surprise: "I never realized it would sell that well."[14]

In response, Stan began answering fan letters in the comic. The chatty column gave readers insider information about Marvel and its staff. On the surface, the jokey interaction with fans seemed frivolous. Over time, however, the easygoing tone became an important link in establishing Lee as the central persona of not only Marvel but the wider comic book industry. Stan seemed like every reader's favorite uncle, always willing to share a wisecrack and behind-the-scenes gossip.

The connection turned many young people into lifelong fans. Through Stan's responses and tone, a reader might feel as if they were in New York City with him and his "bullpen" collaborators, each with a colorful nickname, artistic skills, and quirky personalities. A born showman, Lee used the space to express his newfound happiness. *The Fantastic Four* gamble paid off.

Although *The Fantastic Four* sold extremely well, Marvel did not list the title among its 1961 sales figures since it had been released so late in the year. If the comic was the company's best-selling issue that year, though, one can infer its sales exceeded *Tales to Astonish*, which ranked fortieth with about 185,000 issues sold. In comparison, *Uncle Scrooge* (published by Dell) ranked first with more than 850,000 in paid circulation, while DC's venerable *Superman* stood at 820,000. Based on how publishers reported circulation, *The Fantastic Four* would not appear on the official roll until 1966 when it placed nineteenth at 329,000 copies.

Enthusiastic fans and mountains of mail combined to produce a watershed moment in Lee's career. In 1961, DC's *Justice League of America* won the Academy of Comic Book Arts and Sciences (Alleys) comic book of the year award. A year later, *The Fantastic Four* won the award.

The Marvel revolution took flight.

Although years later Jack and Stan bickered about who deserved more credit for creating the Fantastic Four, they each brought special talents to the process at the time, like all great creative duos, whether musicians, filmmakers, or athletes. Without Kirby's unmatched artistry, the superhero team would not have burst from the page, generating energy and action that a reader could almost feel, whether the void of deep space or the feeling of a man's arm stretching hundreds of yards or bursting into flames. Lee is all words. He delivered a distinct dialogue and narrative patter that left his own unique mark on the characters and their enemies.

By 1961 both men were seasoned professionals, having spent most of their adult lives in the comics. Although they would soon become legends, it is easy to overlook that Stan and Jack felt personally and professionally trapped. Both had been deeply unsatisfied, a mix of anxiety and fear for themselves and the industry. Later—particularly as Lee's career shot skyward and Kirby felt jealous and used—a personal cold war enveloped the duo. But when *The Fantastic Four* hit newsstands, the two barely looked up . . . the writer from his one-finger, clickety-clacking typewriter and the artist from his worn drafting table. They could not have realized they were creating a masterpiece. For them, the comic book superhero team was just another product, one among many that kept them chained to the business.

Headstrong and talented, Lee and Kirby shared many traits—intense workaholics and deeply driven—but with dissimilar personalities. By the time they began working together in the late 1950s, they had nowhere else to turn and were driven by a mix of fear, concern, pride, and passion. The Marvel Method worked based on the talents each willingly put on the table.

> "I think the four characters are really interesting and so are their relationships with each other. . . . Even though they're fantasy, there's a feeling of realism. . . . You just didn't read about stories like that in Superman. . . . The readers could almost think of the characters as real live people." —Stan Lee on the success of the *Fantastic Four* (Tom DeFalco, ed., *Comics Creators on Fantastic Four*)

Years ago, Lee stumbled across his original two-page synopsis of *The Fantastic Four #1* and shared it with *Alter Ego* magazine editor Roy Thomas, Lee's onetime protégé and later replacement as Marvel editor-in-chief. One of the surprises uncovered was that Lee had passed some parts of the script by the Comics Code Authority. Directly in the origin story section, for example, Lee told Kirby that when it came to the Human Torch, the CCA warned he "may never burn anyone with flames, he may only burn ropes, doors, etc.—never people." Thomas speculated that Lee cleared the character because he feared outcry that might delay publication.[15]

This episode reveals two sides of Lee's work as writer/editor. While Stan experienced joy in creating a new kind of superhero team, he had to be business-like and strategic in bypassing the CCA censor. Talking to an early interviewer about "King" Kirby, Lee praised his partner for mixing storytelling and visualization like no one else in the business. He explained that Jack often plotted the comics himself, admitting, "We're practically both the writers on the things."[16] The King also took on the role of unofficial art director, training new artists—really just his style applied to Marvel's superhero lineup.

Lee's budding showmanship grew and his confidence increased as a result of *The Fantastic Four*'s increasing popularity. By the third issue, Stan took the unprecedented step of tattooing the phrase "The Greatest Comic Magazine in the World!!" just below the title. With #4, a slightly altered slogan appeared: "The World's Greatest Comic Magazine!" No one could miss the blaring letters, essentially daring the reader to disagree. Willing to exaggerate, Stan explained, "I figured a line like that would certainly get attention, if only for its flagrant pretentiousness."[17] The declaration drew a line in the sand and told competitors: "We're the best comic book company in the world."

The success of *The Fantastic Four* served as a hurricane-force wind thrusting Lee and Kirby deeper into the psyches of their hero team. Lee remembered that, after ten issues, "We had both gained new insights into the FF and their ever-menacing antagonists. Reed, Sue, Ben and Johnny seemed like part of our own families by now." Stan explained: "I felt comfortable writing their scenarios. It was increasingly easy to imagine what they would say or do in almost any given circumstance, for they had become as familiar to me as my own friends."[18] The family saga intensified as the Fantastic Four continued saving the world, while also confronting the strains on them as individuals and a team.

For many fans, Ben Grimm/Thing was the group's go-to hero. Kirby modeled the hero after himself and added many of the tough-guy characteristics, which he had lived through as a kid on the Lower East Side. According to Stan, Grimm epitomized the duality they wanted to create: "I realized there was no monster, no funny, ugly guy who's a hero. . . . When this guy becomes very powerful, he also becomes grotesque. It had a touch of pathos."[19]

Kirby and Lee also specialized in inventing supervillains evil enough to cause the reader anxiety. For example, they brought back Bill Everett's Prince Namor, the Sub-Mariner, as a misunderstood, majestic villain who just wanted his underwater kingdom to remain sequestered—that is, until he determined that Sue should rule the seas by his side, thus giving Reed constant fits as Namor moved in on his fiancée.

Doctor Doom proved even more interesting, a criminal genius and physically powerful foe who caused global mayhem from Latveria, an imaginary Eastern European kingdom that Lee concocted. In one of their sometimes dazzling and argumentative story conferences, Kirby and Lee talked about a villain that would put the FF to the test. Lee latched onto the name "Doom," but Kirby was skeptical. Lee recalled, "Whenever something is really right, it never takes long to put it all together. Each little idea led to another, more exciting one."[20]

Making Doom as sinister as possible, Kirby sketched him in a suit of armor, with his face hidden behind a cold gray steel mask. The villain first appeared in *The Fantastic Four #5* with a short origin story. The issue begins with one of Lee's soon-to-be famous in-jokes—Johnny Storm reading the new issue of *The Hulk*, which in reality had just reached the newsstands. Johnny teases Ben, "I'll be doggoned if this monster doesn't remind me of the Thing." In dysfunctional family fashion, Ben sets off after Torch, resulting in a broken table. Reed and Sue have to intervene, with Sue dousing her little brother with a fire extinguisher while Reed ties Ben into knots. Reed laments: "What's the matter with the four of us? Whenever we're not fighting some menace to mankind, we end up fighting among ourselves!" Lee's dialogue is heavy-handed, but fans loved seeing the superheroes battle and bicker just like in their own living rooms and dining tables.

After Doctor Doom ensnares the team in its skyscraper headquarters, Reed recognizes that the masked foe is actually his former college classmate Victor Von Doom, "a brilliant science student . . . only interested in forbidden experiments" in "black magic." Doom takes Sue hostage, whisking the team to his fortress. Using a time machine he created, Doom sends Johnny, Ben, and Reed back in time to capture "Blackbeard's treasure." They draw on their superpowers to battle overmatched pirates and seize the treasure. Instead of giving it to Doom, however, Reed realizes, "If Doctor Doom wanted it, there must be some dangerous power which it possesses, and we've got to see that he never gets it!"

Ben, who the pirates think is Blackbeard, decides he likes being an outlaw and orders the pirates to turn on Reed and Johnny. Moments later, though, a tornado rips the ship to shreds, nearly drowning Johnny. Later, they find Ben washed up onshore. He apologizes, "I musta got carried away by being accepted—as a normal man—even if it was only by a band of cutthroat pirates! I—I just lost my dumb head for awhile!" The self-reflective hero/monster provides Lee with a new storytelling style. The monster who wants to be human keeps tensions high. Ben's internal struggle and how it plays out publicly when he appears as a monster adds to the pervasive sense of conflict at the heart of *The Fantastic Four*.

When Doom returns the heroes to his castle through a time portal, he realizes that they tricked him. In retaliation, Doom locks the team in a vault, cutting off the oxygen. Sue, however, turns invisible to thwart the attack, thereby saving her teammates. The heroes escape Doom's fortress, but they cannot capture him. He rockets away on a portable jetpack.

By allowing the villain to escape, Lee and Kirby veered from the traditional comic book plot, not neatly wrapping up the story at the end. Essentially, Lee and Kirby created a comic book that read like a serial or soap opera. The style enabled them to reveal more about the protagonists in each episode, thereby keeping the reader wanting more. As with the launch of *FF #1*, fan mail about Doom piled up in Lee's office. Jack and Stan realized that Doom was "probably Marvel's very top villain, in appearance, in power, personality, and plain sheer reader appeal."[21]

The image of Reed angrily storming away and the seemingly incomprehensible notion of Doctor Doom as part of the team graces the cover of *The Fantastic Four #10*. Despite this intriguing setup, what readers could not have overlooked is the appearance of Lee and Kirby in the lower left-hand corner with their backs to the reader, actually commenting on the issue.

Inside, three team members have to deal with their growing celebrity, avoiding fans who either want a piece of them or think they should be reined in somehow when they attempt to answer Thing's distress signal. Arriving at the apartment of Ben's blind girlfriend, Alicia, they realize that he is not in trouble. However, the mention of Sub-Mariner causes an argument between Reed and Sue. She blurts, "I'm not even sure of my own feelings." Just then, the story cuts to Kirby and Lee at Marvel's Madison Avenue offices, adorned with images of Hulk, Thor, and other superheroes, as the duo creates another supervillain.

Suddenly, Doom walks into the office. He removes his mask, causing Lee and Kirby to recoil in horror. Doom then threatens them, exclaiming, "You are searching for a story—well I shall give you one! Here, phone Mr. Fantastic—say what I tell you if you value your lives!" He shoots a ray out of his index finger, destroying Lee's ashtray as a show of force. Doom waits for Reed to arrive and then ambushes him with sleeping gas. Next, Doom teleports with Richards to his secret lab.

Using telepathy he learned from an advanced race of space aliens called the Ovoids, Doom transports his brain into Richards's body, while Richards is stuck in the Doom armor. Tricking the Fantastic Four into helping him, Doom is able to lock Richards away in an underground chamber that only has an hour's worth of air left. Ultimately, Reed escapes, but he is knocked unconscious by Sue at Alicia's apartment. When the rest of the team (minus Doom in Reed's body) shows up, they realize that he might actually be telling the truth. Johnny and Thing trick Doom into revealing himself, and Reed and Doom are transposed into their own bodies. Doom is accidently hit with a shrinking ray that makes him so small that he vanishes. Thus, the villain is thwarted again.

Drawing themselves into the comic and actually playing a role in the story may have seemed like a farce, but the issue further established that Marvel would be categorically different than the competition. No one could have imagined similar shenanigans at DC. Just as important, the issue introduced Lee and Kirby as heroic figures, able to engage with their creations at will, even being more than a little scared of Doom . . . just as a reader would be in real life. Suddenly, the names adorning the issues—"Stan Lee & J. Kirby"—had meaning. And, as Lee explained, fans called out for the distortion, which he called "perhaps the first super hero take in which our featured players are aware that they are characters in a comic book. It was produced in response to many, many letters requesting such a story, and it was a real hoot for me to script the yarn."[22] Blurring the line between real and imagined showed readers Marvel's playful nature.

"I was tired of doing monster mags. Joan wanted me to make something of myself in the comic book field. The timing was perfect. The elements were all at hand. Kismet." —Stan Lee on cocreating the *Fantastic Four* (Stephen Wiacek, *The Marvel Book*)

Just shy of Lee's thirty-ninth birthday, *FF #1* appeared on newsstands. Created at a watershed moment in his life, as well as Kirby's, *The Fantastic Four* seemed almost a last-ditch effort, as if their careers really did hang in the balance. After the tumultuous 1950s and public backlash against comic books, many people thought the entire industry might collapse. How many more of these boom-and-bust periods could comic books survive?

Instead of a swan song, Lee found himself inundated with fan mail. As he examined the letters, Stan realized that readers in the twelve- to fifteen-year-old age group dug the team's angst. Fans begged for more, which bolstered Lee's flagging spirits.

Ever the curmudgeon and cautious, Kirby was less enthusiastic, not willing to jump on the emotional rollercoaster he had been on with so many other "hit" comics. He continued to write and draw, always churning out pages at an astonishing clip. Lee, however, viewed the letters and cards as vindication of his idea that if he just created a comic book that he would enjoy as a reader, others would too.

The Fantastic Four did more than set the stage for Lee and Kirby to conceive more superheroes—it helped rejuvenate the entire industry. Lee realized that he could assume a different role: trendsetter rather than follower. He placed his trust in his instincts, his storytelling abilities, and Kirby's phenomenal artistry.

CHAPTER 6

SPIDEY SAVES THE DAY!

A new superhero bursts from the page and seems to swing right into the reader's lap. He is masked: only alien-like curved eyes reveal human features; no mouth or nose is visible. His power is alarming—casually holding a ghoulish-looking criminal under one arm, while simultaneously swinging from a hair-thin cord high above the city streets. In the background, tiny figures stand on rooftops, pointing at the hero in astonishment.

The superhero is off-center, frozen in a moment, as if a panicked photographer caught the action on film. The image captures the speed, almost like flight, with the wind at his back. The hero's deltoid ripples and leg muscles flex. Some mysterious webbing extends from his elbow to waist. Is this a man or creature from another world?

The answer is actually neither. Looking at the bright-yellow dialogue boxes running down the left side of the page, the reader learns the shocking truth. This isn't a grown man, older and hardened, like Batman or Superman, one an existential nightmare and the other a do-gooder alien. No, this hero is just a self-professed "timid teenager" named Peter Parker. The world, he exclaims, mocks the teen under the mask but will "marvel" at his new-found "awesome might."

Spider-Man is born.

The 1962 debut of Spider-Man in *Amazing Fantasy #15* happened because Lee took another calculated risk. He trusted his instincts, honed over decades of working in the chaotic comic book industry, which often seemed to run on trial and error more than logic. On the journey from publishing house to newsstands, sales figures were king. Fickle comic book fans frequently switched interests, leaving editors like Lee scratching their heads, attempting to predict the next fad.

Every decision had a price. A new character meant wasting precious hours writing, penciling, and inking a title that might not sell. In an industry driven by talent and deadlines, there were never enough talented artists and writers to spare on a series that didn't sell. The business side of the industry constantly clashed with the creative aspects, forcing fast scripting and artwork to go hand in hand.

Across two decades as a writer and editor, Lee watched genres spring to life, and then almost as quickly, readers would turn their attention to something different. War stories might give way to romance titles, which would then ride a wave until monster comics became popular, and then those would be superseded by aliens. In an era when a small group of publishers controlled the whole industry, they kept close watch over each other's products in hopes of mimicking sales of hot titles.

Lee called Goodman "one of the great imitators of all time." He dictated what Stan wrote after ferreting out tips and leads during golf matches and long lunches with other publishers. If he heard that Westerns were selling for a competitor, Goodman bellowed: "Stan, come up with some Westerns."[1] Every new fad meant immediately switching to that genre. Versatility had been one of Lee's primary strengths, easily transitioning while writing and plotting many different titles. Lee mastered multiple story lines and plots, using gimmicks and wordplay to remember names and titles, such as recycling gunslinger Rawhide Kid in 1960 and making him into an outlaw or the alliteration in *Millie the Model*.

Goodman gave Stan leeway when sales were strong but exerted pressure when sales dipped. The writer bristled at his boss's belittling beliefs: "He felt comics were really only read by very, very young children or stupid adults," which meant "he didn't want me to use words of more than two syllables if I could help it. . . . Don't play up characterization, don't have too much dialogue, just have a lot of action." Stan had little choice: "It was a job; I had to do what he told me."[2]

Despite being distant relatives and longtime coworkers, the two maintained a cool professional relationship. From Lee's perspective, "Martin was good at what he did and made a lot of money, but he wasn't ambitious. He wanted things to stay the way they were." The publishing industry remained highly competitive, but most of its leaders were not stereotypical cutthroat captains of industry. Lee recalled: "He hired a good friend of his to be his business manager, and they would spend two or three hours a day in Martin's office playing Scrabble."[3]

Riding the success of *The Fantastic Four*, Goodman gave Lee a simple directive: "Come up with some other superheroes."[4] For him, the order made sense: superheroes seemed the next big genre, so he pushed Timely in that direction. Yet *The Fantastic Four* subtly shifted the rapport between editor and publisher. With sales doubling, Goodman didn't focus on comics, enabling Stan to wield greater influence and authority. He used some of the profit to pay freelance writers and editors more money, which then offloaded some of his pressure writing, plotting, editing, and approving the company's limited monthly titles. Launching *Spider-Man*, however, Lee did more than divert the talents and energy of his staff. He actually defied Goodman.

For months, Lee grappled with the idea of a new kind of superhero in the vein of the Fantastic Four with challenges that someone with superpowers would experience living in the modern world. The new character, however, would be "a teenager, with all the problems, hang-ups, and angst of any teenager." Lee liked the name "Spider-Man," envisioning a "hard-luck kid" blessed and cursed by acquiring superhuman strength and the ability to cling to walls, sides of buildings, and even ceilings, just like a real-life spider.[5] The more he considered the character, the more important he thought it would be in defining a new kind of superhero.

Lee recalled going to see Goodman: "I did what I always did in those days, I took the idea to my boss, my friend, my publisher," even embellishing the story of Spider-Man's origin, alleging he got the idea "watching a fly on the wall while I had been typing."[6] He outlined the character: teen, orphan, angst, poor, intelligent, and other traits a typical teen might possess. Lee thought Spider-Man was a no-brainer, but to his surprise, Goodman hated it. He forbade Stan from offering it as a stand-alone comic book.[7]

The publisher, according to Lee, had three major complaints: "people hate spiders, so you can't call a hero 'Spider-Man'"; no teenager could be a hero "but only be a sidekick"; and a hero had to be heroic, not a pimply kid who isn't popular or strong.[8] To Goodman, a hero who isn't a hero or even particularly likable sounded like a "comedy character." Irritated, he asked Lee, "Didn't [he] realize that people hate spiders?"[9] To Stan's chagrin, "Martin just wouldn't let me do the book."[10] Goodman hated everything about Spider-Man. Primarily, he believed featuring a teenager would make Timely (and him personally) a laughingstock among publishing executives (a concern that he worried about incessantly).

Realizing that he could not entirely circumvent Goodman, Stan made the executive decision to at least give Spider-Man a try in a low-risk way. The best case would be to place the character on the cover of a series that had bombed up to that point—*Amazing Fantasy*. The series had featured thriller/fantasy stories by Lee and surreal (macabre, surreal, or Dali-esque) art by Steve Ditko. Lee later added "Adult" to the title, hoping that *Amazing Adult Fantasy* would generate interest. Nothing worked. Facing Goodman's condescension and woeful *AF* sales, it seemed as if there were already two strikes against the teen wonder.

Despite these odds and his boss's directive, Stan couldn't stop thinking about the nerdy superhero: "I couldn't get Spider-Man out of my mind."[11] He worked up a Spider-Man plot and handed it over to Jack Kirby. Lee figured that no one would care (or maybe even notice) a new character in the last issue of a series that would soon be discontinued.

In this fast-paced environment, where Lee served essentially as Marvel's managing editor, writer, copyeditor, and overall creative director, he turned to artists that he trusted because they needed little direction and worked quickly. Often, Lee would dictate a story line and then the artist would take that plot and begin to draw the issue. Later, Lee added dialogue and extra information, allowing time to edit or add in what the artist might have overlooked.

With Spider-Man, however, Kirby missed the mark in Stan's eyes. His early sketches turned the teen bookworm into a mini-Superman with all-American good looks, like a budding astronaut or football star. With little time to pause and think about what was essentially a throwaway character, Kirby turned to other projects. Lee put Ditko on the title. He was familiar with the *Amazing Fantasy* style and more suited for drawing an offbeat hero.

Ditko nailed Spider-Man, but Stan wavered on the cover, commissioning Kirby for the task, with Ditko inking. Despite Kirby's last-minute substitution, Lee loved Ditko's version: "Steve did a totally brilliant job of bringing

Jack Kirby's iconic cover for *Amazing Fantasy #15* (August 1962). © 1939–2022 Marvel Characters, Inc.

my new little arachnid hero to life." They finished the two-part story and ran it as the lead in *AF #15*. Revealing both the busy, all-hands state of the company and their low expectations, Lee recalled, "Then, we more or less forgot about him."[12] As happy as Lee and Ditko were with the outcome, they could never have imagined that they were about to spin the comic book world (and popular culture) onto a different axis.

Lee's distinct style established the voice for Spider-Man comic books and the company as a whole. Breaking down the barrier between writer and reader (commonly referred to as "the fourth wall") on the first page of the initial Spider-Man *AF* debut reveals how Lee established a friendly, homespun voice that also gently guided the reader on the hero's journey. This second-person method stood in blunt contrast to the more formal, distant language of other superheroes, primarily the competitors at DC—Superman, Batman, and Wonder Woman.

From the start, Lee lets us in on a secret, explaining that "confidentially" people in the business call superheroes "long underwear characters" and say they are "a dime a dozen." Yet the reader is also informed that this new character is "just a bit . . . different!" At about one hundred words into the story, then, Lee has already formed a relationship with the reader and created the context for Spider-Man as something new. The tongue-in-cheek tone emphasizes how "different" this hero will be in a deliberately easygoing style.

On page 2, Lee shows how adults generally like Parker, including his surrogate parents, Aunt May and Uncle Ben, and his teachers, who are "fond" of the "clean-cut, hard-working honor student!" Yet, as quickly as the reader realizes that Parker is a good guy, Lee shows that his classmates alienate him, particularly in contrast to school stud Flash Thompson. Parker asks a girl out and she refuses, turning instead to "dreamboat" Thompson. As the popular gang speeds off in a red convertible, they laugh at him for suggesting that they go to a science exhibit. "You stick to science, son. We'll take the chicks," one of his classmates sneers. In the next frame, Parker is crying as he enters the science lab, declaring, "Someday they'll be sorry!—Sorry that they laughed at me!"

The elegance in juxtaposing Parker as a regular guy versus the popular crowd makes the teen sympathetic. Most readers can instantly relate because every school has a Flash Thompson who basks in attention and seems especially gleeful in pushing aside the smaller, frail Parker. Again, Lee addresses the reader directly, saying: "Yes, for some, being a teenager has many heartbreaking moments." The writer establishes that Parker has feelings and that it hurts being an outcast.

"A—a spider! It bit me! But why is it burning so? Why is it GLOWING that way??"
—Peter Parker, *Amazing Fantasy #15*

Rather than simply hinging the story on Parker as outsider, Lee exposes his full range of emotions, while the story grows darker and more foreboding. Once the atomic-powered spider bites the teen, he stumbles into his newfound power blindly, later entering a professional wrestling contest to test his strength and make quick money. Parker's lack of confidence causes him to put on a mask to avert the possibility of being a "laughingstock," but he challenges the muscled bruiser Crusher Hogan anyway, who calls the boy "a little masked marvel." Lee's wordplay, using "marvel" here and on the cover, subconsciously creates an association between the character and the future company name, which the writer/editor had already been contemplating.

Almost immediately adults search for a way to exploit the teen's powers. A "TV producer" promises the masked Parker a "fortune" via an appearance on the era's immensely popular *Ed Sullivan Show*. Under the tutelage of the TV man/agent, Spider-Man becomes a sensation, breathing what is described as the "first sweet scent of fame and success." The celebrity goes to the youth's head, though, and when he has the chance to stop a thief that a policeman is chasing, he does nothing, despite his massive powers. Parker, as Lee demonstrates, has strength but not yet the wisdom to transform into a real hero.

Later, when the now-familiar story of Uncle Ben's death unfolds, Parker loses his cool, becomes Spider-Man, and hunts the fugitive. In the only frame in the entire comic that shows his pupils through the mask, Spider-Man realizes that the thief is the same villain he could have stopped earlier. He does not kill the criminal, instead dangling him from a web and lowering him to the police below. However, Lee depicts the anguish the teen suffers and his acceptance of the burden of his actions. In the final frame, Lee wrote the famous line that sums up Spider-Man: "Aware at last that in this world, with great power there must also come—great responsibility!"

> "Aware at last that in this world, with great power there must also come—great responsibility!"—*Amazing Fantasy #15*

Finally able to apply his innovative ideas about voice and style, Lee captured the reader's attention by formulating a hero that had genuinely human traits. Peter Parker, a wallflower kid picked on by his peers for being different, actually grew out of Lee's own feelings of being bullied. "Because I was the youngest and the thinnest, I was never the captain or leader and I was always the one getting pushed around." So, when searching for Parker's voice, Lee explained, "I figured, kids would relate to a concept like that. After all, most kids have had similar experiences. Turns out I was right."[13] Lee put the *AF* issue to bed and scurried off onto the next title that demanded his attention.

The hectic pace did not allow anyone to hesitate, let alone stop to contemplate reader reaction, which may account for why "Spider-Man" is listed in *AF #15* both spelled correctly and as "Spiderman" and "the Spiderman." Lee and his small crew of artists were already off onto new titles, working against constant deadlines. In the early 1960s, it took months before final sales were determined. As a result, publishers nervously waited to find out circulation figures, good or bad.

The only gauge Marvel, DC, and other publishing houses could rely on is the number of letters from fans, an anecdotal frame of reference that might mean they had struck gold. Although Lee turned his attention to other titles, he realized that Spider-Man had found an audience when letters from readers poured into the office, just as they had a year earlier when Fantastic Four debuted. Lee recalled getting about one hundred fan letters a day and sometimes more, which he or his staff dutifully read and answered.

The fateful day sales figures arrived, Goodman stormed into Lee's office, as always awash in art boards, drawings, mockups, yellow legal pads, and memos littering the desk.

Goodman beamed: "Stan, remember that Spider-Man idea of yours that I liked so much? Why don't we turn it into a series?"[14] Rather than scold his right-hand man, Goodman claimed his affection for Spider-Man, telling Lee how much he loved the boy hero.

If that wasn't enough to knock Lee off-kilter, then came the real doozy: Spider-Man not only appeared a hit; the issue in fact was the fastest-selling comic book of the year and indeed the decade. *Amazing Fantasy*, perpetually at the bottom of the sales charts, skyrocketed to number one with issue #15.[15] Although it had been months since Lee and Ditko created Spider-Man, the overwhelming popularity meant that they now could turn the character into a series.

The success of *Amazing Fantasy #15* elevated Lee and Ditko's standing. The new character would soon become the lynchpin of Marvel's superhero-based lineup. More importantly, the combination of the Fantastic Four and Spider-Man transformed Marvel from a company imitating trends to a hot commodity, both hip and relevant.

Because of the long lag between obtaining sales figures and the length of the printing and distribution system, the new Spidey comic debuted six months later. To make way for the new title, Lee had to drop one, since the distribution agreement with Independent News only allowed Marvel to carry eight total titles. A little less than a year after its debut, *The Incredible Hulk* ceased publication due to limited sales. In March 1963, *The Amazing Spider-Man #1* burst onto newsstands.

When *The Amazing Spider-Man* arrived, fans could not believe their eyes. The teen superhero seemed suspended in midair and encased in clear tubing, captured by none other than the Fantastic Four. The Human Torch blazes up to eye level as if checking on the captured hero, while on the ground the Thing shakes his powerful fists, eager for a fight.

Stan with artists Steve Ditko and Jack Kirby. Illustration by Jason Piperberg.

The appearance of Marvel's other breakout heroes—the Fantastic Four—in Spider-Man's debut reveals how Lee hedged his bets and hoped to boost sales by bringing the two hot commodities together in one book. This idea seemed to carry over from the final issue of *Amazing Fantasy*, when Lee told readers to look forward to the next issue, even though the comic book faced cancellation. Sales figures revealed how popular Spider-Man promised to be, but using the Fantastic Four as reinforcement made good business sense and spurred a new creative form along the way.

For the cover image of *The Amazing Spider-Man*, Lee once again turned to veteran Kirby, which worked well, particularly since he was the artist and cocreator of the Fantastic Four. The difference between Kirby's cover and Ditko's work on the rest of the issue is immediately noticeable on the splash page. Here, Spidey seems slightly less muscular and more spider-like. A crowd led by publisher J. Johan Jameson calls out: "Freak! Public Menace!" as the hero retreats to a web, gripping a tendril for balance. Lee's callout to the audience is full of hype and hyperbole: "There's never been a story like this one—because there's never been a hero like—Spider-Man!"

The first *AS* issue carried two separate stories, which was not uncommon in the era's comics. The pieces were connected but had different purposes. The first focused on recounting the hero's origin story, a much-needed rehashing for fans that might have missed the *Amazing Fantasy* issue. The second half brought Spider-Man face-to-face with the Fantastic Four and introduced the first stand-alone villain that the teen hero would face.

The first Spider-Man story emphasizes the plight Parker and Aunt May face with no money, forcing Peter to support them. His efforts are thwarted, though, when his manager writes him a check for his "town hall" show and the bank won't cash it. Then Jameson publishes a headline labeling the hero a "menace" and lectures around town, declaring, "Spider-Man must be outlawed! There is no place for such a dangerous creature in our fair city." The newspaperman counters that his son, test pilot John Jameson, is a real hero.

When the mission goes awry, Spider-Man springs to action, even though the pilot's father is the source of his inability to make money. When the older man calls Spidey out for being a "publicity-seeking phony . . . trying to grab a headline!" the hero responds in Lee's smart-alecky style, saying, "Instead of flapping your lips, mister—just watch and see what I can do!" Within minutes, Spider-Man is hanging onto the shooting missile and replaces a control unit that enables Jameson to land safely.

Rather than celebrate, the newspaper editor resumes his fight, claiming the difficulties were a "plot by Spider-Man to steal the spotlight . . . sabotaging the capsule." Later, Parker is shown listening to a crowd of workers demanding that the hero be "run out of the country" and reported to the FBI. Even Aunt May turns against Spider-Man. The episode ends with Parker nervously wondering if becoming "a menace" is the "only course left for me."

In the second story, Parker decides that he will show off his powers to the Fantastic Four, which will lead to them inviting him to join. Showing off, he breaks into the Baxter Building. When the supergroup picks up his arrival by camera, Johnny Storm quips, "Why didn't he phone for an appointment, like anyone else?" Thing answers: "Cause he's a teen-age cornball show-off, just like the Torch."

Later, the group squares off with the teen, trying to contain him, but battling to a draw. Spider-Man announces his plan, exclaiming, "I'm worth your top salary." Sue Storm tells him, "We're a non-profit organization," while Reed Richards explains, "We pay no salaries or bonuses! Any profits we make goes into scientific research!" Johnny, like Parker a sarcastic teen, says, "You came to the wrong place, pal! This isn't General Motors!" Lee's ear for teen-specific dialogue captures the cadence and sarcasm of the era.

Meanwhile, Spider-Man is about to face his first supervillain—the Chameleon—a highly intelligent criminal who can disguise himself as anyone, even the teen hero. Chameleon orchestrates a plan to frame Spider-Man by stealing secret missile defense plans. The real Spidey escapes from the police and slingshots himself across New York to catch the villain's helicopter. He speeds out in a motorboat to a waiting Soviet submarine, uses his webbing to keep its hatch from opening, and then takes control of the helicopter.

Chameleon then uses a number of tricks to escape momentarily, including impersonating a policeman and forcing the real police to grab Spider-Man. The police realize the ruse, but the hero scampers up a wall "in a fit of white-hot fury" and vows to let the officers catch the criminal rather than help. As Spider-Man flees the scene, he tears up, thinking, "Nothing turns out right. I wish I had never gotten my super powers!" The Fantastic Four members wonder if Spider-Man will eventually turn evil. The ten-page story ends with Lee's narrative: "And the whole world will have to wonder—until our next great issue! Don't miss it!!"

Over the course of the next year, Lee and Ditko introduced almost every one of Spider-Man's significant supervillains, from Vulture and Electro to the Lizard and Doctor Octopus. While battling these criminals provided the comic book with the requisite action, it was the large supporting cast around Peter Parker that propelled the stories. Peter's interactions with Aunt May, Jameson, and a series of love interests made the youth seem more convincing as a teen who stumbled into his role as a superhero.

As a comic book author, Lee used Spider-Man to introduce several innovations that separated him from other writers. Besides narratives directed at the audience, Lee also pulled the reader deeper into the story via thought balloons. As Lee explains, they "let our readers know what a character was thinking as often as possible . . . and add a whole additional dimension to the story."[16] These advances in style and voice shouted at the reader to pay attention, while simultaneously making them aware that a *person* existed within the pages. Lee's easygoing manner let you know that he was a friend and equally excited about what you were reading.

Another Lee and Ditko novelty centered on using New York City as Spider-Man's stomping grounds, having the youth living in a cramped apartment in Queens with his surrogate parents. Lee and Kirby had done the same with the Fantastic Four, plopping them down in Manhattan, but while they jetted around the globe and universe, Spider-Man stayed central to the city, bringing it alive on the pages. For readers familiar with New York, the stories seemed more real at the mention of Manhattan or the Brooklyn Bridge, while others could imagine Spidey swinging through the steel and concrete canyons created by the massive skyscrapers. "Instead of living in a fictitious Gotham City or Metropolis," Lee explained (taking a swipe at his DC Comics competitors), "[Spider-Man] has his digs in good ol' New York City and . . . might be found running after a taxi anywhere from Greenwich Village to the Upper East Side."[17]

Placing all his heroes in and around the Big Apple enabled Lee to accurately depict the setting and gave him another innovation—having superheroes casually (or not so coolly) run into one another. Beginning with *AS #1*, the "guest-starring" notion kept readers thrilled at the idea that Spider-Man could engage with (and potentially battle) the Fantastic Four, the Hulk, or other characters.

The webslinger's growing popularity also enabled Lee to use him to introduce new characters or spruce up existing ones. For example, Spider-Man appeared in *Strange Tales Annual #2* (September 1963), a seventy-two-page crossover with Human Torch. As Marvel continued to move from odd, macabre stories to superheroes, Spidey guest-starred in an issue focused on Giant-Man and Wasp. *The Amazing Spider-Man Annual #1* appeared in 1964, with Lee dubbing himself and Ditko "the most talked about team in comics today!" The comic took the crossover idea to the max, with appearances by every Marvel hero, including Thor, Dr. Strange, Captain America, and the X-Men.

Spider-Man now stood at the center of a comic book empire. Stan could not have written (or planned) a better outcome.

All this from a risky run in a dying comic book!

CHAPTER 7

CREATING THE MARVEL UNIVERSE

"A monster!" Martin Goodman turned on his heels, shaking his head. Following the success of *The Fantastic Four*, the publisher wanted Stan and Jack to create another superhero team. When Lee told him that he had a different idea, a solo book centered on what he described as an "offbeat" monster, Goodman sighed and walked away. Lee watched his boss leave the room, imagining the powerful behemoth that he and Kirby had been kicking around. "I had been wracking my brain for days, looking for a different superhero type, something never seen before," Lee said.[1] The new character had to have superstrength but not mirror the Thing or DC's Superman.

Stan considered different classic stories and narratives. Like other great artists of that era, whether Bob Dylan transforming traditional folk songs into protest anthems or John Updike turning the Peter Rabbit story into a 1960s existential everyman named Rabbit Angstrom, Lee turned to classics. The result would be an almost invincible monster as antihero.

Stan and Kirby cocreated the Hulk out of traces of Mary Shelley's *Frankenstein* and Robert Louis Stevenson's *Dr. Jekyll and Mr. Hyde*. Then, to add drama, Lee contextualized the origin story with heavy doses of Cold War anxiety. As the world contemplated nuclear annihilation, Lee made weapon testing the cataclysmic event that turns a brilliant young scientist into a rampaging behemoth. Introducing the Incredible Hulk, a brooding, somewhat terrifying monster and convoluted antihero to the Marvel family, Lee and Kirby took another intellectual leap forward, deducing that fans would gravitate to the giant's failures and frailties, just as they had with the Fantastic Four.

The ongoing success of *The Fantastic Four*—measured by mountains of fan mail, critical acclaim, and later sales data that confirmed the heady circulation numbers—and the quick introduction of Hulk, Thor, and Iron Man, along with other heroes, set off a two-year run that changed the way people looked at comic books. After toiling in comic books for decades, Lee and Kirby became celebrities. Stan gave them monikers that readers would soon adopt: Jack "King" Kirby and Stan "the Man" Lee.

As a creative duo, Lee and Kirby caught a star as it shot skyward, able to bring dazzling characters to life and create stories drawn from the real world. These heroes were different—they spoke differently, inhabited a world that seemed authentic and right outside the window, all the while turning on fantastic plots and strong visuals. Stan and his artist cocreators churned out a succession of superheroes that captured the attention of rapt fans and turned others into first-time readers. After decades, Lee now headed the hottest comic book publisher in the business. His voice brought superheroes to life for eager readers.

> "We refer to Jack . . . calling him Jack 'King' Kirby, but actually I mean it. I think that this guy is absolutely . . . in this particular field, he's the master." —Stan Lee on artist and cocreator Jack Kirby (Danny Fingeroth and Roy Thomas, eds., *The Stan Lee Universe*)

Many of the letters from fans, Lee recalled, screamed for "more innovative characters." When he sat down and stared at a blank piece of paper in his typewriter, he considered these missives. He drew on what he considered the craziest idea possible. "Think of the challenge it would be to make a hero out of a monster," he prompted himself. "We would have a protagonist with superhuman strength, but he wouldn't be all-wise, all-noble, all-infallible."[2] That monster would have elements of Frankenstein's creation but turn the idea on its ear by making the townspeople chasing him the real monsters, while the monster would turn heroic, though always misunderstood.

Readers picking up *The Incredible Hulk #1* could get a sense of the character on the splash page. Kirby drew massive, tree-trunk arms but also faraway, almost pleading eyes, capturing the Hulk's pathos and internal strife. A few pages later, when brilliant but meek scientist Bruce Banner endures gamma bomb rays and transforms into Hulk for the first time, the monster bats young Rick Jones away, demanding, "Get out of my way, insect!" Via Kirby's masterful artwork, Hulk (initially with gray skin) seems to burst from the page, charging at the reader. "Lee had come up with the perfect vehicle for exploring the notion of what it would be like to possess super powers in the real world," one comic book historian explained. "Kirby's chunky, monster style art" gave the hero/monster energy, adding to the existential angst and inner id that Hulk represented.[3]

This single panel embodies the character, as well as the achievement of its creators. The reader almost feels like they are inside the art, feeling Jones's feet lift off the ground. In terms of capturing the giant's bewilderment, Lee decided to use the word "insect," which provides immediate insight into the Hulk's strength and feelings about "normal" human beings. He shreds the wall of the military base to escape, then demolishes a jeep that runs into him. "Have to go! Have to get away . . . to hide," Hulk murmurs as he "storms off, into the waiting night."

Just six months after the debut of *The Fantastic Four*, *The Incredible Hulk* shot out of the gate in May 1962 but later struggled. Readers lost interest, perhaps giving credence to Goodman's criticisms. Lee couldn't provide the comic with room to grow because the egregious distribution contract limited the number of titles Marvel could ship. Once Spider-Man's popularity was cemented, he had to cancel the Hulk to make room for the first issue of *The Amazing Spider-Man* in March 1963, less than a year after the rampaging hero's debut.

The failure of the Hulk book also highlighted the incredible pressure on Lee. Goodman reviewed the sales figures, always urging his editor to cancel titles that performed poorly. In only six issues, Lee had made wholesale changes to Hulk: he transformed at nightfall, then later when angry; next, he kept modifying the character's intelligence, sometimes making Hulk imbecilic and other times having him keep Banner's supergenius capabilities. The strangest Hulk occurred in the final issue when Hulk transformed but kept Banner's human-sized head. This version had to don a Hulk mask to keep his identity secret. When he faces off against Metal Master, he exclaims: "Don't look so surprised, peanut! Everyone on earth isn't a puny weakling!" Clearly, the rails were off, and Lee took the revisions into absurdity.

Stan used creative methods to get characters back in print, though, especially when fans demanded more (the case with the Hulk). In October 1964, Lee featured the green goliath in *Tales to Astonish #60*, one book featuring two separate superheroes: a renewed Hulk and Giant-Man. Since early comics were anthologies containing several different stories, like the ones Lee worked on early in his career with Simon and Kirby, he kept that idea going with team-up books.

Hulk starred in *Tales to Astonish* and other titles, including *Spider-Man* and *Avengers*. When Marvel's popularity surged, the new *The Incredible Hulk #102* took over for *Tales* in March 1968. It had taken years, but one of Marvel's premier superheroes would carry on the existential mantle, growing more popular as he appeared across varying media, including animated television and licensed goods, such as lunchboxes, T-shirts, and action figures.

Realistic superheroes were Marvel's strength, but dating back to the late 1930s and Superman's tremendous impact, the industry revolved on near-invincible characters that possessed unimaginable powers. Lee understood that he needed a superhero "bigger, better, stronger" than his current creations. After dozens of failed attempts, from outlandish concepts like "Super-God" to mountains of discarded doodles and sketches in his loopy, left-handed scrawl, Lee figured, "since we were the legend makers of today, we'd simply take what had gone before, build on it, embellish it, and come up with our own version." Instead of "God," Lee focused on Norse mythology to create a "god" with a small "g" that would unfold the "continuing saga of good versus evil—god-wise," just the kinds of stories that human beings had been telling for centuries.[4]

The Norse god that Lee and Kirby birthed would be named Thor and powered by the magical Uru hammer. The hero debuted in *Journey into Mystery #83* (August 1962), replacing *The Fantastic Four* in its former slot as a bimonthly when the superhero team became a monthly. Goodman's distribution deal still hampered the company, limiting Marvel to eight monthly titles. As a result, Thor and other new creations debuted in existing anthology books rather than solo efforts. The upside was that Lee could develop a new superhero slowly and gauge fan interest prior to committing full-time resources.

Given the publication schedule, Lee had to alternate between teen and Western titles and superheroes. He searched for other writers to fill in the gaps. For Thor, he gave scripting duties to his younger brother, Larry Lieber (who kept the family name). "Stan would give me a plot, usually typed," he explained. "Then he'd say, 'Now, go home and write me a script.'" Initially, Lieber worried about his ability to write because he "thought like an artist," yet Stan, he claimed, "did teach me" to write, providing him with insight about how to make stories positive and exciting using strong language. "Everything he said was much better than what I wrote," Lieber claimed. "I learned a lot from him."[5]

Teaming his younger brother with Kirby as penciler worked well. Lee and Kirby discussed plot points, and Jack expanded them because he was particularly proficient in the kind of mythic tales Thor necessitated. Soon, though, Lee took over the writing completely, in part because he liked the character and wanted Lieber to take on more Western titles, which remained extremely popular, even in the superhero age.

Writing *Thor* enabled Lee to draw from his study of Shakespeare, which he had read as a kid. Other sources, like Edgar Allan Poe and the swashbuckling works of Alexandre Dumas, allowed Stan to try different dramatic voices, giving the Norse god added depth. From a lifetime of watching movies, he understood the significance of rhythm and pacing, applying it to his superhero style. He also looked to Arthur Conan Doyle's Sherlock Holmes, deciding that he epitomized the ultimate superhero because "a superhero should be believable. There was never a more believable character than Sherlock."[6] Many of Lee's creations were implausible, but their torment and anxiety appealed to growing numbers of high school and college readers.

When Lee told Goodman about his desire to create a superhero who was also a handsome tycoon and weapons manufacturer modeled after Howard Hughes, Goodman said flatly: "You're crazy."[7] Insane—or crazy like a fox—Lee figured that Goodman hadn't said no, so he cocreated Tony Stark/ Iron Man with artist Don Heck.

With the Cuban missile crisis still fresh in people's minds, as well as President Dwight Eisenhower's harsh words about the growth of the military-industrial complex in his farewell address, Lee thought Stark should be the antithesis of other superheroes: wealthy, suave, handsome, without a care in the world, but also a weapons dealer. For Iron Man, Lee drew on technology but also placed the hero's origin story in a then little-known nation on the other side of the world—Vietnam—long before anyone in America really knew about the country. Iron Man first appeared in *Tales of Suspense #39* (March 1963).

Iron Man peers out from the cover in gunmetal gray, looking stiff, more robotic than human, and with few distinguishable facial features—slits for eyes and a mouth slot. Littered with Lee's excitable tone, the reader is asked to speculate about "the newest, most breath-taking, most sensational super hero of all" but also told that the character comes from the same "talented bull-pen" where the other famous Marvel superheroes "were born." In early 1963, trust was already a defining matter for Marvel readers. Lee asks them to have faith in the new hero (and essentially Lee's role as leader of this flock).

Stark is a scientist but also a "glamorous playboy, constantly in the company of beautiful, adoring women." Much of the plot (created by Lee but written out by Lieber) is told in flashback, tracing Stark's transition from Hughes-like industrial leader to armored superhero. A booby trap in the jungle leads to Stark's capture by the enemy. Later, at the "guerrilla chief's headquarters," the reader learns that Stark is alive but expected to die because shrapnel is lodged near his heart. The guerrilla leader Wong-Chu determines that he will trick the American inventor into creating bombs until the moment he dies from the steel moving closer to his heart.

Realizing that his time is limited, Stark declares: "This I promise you. . . . I shall build the most fantastic weapon of all time!" Then he begins crafting a suit designed to keep him alive and defeat Wong-Chu's forces. With the help of Professor Yinsen, a renowned physics professor imprisoned for not helping build weaponry, Stark creates the Iron Man suit using his powerful transistor design. Yinsen fits the suit on the American just in time, stirring Stark back to life just as the guerrilla's forces kill Yinsen. Iron Man declares that he will avenge the professor and flies into the shadows to hide until he can concoct a plan.

Iron Man's debut in *Tales of Suspense #39* (March 1963). © 1939–2022 Marvel Characters, Inc.

Confronting Wong-Chu, the superhero tosses him aside, then uses a transistor to reverse the trajectory of bullets, scattering his forces. After using his "electrical power" to get a heavy cabinet off himself, Iron Man shoots a stream of oil at an ammo dump the leader is trying to reach. He then lights the oil on fire, blowing up the villain. Iron Man frees the other prisoners and walks away, covering himself in a long brown jacket and fedora. The superhero ponders his new fate as Iron Man, asking, "Who knows what destiny awaits him? Time alone will provide the answer! Time alone . . ."

The partnership between Heck and Lee in bringing Iron Man to life centered on Heck learning and adapting to Lee's new storytelling mode, which seemed foreign for many artists who had worked at other publishers. As a matter of fact, when Heck first got a story synopsis from Lee, he balked at the process. Later, though, he grew to enjoy the creative freedom and trust that developed. "Stan would call me up and he'd give me the first couple of pages over the phone, and the last page," Heck remembers. "I'd say, 'What about the stuff in between?' and he'd say, 'Fill it in.'"[8] While some artists found it difficult to adjust, Heck and many others flourished. The Marvel Method is similar to the way many television and Hollywood scriptwriters work: many smart minds tackle a script after the central idea has been established. The process adds depth and nuance, even if the initial idea is birthed by one person on the team.

The character Steve Ditko and Lee created as a companion piece to the Human Torch grew out of Stan's childhood listening to a radio program called *Chandu, the Magician*. Lee and Ditko's version became Dr. Strange, capitalizing on Ditko's psychedelic imagery and magical vision of the enchanted world. The story centered on Stephen Strange, an arrogant surgeon who suffers a debilitating injury to his hands, rendering him unable to operate. After hitting skid row, he journeys to visit the "Ancient One," a mystical healer. After studying with the wizard, Strange becomes a supreme sorcerer, returning to set up shop on Bleecker Street in Greenwich Village. Unknown to the world at large, which sees him as a fraud, Dr. Strange battles the dark arts invisible to the naked eye, thus protecting people from evil they cannot see.

Since Dr. Strange is essentially a magician, Lee's dialogue rose to an elevated tone, not in a corny way that people expected from carnival barkers, like "hocus pocus," cartoony kind of stuff. Instead, Lee reveled in the character and the new words Dr. Strange demanded. "I can lose myself completely while putting them together, trying to string them on a delicate strand of rhythm so they have a melody all their own," he explained. "When it came to Dr. Strange I was in seventh heaven. . . . I had the chance to make up a whole language of incantations."[9] Reading the comic, one can immediately hear Lee's cadence and voice in their ear. He gave Strange interesting speech traits and catchphrases, like his frequent "by the hoary hosts of Hoggoth," always alliterative and beguiling.

It did not take long for older teens and college students to catch onto Lee's words and Ditko's groovy artwork. Many dissected Dr. Strange's odd cadence and tried to assess the literary origins. Lee barely had the heart to tell them that he made most of it up. If it were derivative, the phrases and symbols came from reading science fiction as a kid. When Ditko abruptly left Marvel, Lee continued writing the series with artists Bill Everett, Dan Adkins, and Marie Severin. The mystical sorcerer attained an important place in the Marvel universe. Dr. Strange took on villains that embodied evil itself, such as the dreaded Dormammu and the Living Tribunal. By occupying this dark realm, a case could be made that Stephen Strange became Marvel's most powerful superhero.

The Fantastic Four surprised everyone when it became a hit, so Goodman never let go of his idea that Lee should come up with another superhero team. The publisher reworked the company's distribution deal to publish additional titles each month to capitalize on Marvel's popularity, even though rival DC owned the distributor. No one thought that Goodman and Lee would actually catch up to the market leader, so the thinking was that merely allowing a few extra titles a month would just make both sides more money.

Lee gathered information from fan mail asking for teams of Marvel's heroes. He determined the group would consist of its most powerful characters. Since Kirby drew so many of the heroes in their other comics, Lee tapped him for *The Avengers*, composed of Thor, Ant-Man, Hulk, Wasp, and Iron

Man. Finally, Lee had the roster of superheroes that could form a potent counterpoint to DC's group.

Stan and Jack gave the Avengers an aura of superiority, as if this super-group were the best-of-the-best in the Marvel universe, yet they also added the realistic characteristics that had pushed sales skyward for other titles. Similar to the Fantastic Four, the members of the Avengers wouldn't always get along or agree. They too resided in New York City, in a building donated by Tony Stark. Lee called these points the "fashioning of a world for the characters to live in" and a "mood of realism to be created so that the reader feels he knows the characters, understands their problems, and cares about them."[10]

The action jumped off the cover in *Avengers #1* (September 1963)—Thor's swinging hammer, Ant-Man and Wasp swooping in, and Hulk and Iron Man prepping for a battle. The reader only sees Loki, the "god of evil," in a glimpse from behind, as if a camera has taken a snapshot over his right shoulder. The perspective makes it seem that you are there viewing the confrontation firsthand. Although Kirby's Thor and Hulk look like cousins (based on the way Jack drew character faces), the cover's layout provides a brilliant introduction to the new superhero team.

Inside, Loki unleashes a sinister plan to draw out his brother Thor using the Hulk as bait. All the heroes respond to a distress call from Rick Jones's Teen-Brigade after the guest-starring Fantastic Four can't help because they are off on a separate mission. Eventually, the heroes find Hulk, who has disguised himself as Mechano, a superstrong robot performing in a travel-ing circus (the monster is in an odd brown jumpsuit, orange shoes, and has white makeup around his mouth). Thinking that Hulk derailed a passenger train, they attempt to stop him.

Meanwhile, Thor returns to Asgard to confront Loki. After fighting his brother and then thwarting a series of traps, Thor returns Loki to Earth, revealing the plot to the other superheroes. When the god of evil turns radio-active, it seems he will fight Thor again, but Ant-Man and Wasp trap him in a lead-lined container designed for trucks to "carry radioactive wastes from atomic tests [and] dump their loads for eventual disposal in the ocean." After stopping Thor's evil brother, the group decides to band together, convincing the Hulk to join. Lee's final panel announces "one of the greatest super-hero teams of all time! Powerful! Unpredictable! . . . A new dimension is added to the Marvel galaxy of stars!"

The second issue of *The Avengers* begins with Thor criticizing the Hulk, who then threatens him. Here Lee places the supergroup directly within the realistic confines of his other characters. Thor and Hulk itch to fight one another, forcing Iron Man into the mediator role. Wasp pines for Thor, whom she calls "adorable" and "handsome." Their foe, the Space Phantom, can assume the identity of others, so he appears as the Hulk, starting a fight inside Stark's mansion. Hulk gets away and is later confronted by his teen sidekick Rick Jones, who mistakenly tells him that he can turn back to "Doctor Don Blake when you want to!" (a Lee slip-up that demonstrates the fast pace of comic book production since Blake is Thor's secret identity). Summoning the Norse god, the Avengers defeat the Space Phantom but, in the melee with Hulk, reveal their suspicions of the green goliath. As a result, he quits the Avengers and leaps off into the future.

Only two issues into the series and Lee has transformed the team (also adding Giant-Man) and presented Hulk as a nearly indestructible force. Over the next several issues, the group will battle Hulk when he teams up with Sub-Mariner. Later, the Avengers find Captain America and bring him into the fold. In a callout box, Lee trumpeted the return of the red, white, and blue supersoldier, telling the reader that Kirby had drawn the original and that his first story was a Cap tale: "Thus, the chronicle of comicdom turns full circle, reaching a new pinnacle of greatness!" Lee also urged fans to "save this issue," more or less pushing the notion that comic books could be collector items, explaining, "We feel you will treasure it in time to come!"

The Lee/Kirby creative team set 1963 ablaze with quirky superheroes that seemed like real people who happened to stumble into tremendous powers and then had to deal with the ramifications. Fearing that readers might get tired of accidental heroes, they reworked the formula, creating a new team made up of individuals born with "unique abilities." This team, Lee recalled, would be "mutants . . . an aberration of nature." Together, he and Kirby created two groups—one good and one evil—which Lee thought had "an air of freshness and surprise."[11] He stumbled on the word "extra," as in the extra powers the characters possess, after Goodman shot down his original title, "The Mutants," for being above the heads of young readers. The publisher agreed to "X-Men" (as if that made more sense), so Kirby and Lee sat down to brainstorm, plot, and plan.

The world that Lee and Kirby created centered on the idea that human beings continued to evolve and some people were born with special powers that came to light at puberty. They reasoned that teenagers with amazing powers would delight young readers. Such mutants, like Cyclops, who shot laser beams from his eyes, and Jean Grey, who had telekinetic powers that enabled her to move objects at will, attended Professor Charles Xavier's School for Gifted Youngsters. There they learned to harness their abilities and then utilize them for good.

The *X-Men* series enabled Lee to delve into the alienated feelings that many teens experienced, while also providing the group with kinship via their relationship with Professor Xavier, a father figure for them. The school turned into an extended family for the youngsters, many of whom had faced discrimination for having abilities that "regular" humans could not comprehend. But their powers were a blessing and a curse. Only the wise counsel of Professor X and their experiences battling evil as a team could provide them with a semblance of normality, which always seemed fleeting.

Running from 1963 to 1970, *X-Men* never really generated strong sales, despite Lee's high hopes. He and Kirby faced tremendous pressure to work on the comics that sold well, so when Jack asked for a replacement, Lee granted his request. Later, Stan moved off the book to concentrate on better-selling titles.

Once the superhero business took off, Lee created an internal system that centralized his control over the creative side of the comic books division. Some of these work responsibilities were the continuation of what he had been doing in art, editorial direction, and general management, but other aspects grew out of necessity, since Marvel as a publisher grew and transformed as it became more popular. Stan may not have been trained to be a manager or talent scout, but his years in the business honed these skills.

Lee's unique ability with dialogue mirrored the voice and style of early 1960s popular culture and brought that voice into comics. As a result, Marvel readers get some of the humor and satire that actor Peter Sellers brought to

The Pink Panther (1963) and *Dr. Strangelove* (1964) and also full-throttle heroic characters, like Ian Fleming's James Bond, whose action-packed films like *Goldfinger* (1964) encompassed a mix of sophistication, violence, and superhero-like deeds by the British secret agent. Lee found a groove with realistic superheroes that balanced great power with existential angst. He explained: "We try to write them well, we try to draw them well; we try to make them as sophisticated as a comic book can be. . . . The whole philosophy behind it is to treat them as fairy tales for grown ups and do the kind of stories that we ourselves would want to read."[12]

As editor/art director, Lee guided Marvel's voice and style by employing trusted artists and writers. Stan deliberately indoctrinated them into Marvel's distinctive process. For example, he recognized the beauty in the artwork of George Tuska, a stylist who some insiders felt had the most unique ability in all of comics. Tuska soon became one of Stan's favorites. According to *Daredevil* artist Gene Colan, "Stan always would hold [Tuska's] work up as the criteria of how he wanted the other artists to draw." Lee's management style enabled Marvel to be distinctive yet also gave his artists a template that emphasized the work he demanded.[13]

In a business frequently cold and ruthless, Lee cultivated talent. On one hand, he had to, since Marvel lagged behind DC. He needed talented freelancers to implement his vision of comics that readers would hold to a higher standard. Early in his career, for example, Colan could not land a position at DC. Yet Lee was different, Colan remembered: "Stan could see something in my work that no one else could see. . . . That's what really got me started, Stan's faith in my ability. Although it wasn't completely there at the time, I was too young and had a lot to learn."[14]

Lee needed artists to work fast. Colan remembered Lee giving the artists "unprecedented freedom," which made them happier. "I'd talk with Stan about a plot over the phone, and I'd tape record his whole idea—it'd just be a few sentences." Lee would say: "This is what I want in the beginning, the middle, and what I want in the end. . . . The rest is up to you." For Colan and other trusted artists, this was an exciting precedent. "I had all the characters work for me, what they looked like was up to me—except those that were already established. But whatever I did, I could do."[15]

Despite his growing public persona that eventually made him the face of comics, the day-to-day Stan understood marketplace volatility and how it impacted freelancers. As a result, many artists grew into steadfast Lee fans.

The camaraderie had important ramifications: artists worked long hours to meet Marvel's needs. In return, Stan rewarded them with steady work. Colan, for example, spoke about the grueling hours necessary to produce two complete pages daily (about two full books per month)—a schedule well more than forty hours per week.

The core group of freelance writers Lee took under his wing received a master class in comic book writing. Dennis O'Neil, a former journalist who started his career as a staff writer at Marvel (later famous for work on *Daredevil*, *Batman*, and *Green Lantern*), explained, "That first year working for Marvel, my job was to, in effect, imitate Stan." For the young writer and his colleagues, the message was clear: "Stan's style really was Marvel."[16]

For O'Neil, Roy Thomas, and the other writers, Lee served as a commanding general but with a level of benevolence that many leaders did not possess. He didn't spend much free time mingling with staff—primarily based on how much older he was than his staffers—but their admiration ran deep. The Marvel team comprised Stan's first "true believers." According to O'Neil, "I learned the basics by imitating Stan, and he was, by a huge margin, the best guy to imitate back then." The writers felt they produced revolutionary work under the guidance and training of the industry's pioneer: "the best comic book writer in the world."[17]

Lee's eye for talent, though, is clear from what the writers and artists he commissioned would later achieve. In the years that Marvel began its ascent on the back of the characters Lee, Kirby, Ditko, and others created, the company served as a kind of comic book university, teaching the next generation how to build and expand what would become famous as the "Marvel Method." The new style of creating a comic book actually grew out of Lee's determination to keep freelance artists working. If they had to wait around while he finished writing a script, they were losing money.

Marvel's success with superheroes upped the pressure on everyone in the creative process to perform at a faster rate, even Lee, who neared the limits of how quickly a person could write. He famously hired three secretaries and would dictate stories to them in order, running through one as the other two typed out the notes.

"In the beginning, I was writing almost all of the stories for Marvel. I couldn't keep up," Lee explained. Production demanded that all the various creators be kept constantly busy. For the freelance artists, the need was much more basic: if you aren't drawing pages, you aren't getting paid. He remembered that they would pace around after they dropped off their work, always wanting more. Lee simply had no way to keep up, so he changed the system: "I couldn't stop what I was doing. . . . [Instead] I would tell him generally what I wanted. He would go home and draw it any way he wanted, bring the illustrations back to me, and then I would put in the dialogue and the captions."[18]

> "I think we have finally made the first inroads in elevating the comics just a little bit. I think they're beginning to become a form of literature." —Stan Lee remark to Jack Kirby and Martin Goodman (John Morrow, *Kirby and Lee: Stuf' Said!*)

Without really planning a new system, Lee came up with the Marvel Method, as he explained it, "purely through need." The process amplified the strengths of the artists. "These guys thought like movie directors. They were really visual storytellers," Stan explained. As a result, he could give them latitude to interpret what he wanted from a quick story conference or brief phone call. "When I would give them a plot, they knew how to break it down—how to begin it, how to end it, where to put the interesting parts." When the artists missed the mark, Lee found he could intensify the artwork with sound effects or extra dialogue. "It started as an emergency measure—it's the only way to keep these guys busy—but I realized that you get better stories that way."[19]

Marvel's successes in the early 1960s took place as Lee and Kirby cemented their creative bond. The most logical and straightforward aspect of their relationship centered on mutual respect. Later, though, their decades-long entanglement grew convoluted. There were inherent difficulties in the many twists and turns Jack and Stan experienced. When the superhero boom began, Kirby worked for and reported to Lee, a reversal from the brief time he had been Stan's boss when the writer/editor started as a teenager. The shift—and success on the near horizon—also brought ego into the equation. Most of the now-famous superheroes were created in a time when almost no one cared who originated a particular character. Later though, the birth of the Marvel universe would become a hot topic worth billions of dollars. Stan and Jack both believed deeply in their roles as architects and creators.

In the early to mid-1960s, they could not have grasped just how dependent they were on one another. And they couldn't have anticipated the success with superheroes and how that would put Marvel's future directly on their shoulders.

Perhaps even more pointedly, neither realized the other's immense frustration. They both detested many facets of the industry and its continuous boom-or-bust cycles. Stan and Jack were friends with a long professional history, but their friendship did not carry over to sharing intimate details about their current or future hopes and dreams. If either actually opened up to the other, it may not have changed their relationship, but it may have enabled them to appreciate that they shared more in common than they ever realized.

Clearly they needed each other professionally. Jack was an unbelievable talent and had an unlimited creative mind. Stan captured the emerging voice of the 1960s. As editorial and art director, Stan resolved that Kirby's artistry would serve as the company's signature style, just as his writing became the de facto voice. Artist Gil Kane, who worked for Marvel on and off for decades, most memorably drawing many covers in the 1970s, recalled:

> Jack's point of view and philosophy of drawing became the governing philosophy of the entire publishing company and, beyond the publishing company, of the entire field. . . . They would get artists, regardless of whether they had done romance or anything else and they taught them the ABCs, which amounted to learning Jack Kirby. . . . Jack was like Holy Scripture and they simply had to follow him without deviation. That's what was told to me, that's what I had to do. It was how they taught everyone to reconcile all those opposing attitudes to one single master point of view.[20]

The entire Marvel line revolved around the Kirby style. For example, Jim Steranko passed the Marvel employment test by inking two of Kirby's penciled pages for *S.H.I.E.L.D.* He then worked with Kirby on three Nick Fury issues as a kind of apprenticeship. According to writer Chris Gavaler, "Becoming the Marvel house style seems to have required Kirby to regularize his layouts, presumably so they could be more easily imitated. Variation and innovation are not qualities easily taught, and they do not produce a unified style across titles."[21] Yet Steranko built his later reputation on irregular page layouts, which introduced art deco, postmodernism, and new wave impulses into Marvel's pages.

All DC could do was try to keep pace with Marvel. By the time DC recovered—sort of—by producing its own colorful, exciting covers, Marvel's creative leap enabled it to take over the top spot in the industry. In the battle between Marvel and DC, readers voted with their nickels, dimes, and quarters.

As a result, an innovative, colorful, and exciting character like Metamorpho, created by DC mainstays George Kashdan and Bob Haney in late 1964, seemed merely a Marvel clone. The Metamorpho cover (*The Brave and the Bold #57*) mirrored the kind of language that Lee popularized, exclaiming: "See the amazing powers of the world's most fantastic new hero." The book also used dynamic imagery and colors, yet Marvel had already created a beachhead in the war over what readers deemed "hot." Lee wanted to add to its roster to keep the forward progress. "I was like a crapshooter rolling one great pass after another," Lee said. "You just don't stop when you're on a winning streak."[22]

Yet Stan still believed the superhero boom would eventually end, just like the other cycles he had experienced. As a result, he moved fast to generate new titles and new characters, keeping freelancers hopping, driven by his endless supply of optimism and energy. Under relentless publishing deadlines, Lee had to live and breathe the constant balance of creativity and commerce, artwork versus commodity. Under his leadership, Marvel would spend the rest of the decade solidifying its universe.

CHAPTER 8

THE SUPERHEROES

"Face front!" Stan Lee's demand that readers snap to attention kicked off the "Marvel Bullpen Bulletins," a feature that ran in the back of all December 1965 issues. It replaced the "Merry Marvel Bullpen Page," which had debuted in August. Filled with "news" and "gossip," along with a checklist of current issues for sale with synopses, the yellow shadow boxes quickly became a mainstay.

No matter where a reader lived or whether they could even envision what the Marvel headquarters might have looked like, the Bulletins made them feel like part of the family. Some gravitated to the insider perspective that might detail who inked a particular issue or to find out the latest scoop on an artist's personal life. Others yearned for the merchandise offers, like the Spider-Man or Dr. Strange T-shirt at $1.50. Certainly young readers viewed the missives as personal correspondence from Lee, the coolest guy in the country.

Regardless of why buyers loved the Bullpen Bulletins, the page gave Stan room to hone and craft his voice as the main man behind Marvel. At the same time, the columns demonstrated his savvy strategic sense: Lee knew heightening audience engagement would result in greater reader dedication. From reading thousands of letters over the years, the editor knew that his interaction increased sales.

His voice became Marvel's hallmark. "It was a little thing," Lee said, "but it was trying to give a feeling of warmth, a feeling of friendliness. . . . It seemed to work." For teens and college-aged fans, the wink-wink, tongue-in-cheek tone spoke to their antiestablishment notions and seemed discernibly different from what they typically heard from adults. "It was all spontaneous," Lee remembered. "When I was writing a story, I'd think of something. So I'd throw it in."[1] His success with superheroes and their angst-ridden personas proved that if he trusted his instincts, good things would follow.

The chance to buy Marvel merchandise drew others to the Soapbox. The cost was fairly meager at a buck or so, which seemed just within (or maybe outside) their reach. How many days of lunch money did a kid need to secret away in order to afford that Dr. Strange shirt? Others gravitated to the list of new members of the Merry Marvel Marching Society fan club, finding others across America who shared their interest. The insider perspective turned Stan into the comic book nation's favorite uncle. He described the relationship as "part of an 'in' thing" and "sharing a big joke together and having a lot of fun with this crazy Marvel Universe."[2]

Utilizing a singsong, chatty style, Lee also turned up the wattage on his own celebrity status. The "Stan the Man" voice and persona came through in comic book dialogue and editorial content: "If I got a kick out of it, maybe a reader would, too," Lee reasoned. "Even in writing the credits, I'd try to make them humorous, because I enjoyed doing that."[3] Stan also awarded select fans who wrote intriguing letters or otherwise caught his fancy a "Marvel No-Prize," literally no prize, but public recognition all the same. He sent them an empty envelope, even mockingly stamping it "Handle with Care." The sillier Stan acted, the more fans seemed to enjoy the shtick. More importantly, sales climbed.

Lee also introduced the other bullpen members to readers on a first-name basis, giving them personalities, which translated into a deeper connection. In these narratives, Stan is always "Smilin' Stan Lee," a slightly wacky, permanently overworked editor, who is keeping the whole place running by the seat of his pants. He explained the goal: "Give our fans personal stuff, make them feel they were part of Marvel, make them feel as though they were on a first-name basis with the whole screwy staff. In a way, I wanted it to be as though they were getting a personal letter from a friend who was away at camp."[4]

The page provided readers with mental images of sitting down next to the famed comic book chief as he regaled them with stories of Jack "King" Kirby or "Jolly" Joe Sinnott. Marvel filled readers' dreams with visions of the Hulk and Iron Man, while news from the bullpen turned readers and the creative staff into long-lost friends. The tone gave fans in small towns nationwide the impression that Lee was their comrade and that Marvel's superheroes—despite one's better judgment—might just be real.

Lee's mad dash over the previous four years resulted in a superhero frenzy and Marvel's repositioning in American popular culture. The company and its editor stood at the epicenter of cool. Other publishers jumped onboard the superhero wave, from Charlton Comics (hiring Steve Ditko after he left Marvel and granting nearly complete editorial control over his conservative Ayn Randian creations) and Tower Comics (which doled out work to high-profile artists, such as Wally Wood and Gil Kane) to the venerable Archie Comics (which launched its own group—the *Mighty Crusaders*). The new entries attempted to mimic Marvel but often produced derivative content and cover art. Publishers yearned to emulate Jack and Stan but couldn't capture the magic.

In 1965, Lee and his creative gang launched a series of changes and gradual modifications to the hero genre, building a more cohesive, unified cosmos to solidify the growing fan base. For the next several years, the goal would be to increase depth, nuance, and context. Lee believed that intensifying the relationships between characters and intertwining the superhero worlds would ensure progress and, more importantly, create stronger bonds between the characters and readers.

"Comics are a team effort. I can say I created Spider-Man, but Steve Ditko, the artist who worked on it with me, will say: 'Hey, what about me? I drew it, and I helped with some of the plots.' And that goes for the inkers, colorists, letterers, and editors. It's such a complex process, how the hell do you know whom to pay for what?" —Stan Lee on creating comics (John Morrow, *Kirby and Lee: Stuf' Said!*)

Marvel's existential heart continued to center on the authentic, daily challenges as ordinary people gained larger-than-life powers. Lee quickly utilized the most human of human problems—the trials and tribulations of romantic relationships. Both Lee and Kirby had long histories in teen romance comics. Kirby and Joe Simon basically invented the genre in 1947. Lee also had deep experience, serving as the primary writer for *Millie the Model*, as well as its many offshoots that were aimed to attract female readers. Indeed, *Millie* could be considered the most successful nonsuperhero title Marvel ever produced.

The romantic interlude that drew the most interest was the marriage of Reed Richards and Susan Storm in *Fantastic Four Annual #3*. Kirby dazzled readers with the oversized issue, which also contained reprints of two popular past issues. The cover featured a free-for-all: almost every hero from the Marvel cosmos attended the star-studded event, as well as countless villains hoping to crash the festivities. While the two sides battled, a glum Sub-Mariner watched over the proceedings—his heart clearly broken. Inside, Lee called the issue "the most sensational super-spectacle ever witnessed by human eyes!!"

The Baxter Building is surrounded by adoring fans (including teen beauty Patsy Walker, another long-time Marvel character) but also under constant attack. The Thing tries to ward off the bad guys but needs the help of Nick Fury, the X-Men, Dr. Strange, and a host of others. Richards ultimately saves the day, and the episode ends with the wedding kiss ("No mere words of ours can truly describe the tenderness of this moment . . . so we won't even try," Lee wrote). Then two interlopers in top hats and stylish overcoats attempt to crash the reception but are stopped by Fury and his men. The trespassers are Lee and Kirby, only seen from the back. Not even the Fantastic Four creators could get into such a lavish celebration.

Also that magical year, Mary Jane Watson first appeared in *The Amazing Spider-Man #25*, but Ditko strategically hid her face, confusing the reader. Heightening the anticipation, other characters exclaim: "She's a friend of Peter's? She looks like a screen star!" Yet readers wouldn't actually see M. J. for years. At the end of 1965, blond beauty Gwen Stacy also debuted. As with M. J., it would take the hapless Peter Parker years before dating her. When they initially meet, Parker is so wrapped up with Aunt May and keeping his Spider-Man persona secret that he basically ignores her.

Marvel creative teams employed tactics seemingly out of soap operas to create ties between characters and fans. Since Lee's superheroes were purposely realistic, the notion that they were entangled in difficult relationships deepened the emotion.

In addition to guiding Marvel's art, writing, and production with a small team of full-time staffers and a growing crew of freelancers, Stan also expanded the brand. There were simply too many things to grab people's attention, ranging from the overtly commercial, like the national sensation caused by the arrival of the Beatles, to the overtly political, like Martin Luther King's 1965 civil rights march in Alabama and the growing presence of American troops in Vietnam. Comic books might have a difficult time competing with these global topics, but the flip side was that comic books could then be marketed as a pleasant diversion from real-life difficulties.

Marvel also utilized sophisticated marketing, advertising, and public relations in the mid-1960s. A 1965 flyer aimed at distributors used Lee's amped-up patter in a direct appeal to dealers, exclaiming: "When fans EYE them, they BUY them!" While newsstand owners may or may not have bought into the exaggerated language, they couldn't have missed the dramatic sales growth. In 1960, Marvel sold about 16.1 million copies, but that number grew to 27.7 million in 1964, and the company expected to top 35 million the next year.[5]

The marketing brochure underscored what insiders knew about Marvel's successes: the superhero "secret formula" that Lee and his colleagues launched had created a vast Marvel audience, which included more older readers, college students, and adults. One of the critical aspects of Marvel's reach, according to the flyer, centered on superheroes "bringing in a brand new breed of reader. . . . Marvel fan clubs are springing up at every COLLEGE and UNIVERSITY from coast-to-coast." Although Marvel's marketers assumed that newsstand operators would be duly impressed with that information, the company boasted of already having fifty thousand members within the handful of months after its launch.[6]

With sales booming and the end of restrictions on how many titles Marvel could publish each month, Lee sat atop a company with dozens of titles coming out on a monthly or bimonthly schedule. When the lineup expanded, editorial director Lee had to commit to writing a new series or find someone to take it over. Consequently, Lee had to tap into alternative sources—writers from fan magazines, journalists, and some Marvel readers that pushed until they got Stan's attention. Stan continued to hone the dialogue style that had become Marvel's trademark, not just because he had so much to write himself but because he was also responsible for controlling the editorial and artistic direction. The relentless pace and increased number of titles forced the development of new processes to cope with the pressure.

Denny O'Neil spoke about Marvel's style and tight deadlines clashing in July 1966, when the publishers upped production to take advantage of the surge in superhero popularity based on the *Batman* television series. "I did *Daredevil #18* because Stan got into a deadline bind. Romita had done the art and put notes in the margins, but Stan didn't have time to do the script."[7] Yet, according to O'Neil, Lee worked harder than the writers he hired, ultimately putting in innumerable hours to develop the Marvel universe for its eager fans.

Lee's effort and persistence became company lore, inspiring those he hired to put in similar grueling hours. For example, even a citywide blackout could not stop Lee from completing his pages. During the first significant power outage in New York City in 1965, O'Neil and assistant editor Roy Thomas gave themselves the night off. Yet, they recalled, their boss sat at home writing by candlelight. "The pages had candle wax dripped on them," O'Neil says, though it's difficult to know whether we should take him at his word or if this is yet another Stan-inspired legend.[8]

For Lee, plotting took little time. He charted the different books out—perhaps ten to twelve a month—then gave them to the artists to draw. When the artist delivered the work, Lee sat and put the words down. However, Lee's various roles necessitated that he also keep an eye on the art and covers. "While I was putting the copy in," he explained, "I'd be making notes on changes that the artist should make in the artwork." Sometimes, Lee said, he had to deviate from the original plot because the artist took the story in a different direction. Kirby, for example, would change the plot to suit his needs, and Lee would piece together the dialogue, which he likened to completing a "crossword puzzle."[9]

Marvel's offbeat superheroes turned it into the hip 1960s comic book house, but DC still controlled the industry based on sales figures. DC counted on its heroes—Batman, Superman, and Wonder Woman—while Marvel countered with Spider-Man, Thor, and the Fantastic Four. Readers seemed to be moving toward Marvel, but then the ABC television series *Batman* debuted in January 1966. In a unique programming move, the show aired two nights week—Wednesday and Thursday—in half-hour segments.

Batman's instant success enabled DC to regain some of its swagger. With actor Adam West as the Caped Crusader and Burt Ward as his youthful sidekick, Robin, the series mixed camp and action to appeal to television audiences. Using a steady stream of one-liners and plenty of "POW," "BAM," and "ZONK" graphics, the show delighted audiences across age groups. The music alone gave the program a lift, a mix of 1960s pop-infused songs mixed with Batman-specific tunes that stuck in listeners' minds like an earworm. *Batman* also took advantage of the color television craze, using bright color schemes to bring characters to life.

After half a decade searching for the magic decoder ring that would open an inroad to Marvel readers, DC seemed to finally attain the voice that Lee brought to comics. *Batman* captured the nation's fascination with superheroes, especially in its satirical tone, which Lee had brought to the medium.

Chadwick Boseman (1976–2020) portrayed Black Panther. He was the first Black actor to headline an MCU film. Illustration by Jason Piperberg.

In many respects, the snarky banter of the two heroes seemed closer in alignment to Spider-Man or the Fantastic Four than anything DC had recently produced.

All the major publishers saw sales increases, with some attempting knockoffs, like Harvey Comics' superheroes *Spyman* and *Jigsaw* and Tow Comics' *Dynamo* and *Noman*. Marvel attempted to counter *Batman* to some degree by beginning Thor's solo run in March 1966, then debuting the Black Panther, the first African American superhero, in *Fantastic Four #52* (July 1966). Today's fans who saw the remarkable Chadwick Boseman play T'Challa in the MCU may not realize what a gamble the Black Panther was for Stan and Jack. For much of the country, racism was the norm, so the courage to introduce a black superhero should be valued. *Black Panther* (2018) later became the first Marvel film to win an Academy Award, and ticket sales exceeded $1.3 billion. Boseman tragically died on August 28, 2020, of colon cancer.

> "Black Panther would not exist if not for Stan Lee and artist Jack Kirby taking a quote-unquote 'risk' bringing in an African—not even African American, an African—character to their stories who was smarter and wealthier and more technologically advanced than any other hero. This was at the height of the civil rights movement, and that's astounding." —Kevin Feige, president of Marvel Studios and producer of the MCU (*Entertainment Weekly* special on Stan Lee, "Heroes Made Human")

Lee and Kirby did not let the Bat-mania thwart their efforts to further build up the Marvel universe. As a kind of counterbalance, they introduced a three-part trilogy in *The Fantastic Four #48–50* (March-May 1966) that had the supergroup battling Galactus, an omnipotent superbeing who sustained life by devouring entire planets. The epic plotted Marvel's most powerful villain against Earth's powerful superhero team. A comic book arc couldn't compete head-to-head against a popular television series, but Marvel hoped to at least increase sales and entice new readers.

Lee's aggressive antics began to work but took some time. As late as July 1967, almost six years after *The Fantastic Four* debuted, *New York Times* reporter Leonard Sloane correctly deduced that millions of people read comic books but believed most adults did not respect the medium. He outlined how advertisers thought of the average comic book reader: as members of "special audiences . . . children, servicemen and semi-adults (. . . those over 18 who may not always think at the same level as their chronological age)."[10] Yet Marvel letter pages and the mail stacks were filled with articulate, passionate messages from educated readers nationwide.

In the mid- to late 1960s, comics, unlike other consumer-focused magazines, still generated most of their revenue from circulation, not advertising, but the latter was still significant. Sloane cited the still-number-one-ranked National Periodical, which published forty-eight titles a month that led to about seven million in monthly circulation. Advertising income, however, remained relatively small, only growing from $250,000 to $500,000 between 1962 and 1966. Comic book executives usually claimed that their selectivity kept the ad revenue down. Many companies (including Marvel), however, decided to run small print ads for a variety of products, from novelty toys and mail-order gimmicks to hobby kits.[11] Many large corporations would not run ads in comic books, so publishers attempted to make up for the lack of direct advertising revenues by licensing characters to other companies.

In contrast to DC, Marvel's monthly circulation hit about six million, according to Sloane, but the company launched a campaign to run ads for products targeted at older audiences, like shaving cream. Lee equated the quality of the stories and the artwork with the class its audiences expected, explaining: "We editorialize. We try to back the soldiers and try to tell the kids not to drop out of school. We stand for the good virtues."[12] The decision to intentionally target older readers had been Lee's top concern. A little more than midway through the decade, his determination started to pay dividends.

Lee also studied Marvel's merchandising opportunities. The *Batman* success led to DC licensing the character to ninety companies, pulling in about $75 million in sales, but some experts claimed the figure reached $150 million.[13] Lee's tasks multiplied as Marvel grew more popular, yet Goodman kept the staff small and expected more from his chief editor/art director.

Stan recognized television's increasing significance, confident that superhero sagas would be a perfect fit. Goodman had stumbled and bumbled with Marvel licensing in the past, so it did not really surprise anyone when he basically gave away the company's animation rights. Figuring that the production part of the company should be run by someone young, the publisher turned the department over to his son Charles (Chip) Goodman, anticipating that he would use the position as stepping-stone to taking over the family business.

Audited circulation figures revealed that Marvel sales jumped from eighteen million in 1961 to about thirty-two million in 1965. The surge in popularity attracted television executives, who attempted to dissect the company's secret appeal. No one could put their finger on it exactly but usually pointed to the antihero themes and Stan's ability to understand the youth market.

In September 1966, the animated *Marvel Super Heroes* debuted, featuring a group of stories based on Captain America, Thor, Iron Man, Sub-Mariner, and Hulk. Ads ran in all comic book titles the following month, listing the twenty stations carrying the cartoon, including big media targets: New York City, Chicago, and Los Angeles. In total, close to fifty aired the show, including overseas channels in Brazil, Puerto Rico, and Venezuela.

Produced by Grantray-Lawrence Animation, the cartoon version used color photostat reproductions of actual comic books—rather than original animation—which created a seven-minute chapter that could then be played back-to-back or chopped up and fitted into other children's television programming. In total, the company generated 195 segments for the initial syndication effort stretching from September to December 1966.

The crude method reduced the animation quality of *Marvel Super Heroes* but did showcase the exquisite artwork of Kirby, Ditko, and the rest of Lee's team. In each shot, there is usually only one object animated. Sometimes it is Captain America's shield looping through the air, while other times it is the character's eyes blinking or lips moving as they speak. The *Marvel Super Heroes* theme song provided a brief overview of each character, then led into the next segment, with voices merrily singing, "The Marvel superheroes have arrived."

Hanna-Barbera Productions launched *The Fantastic Four* in the fall of 1967 on ABC. The show began with a bang: a signal arching into the nighttime sky and then bursting into a vibrant "4," which called the superheroes to their Big Apple headquarters. The minute-long introduction took the viewer through a condensed version of the group's origin story, showing them battling a variety of bad guys. Aimed at young viewers, the show emphasized the superstrength of the heroes and made the villains dangerous but somewhat campy. The writers aped some of Lee's style, showing its early infiltration into mainstream popular culture, as well as the sustained influence of Adam West's gonzo Batman.

The inevitable boom-and-bust mentality that seemed to plague comic books continued, however. Although the Marvel cartoons were popular, sales nosedived in 1967 when the televised *Batman* show sputtered, limping through a final year and basically pulling comic books sales down in its wake. DC remained on top, but total circulation industry-wide decreased. *Spider-Man* was Marvel's highest-selling comic but only placed fourteenth on the annual list of top sellers.[14] Overall, Marvel did better than most of its competitors who saw deeper circulation decreases. The fact that Marvel remained consistent revealed how hipness and good marketing could overcome broader market forces.

The late 1960s were full of changes for Stan personally. He moved J. C. into an apartment in the city so she could study acting. Later, after living part time in the city, he and Joanie also found a place on Sixty-Third with a large terrace, which had been her prerequisite. After about two decades of suburban life, the couple now lived in the heart of the Big Apple.[15]

Lee's popularity continued to grow with college students—as a speaker and as de facto head of the one hundred or so campus chapters of the Merry Marvel Marching Society fan club. His fame, though, caused tension with Goodman. "I began to think he almost resented the success of our comics line," Lee remembered. "I felt it wouldn't displease him to see sales slip and have my confidence taken down a peg."[16] It was a double-edged sword for Martin: Lee was too valuable and popular to fire, but his fame caused resentment.

One of Stan's highest-profile appearances was on the popular *Dick Cavett Show*. The host seemed to doubt that comic books were of much value, so Stan countered by positioning comics as a significant part of "the age of the offbeat." Marvel superheroes specifically represented the decade because they had human feelings and problems while they saved the world from all-powerful aliens, supervillains, and other crises. Lee explained to Cavett—at the time one of the nation's great promoters of both high- and lowbrow culture—that in Marvel fandom, "our most popular heroes are the most wackiest." He singled out Hulk ("a green-skinned monster") and Spider-Man as representative of the quirky era.[17]

While Cavett and Pat McCormick (his comedian sidekick) poked fun at Lee and comics in general, Stan kept his cool, explaining that Spider-Man's popularity rested on his status as an "anti-hero hero" who "gets sinus attacks, he gets acne, and allergy attacks while he's fighting." Prior to a commercial break, McCormick fired the kind of zinger that Lee had battled his entire career, snickering: "One thing I like about those comic books is that they're easy to turn while you're sucking your thumb with the other hand."[18]

A comedian like McCormick might have been able to play the dumbed-down nature of comic books for gags, but Lee stood at the center of a new comic book universe—one that he and his colleagues created. When Jenette Kahn, later the head of rival DC, was asked what she considered the "most significant event" in the post-1950 comic book world, she pointed to Lee, explaining:

> Comic book characters pick up the unconscious trends of the time and become the spokesmen for those trends. That's why people can identify so fully that the characters can become part of the mythology. Stan Lee's characters did that in the sixties. He picked up on anti-Establishment feelings, on alienation and self-depreciation. . . . Stan came in with characters with bad breath and acne, punkier, younger, when young people needed symbols to replace many of the things they were rejecting.[19]

In a flurry of creativity over a relatively short span, Stan upended American popular culture and forever changed the way people looked at heroes and storytelling.

While Lee fixated on art, word balloons, continuing story lines, and the countless other responsibilities he faced, Goodman searched for an exit strategy. By the late 1960s, large corporations had started to gobble each other up in a series of mergers and acquisitions. For Goodman, merger-mania provided the perfect opportunity to cash out.

At the midpoint of 1968, a budding corporate mogul and lawyer named Martin Ackerman approached Goodman about selling both the men's magazines and the comic book division. Ackerman ran a handful of photo stores, pharmacies, and other concerns under the banner Perfect Film & Chemical Corporation. He fancied himself a major business figure, chomping away on cigars and bossing around staff and underlings despite his diminutive stature. Ackerman had extended a $5 million loan to Curtis Publishing, under the stipulation that he would serve as president. What he really wanted was to control the distribution firm Curtis Circulation. Buying Goodman's Magazine Management collection of periodicals and comic books ensured that Ackerman would have the content necessary to distribute, a kind of double-dipping that gave him more revenue and control—an early example of the adage "content is king."

Goodman, though wracked with internal strife, ultimately demanded a cash deal, selling the whole enterprise for about $15 million. When he made the sale, however, Goodman pulled Lee aside, promising Stan "warrants," which he said were like stock options. Not only would Goodman get rich, but he explained that Lee would, too. "My pot of gold had arrived," Lee thought, "and I didn't even have to ask!"[20] As the deal got finalized, however, Goodman not only didn't give Lee options; he never mentioned them again. He then signed a deal to remain publisher of Magazine Management, while his son Chip became editorial director (with the assumption Chip would eventually replace his father).

Ackerman and his underlings, according to Lee, "told Martin they wouldn't buy the company unless I signed a contract to stay on."[21] The new owner saw Lee as the vital cog in the purchase, but Stan didn't press Goodman for a large raise or other long-term financial gains. He unwisely trusted his longtime boss to take care of him.

The sale called for a party. "I'll see to it that you and Joanie will never have to want for anything as long as you live," Goodman told Lee while celebrating at the publisher's house the night after the sale.[22] Ackerman celebrated too: he bought a $1.5 million private jet and a snazzy Park Avenue apartment. Placing his faith in Goodman, Lee didn't press for a big raise or threaten to leave Marvel when he could have demanded a hefty fortune to not run to DC. The three-year deal he eventually inked bumped up Lee's salary, but he never trusted Goodman again.

Although Ackerman's Curtis Circulation took over Marvel's distribution, erasing the disastrous deal Goodman had been forced to sign ten years earlier, the entire industry reset somewhat as sales flattened. Goodman took a heavy-handed approach, threatening layoffs and cancelling titles, including the beloved *Doctor Strange*. The publisher even demanded that comics drop a page (from twenty to nineteen) in an effort to save money. The interference made Stan angry. He contemplated quitting. Chip Goodman also illogically shut down the Merry Marvel Marching Society fan club, which Lee believed had energized and coalesced its most loyal readers.

Once again, Lee felt trapped. His primary aim was to build Marvel into the largest comic book publisher, but the sales slump made him a bit vulnerable. Goodman had not come through on his promises and, as a matter of fact, began hinting at another round of mass layoffs, which Lee would be forced to orchestrate. Stan yearned for a way out: "It's time I started thinking of other things," he said, considering a range of options, from writing a play to screenwriting or even poetry.[23] Film seemed the most logical avenue. He even dreamed of taking Kirby and artist John Buscema to Hollywood with him—the artists working on set designs or storyboards while he crafted scripts.

With Lee considering options, the company's new owner felt its first tremors. In a shocking move, Perfect's board of directors ousted Ackerman. The combination of pressure from running Curtis and his flamboyant spending habits were too much to handle. They replaced Ackerman with Sheldon Feinberg, another aggressive young executive with a law background. Feinberg changed the company name to Cadence Industries. He also launched a campaign to reduce its enormous debt. No longer the captain of the ship, Goodman fell in line, ordering Stan to cut costs by publishing reprints so he didn't have to pay freelancers for new pages. Inching ever closer to the end of the decade, Feinberg had quite a task ahead. Lee tried to keep the Marvel bullpen in high spirits, but the business side of the corporation controlled decision making.

The early 1960s hinged on creating new characters and establishing the Marvel universe. In the latter part of the decade, Stan and his crew shifted to deepening story lines via interconnected tales and more emotion. Lee also expanded the line through solo titles for Captain America, Hulk, and Iron Man.

While many publishers watched sales drop, Marvel's stayed constant during the downturn. When it upped monthly production, the additional revenue staved off mass layoffs, thus keeping Lee from firing coworkers and staff members he considered like family. At least the good cheer and hipness factor remained with Marvel. DC went through tougher times, being sold to Kinney National, yet another corporate conglomerate, and unable to figure out how to compete with its smaller rival.

As 1968 unfolded, Lee and Marvel would get increasingly caught up in world events. No one could ignore Vietnam, campus unrest, civil rights protests, or the campaigns for women's rights. On the *Dick Cavett Show*, Lee discussed an earlier *Thor* issue that had the Norse god criticizing college students for dropping out when they could "plunge in." At the time of the interview, however, the significance of the protests had changed. Lee could no longer use a superhero story to write "a good little sermon." "Youth today," he told Cavett, "seem to be so much more activist, which I think is a very healthy thing."[24]

In 1968, the comic book business was unrecognizable in comparison to where it began the decade when *The Fantastic Four* launched. All the new solo titles necessitated an increased universe of intricately woven plots and new characters to fill the superhero books. Lee feared that Cadence executives might shut Marvel down at any moment, yet he soldiered on, hoping that the superhero universe he created would endure the bumps and jolts of a chaotic new age.

CHAPTER 9

AMERICA'S POP CULTURE AMBASSADOR

What Stan Lee understood better than anyone else associated with Marvel—from his boss Martin Goodman and the Cadence executives overseeing the company to the newest assistant editor or freelance letterer—was that if the company had a spokesperson with stories as large-as-life as the Marvel superheroes, then that person could be almost as significant as the creations. Regardless of who drew, inked, or colored the comics, Lee had been the voice of Spider-Man, Thor, the Fantastic Four, and others. His writing created the sound of Marvel Comics.

When journalists attempted to experience the hubbub firsthand, Lee seized on their interest. Reporters may have expected Stan to be younger, but they recognized that the enthusiastic, witty, quote-a-minute Lee had tapped directly into youth culture. When the press looked for a spokesman to contextualize Marvel's rampant success, Lee jumped at the chance. The new role not only played to his ego but also allowed him to try out some of the acting chops that he not-so-secretly harbored.

Stan also grasped the monetary and branding value of serving as the company's primary face. If the role made him essentially indispensable, then that position amounted to job security. He carried a deep aversion for unemployment or even the hint of being underutilized. With his father's humiliation a painful memory, that idea shook Lee to the core.

In addition, the spokesperson role ensured that Marvel remained in the public eye. Stan did not have to be a supergenius like Reed Richards to realize that the superhero craze would lead to an increased number of entertainment options that would build on Marvel's reputation *and* Lee's. The public reaction to the superhero characters he helped create stacked up on his desk in the form of three hundred to four hundred fan letters daily. In some sense, Lee realized, he could become a real-life "Mr. Fantastic" just by capitalizing on his natural strengths and gregarious personality.[1]

Ironically, as Lee's position expanded, he subsequently became further entrenched as a company man. He realized that his fate—as always—remained deeply entwined with Marvel. Although many comic book insiders would accuse Lee of self-aggrandizement for assuming this self-created mantle, he smartly moved in a direction that capitalized on his talents. He was never going to be an inspirational chief executive—he wasn't completely interested in the business aspects—but he could rally crowds and fans. He could just as effectively talk up comics to worried parents or curious journalists.

After spending decades toiling in virtual obscurity and chagrined when people learned of his occupation, his tables turned when Marvel found itself at the center of the cultural zeitgeist. Lee leapt at the prospect of establishing himself as a brand (within and outside Marvel).

Goodman remained the prototype business leader, keen on revenue and profit. He lacked the sense of pure creativity needed to appreciate the work of Lee, Kirby, and the Marvel bullpen, but he built a financial infrastructure that enabled them to flourish. And he continued to serve as a foil to Lee, even as Stan's power increased and Goodman's lessened. Stan may have bristled at the many financial moves, but he understood that Goodman and the Cadence management team played a critical role in the company's success.

The expansion of titles per month meant that Stan had to corral a growing team of staffers and freelancers. Titles had to hit publication deadlines. Missing the mark cost the company money in penalty fees and potential sales. The ironic aspect of Lee's concentration on marketing Marvel was that it took place after so many years. "I had to write just about everything," he recalled. "I was the editor. I was the art director. I was the head writer. So because of that, for better or worse, I had my personality stamped on those comics." It is important to remember that the front-end creation—from writing to artwork and production—was the glitzy outcome that required a great deal of behind-the-scenes effort. "I was designing covers, writing cover blurbs, writing ads, the soapbox column, the Bullpen page," Lee explained.[2]

The persona Lee fashioned—part sarcasm and large dollops of self-deprecation—created a voice that permeated Marvel. The popularity of Spider-Man, Hulk, Iron Man, and the others went beyond mere fandom to a kind of cult status and made Marvel a major cultural influence. Yet, even though it became hip, Marvel still trailed DC Comics in total sales. In 1968, for example, DC Comics published forty-seven titles with sales of approximately seventy-five million, while Marvel had twenty-two titles and fifty million (although in an August 1968 interview, Lee claimed sixty million). Even though Marvel published fewer than half the number of titles that DC did, its sales were at least two-thirds as much, making the company in some way more successful.

> "Well, just between us, we believe in our cavortin' characters a lot more than we believe in some people we know, and we do have a motive—a purpose—behind our mags! That purpose is, plain and simple, to entertain you! . . . If we can also do our bit to advance the cause of intellectualism, humanitarianism, and mutual under-standing . . . that won't break our collective heart one tiny bit! That's it, pussycat! Thanks for listenin'!" —Stan Lee, first Soapbox column ("May 1967," Brian Cunning-ham, ed., *Stan's Soapbox: The Collection*)

In countless speaking engagements and interviews, Lee continued to hone his persona. Simultaneously, he never missed a chance to recognize Marvel fans and his creative team (then numbering around thirty-five staff and freelancers). "Marvel readers must be among the most fanatical in the land," he claimed. "They ask questions, find mistakes, [and] make suggestions."[3] The letters and interaction with fans at comic industry gatherings gave him direct insight into his target demographic, from the obsessed diehards who chided Lee for every *Spider-Man* frame that left out some minor detail to the casual observers attempting to understand how comics got so popular.[4] Stan rarely shied from explaining how innovative or creative Marvel's new work (and by extension his writing) stood in comparison to past characters and publishers, particularly DC, which he constantly chided as a monument to an outdated era.

Lee sincerely believed in the educational and cultural value of comics, so his basic earnestness led to an authenticity that people accepted, particularly when delivered in the corny, self-deprecating style that he perfected. He grasped that fans wanted Marvel books to engage with real-life socioeconomic and political topics. Staying flexible and listening to fans, Stan explained: "They want a whole ethos, a philosophy, within the framework of the comic character. They seem desperate for someone to believe in. . . . I don't want to let them down."[5] In the late 1960s, Lee's willingness to have Spider-Man, Thor, and others address pertinent issues helped legitimize comic books for wider audiences.

Although Lee could be criticized for not taking a more progressive tone, given that he had the youth market at his feet, he often dropped his self-deprecating mask and spoke to readers about serious issues. In late 1968, for example, he used a "Stan's Soapbox" column to speak out against bigotry and racism, which he labeled the "deadliest social ills plaguing the world today." The kind of hatred spread during that era prompted Lee to declare that it was "totally irrational, patently insane to condemn an entire race—to despise an entire nation—to vilify an entire religion." Instead, he urged Marvelites to be tolerant.[6]

Similar thinking led Marvel to create several African American characters, including Robbie Robertson, a city editor at the *Daily Bugle* in Spider-Man. More importantly, he and Kirby cocreated Black Panther, the superhero guise of T'Challa, the prince of a mythical African country. Marvel also introduced the Falcon, another black superhero but this time an American. After debating about what to do with the Black Panther, Lee confessed to hoping that the fan mail would provide him with insight about how to proceed. In 1970, Lee claimed that he wanted to offer black heroes earlier, but "the powers-that-be" were "very cautious" and would not allow it.[7] Whether this finger wagging was aimed directly at Goodman or Cadence, Lee did not feel that he had to hold back.

In March 1970, Lee again turned to the Soapbox to lay out Marvel's policy on "moralizing." While some readers simply wanted escapism, Lee countered: "I can't see it that way." He compared a story without a message to a person without a soul. Stan explained that his visits to colleges led to "as much discussion of war and peace, civil rights, and the so-called youth rebellion as there is of our Marvel mags." All these pieces, Lee said, shape our lives. No one should run from them or think that reading comic books might insulate someone from important societal matters.[8]

> "We believe that Man has a divine destiny, and an awesome responsibility—the responsibility of treating all who share this wondrous world of ours with tolerance and respect—judging each fellow human on his own merit, regardless of race, creed, or color. That we agree on—and we'll never rest until it becomes a fact, rather than just a cherished dream!" —Stan Lee, Soapbox column (Brian Cunningham, ed., *Stan's Soapbox: The Collection*)

Despite the attention and outpouring of fan affection bordering on cult-like devotion, Lee couldn't shake feelings of inadequacy. He continued to receive off-putting reactions from adults who worked in mainstream jobs. As a result, Stan still searched for legitimacy. No accolades seemed enough to erase those initial negative perceptions of being "just a comic book writer."

Often, when Lee faced challenges, his answer was Spider-Man. From a literary standpoint, the character tapped into 1960s existentialism—an average person who fell victim to an accident, thus transforming his life. The radioactive spider that injected its venom directly into Peter Parker's bloodstream enabled the boy to become a superhero, but the venom did not cast aside Peter's insecurities, anxieties, or basic humanity. As a matter of fact, a moment of indecision and exaggerated hubris led to the death of his beloved Uncle Ben, leaving the boy reeling. The dichotomy between arrogance and humility made the character compelling.

As a symbol of the 1960s and its collective unrest, which resulted in a kind of split personality between protest and conservatism, Spider-Man was another iteration of the figures populating books, film, and celebrity tabloids. Peter Parker occupies the same city that drove young Holden Caulfield to the brink in J. D. Salinger's *The Catcher in the Rye*. Similar to Caulfield, Parker questions his place in the world. While Lee knew the character resonated with younger audiences, he believed that more mature readers would connect with the character as well. Stan just needed to get the superhero in front of a larger audience. The growing college-aged population gobbled up *Catcher*, just as it devoured Marvel comics.

In July 1968, in hopes of thwarting some of the criticisms he faced about being in an inferior industry, Lee launched *The Spectacular Spider-Man*, which was not only magazine-sized but black and white, like the popular underground comics. More than fifty pages, the magazine cost thirty-five cents, nearly triple the newsstand price of regular comic books (twelve cents).

The first issue featured a rewritten and redrawn origin story and a Lee original: "Lo, This Monster." The covers were distinctive as well. Harry Rosenbaum, an artist who did cover art for men's adventure magazines, painted an image of the hero in acrylic paint, making it deeply textured. The second issue presented a striking cover by artist John Romita that showed the Green Goblin zapping Spidey with a colorful yellow burst. The energy of the Romita cover exploded from the page, quickly becoming a fan favorite.

In a Soapbox update, Stan called the magazine "a real, glitzy, status-drenched, slick-paper publication" that readers could find "amongst the so-called 'better' magazines at your newsstand." Lee declared it "possibly Marvel's finest achievement to date," as well as a "Marvel milestone" that would go down in comic book history. The editor-in-chief saw the magazine as a chance to bridge to adult readers (featuring more mature themes/topics).

What Lee didn't anticipate is that the new adult-oriented comic seemed to occupy a no-man's land between youngsters and older readers. No amount of bluster could save it from bombing. For average fans, *The Spectacular Spider-Man* cost too much. The foray into black and white did not help either. The second issue went back to interior color, but it was too late. That second issue with the beautiful cover would be its last, though Marvel rehashed the Lee story later in 1973 in *The Amazing Spider-Man #116–118*, with revisions by writer Gerry Conway. Another story from the second issue featuring the Green Goblin would later be repurposed (as Marvel so frequently did) in *The Amazing Spider-Man Annual #9* (1973).

Although the failure delivered a blow to Lee's notions of crossing into mainstream success, the magazine didn't diminish Spider-Man's overall popularity. Nonetheless, Lee still reeled with frustrations. Since the late 1940s, he had attempted to gain legitimacy by self-publishing material for older readers or moonlighting for Goodman's adult-oriented magazines. On the outside, Lee seemed upbeat and passionate about comics and superheroes, but he had internalized the negativity, hiding deep fears about working in an industry that others deemed distasteful.

In early 1970, Kirby's contract expired around the time Goodman sold the company to Perfect Film. They had little interest in re-signing Jack for the big money he anticipated. Moreover, Goodman didn't support him. Kirby correctly gauged that it was his turn to get paid for all that he had done to build Marvel, but according to Mark Evanier, no one would talk to him or his lawyer about a new contract.[9] Eventually, Jack turned to Lee for help, incorrectly assuming that the editor had that power. Though Kirby thought Stan sandbagged him, there is no evidence that he could have swayed Goodman or the management team.

The contract impasse drove another wedge between Stan and Jack, one that, in hindsight, seemed based on misjudgment rather than malice. The irony of the relationship between Kirby and Lee is that the two are tied together forever in comic book lore, yet their complexities turned the relationship indifferent, begrudgingly cordial, sour, and even hostile.

Jack seemed to care less about the fame that came with creating successful superheroes and comic books—he was a craftsman. His desire centered on earning a living and getting treated fairly—receiving an equitable share of the money others were making off his art, ideas, and reputation. With Kirby, the feeling emerges that no matter how financially sound he might have been, the haunting recollections of his youth in the Lower East Side slums would never be far from his mind. "All of Kirby's work in the '60s was for Marvel, and he was always terrified that he would stop getting assignments," Joe Simon explained. "It was a big deal for him."[10]

Both Kirby and Simon, like Lee, had lived through the hardscrabble Great Depression, which fundamentally colored their views of work and money. According to Simon, Kirby put a lot of pressure on himself to provide for his family at least in part because his own parents had been poor. "He had to bring the money home for Roz, put food on the table for the kids."[11] Kirby's demons regarding money hovered ominously over his worldview. This kind of intimate relationship with poverty never leaves a person. Yet his $35,000 freelance salary in 1970 (about $220,000 in current buying power) allowed him to make a decent living, but one could certainly argue that he should have been making multiples more, perhaps millions.

Despite their shared history of growing up poor, for Lee, recognition was a far greater desire than the financial safety Kirby sought. Stan drew from lessons bestowed on him as a child—a mother that demanded perfection and success and the toll financial hardship had on his family. Adulation was the check Lee needed to cash.

Though forever linked as a creative duo, Stan and Jack's complex relationship suffered from different desires—one wishing for fame, the other for financial security. Thus, Kirby's frustration with Goodman's penny-pinching and reneged promises, as well as lingering exasperation with Lee, led him to reject a new contract with Marvel in 1970. Instead he boarded DC, where Carmine Infantino ran the editorial ship. Kirby was given free rein to develop a new superhero universe dubbed "The Fourth World." At DC, the artist/writer created three new titles that enabled him to tackle the biblical, existential, and science fiction machine-driven questions that were at the center of his mythical worldview.

Comic books became big business and successful across other mediums, demonstrating how central superhero narratives were in contemporary American culture. Envious of the way Superman and Batman had moved from radio to film and television, Marvel made similar plans. Historically, the emphasis had been on creating demand for comic books first. In the new era, publishing executives realized television and film would drive licensing.

For Lee and the corporate honchos in New York, the ultimate dream centered on a series of Marvel movies and television shows. Increasing audience size would establish the characters for successive generations. Wider exposure would lead to greater demand, thereby generating a catalog of profitable licensing deals.

The early *Marvel Super Heroes* animated program (produced by Grantray-Lawrence) proved that even a crudely done show would find an audience. Logic dictated, based on the ever-growing popularity of Spider-Man, that the webslinger would be next. In late 1967 and 1968, Grantray-Lawrence led production efforts, but the struggling studio went into bankruptcy. When famed animator Ralph Bakshi took over, the Spider-Man series aired on ABC and proved a hit, running until 1970.

Animation juggernaut Hanna-Barbera Productions created a Fantastic Four show for ABC (airing 1967–1970). The new program ran alongside

Spider-Man, giving audiences an extended dose of superhero stories. Lee and Kirby's original comic books were truncated to fit into thirty-minute time slots and watered down so children could easily follow along. Considered one of the first Saturday morning educational cartoons, each episode had a segment dedicated to Mister Fantastic explaining a scientific term or concept.

Producers downplayed Kirby's ominous depiction of Doctor Doom and made Galactus less imposing, but these stylistic changes were offset to a degree by the enthusiasm of the voice actors, including film and television star Gerald Mohr voicing Reed Richards. This formula—making some characters more generic and operating within the technology boundaries (in this case, clunky animation)—seemed to hinder how production companies brought Marvel to the screen. Publicly, Lee supported the show but had little to do with it otherwise. The lack of control irritated him. He believed that if Marvel created its own programming, like Disney, its superheroes would rival Walt's famous mouse and princesses. The urge to start a production company began to gnaw at Lee.

In 1971, a *New York Times* reporter estimated that about three hundred million comic books were published annually.[12] Considering even a conservative pass-through rate equating to four others reading each comic sold, that means around 1.2 billion comic books were read at a time when the total world population stood at 3.7 billion. Despite lingering questions about their negative consequences on younger readers, comic books were a central component of mainstream culture with Lee as their pivotal figure. In the eyes of many, the name "Stan Lee" was synonymous with comics, a kind of Johnny Appleseed that toured the nation spreading joy and expounding on the importance of comic books.

In May of that year, Lee showed how comic books could be used for good in *The Amazing Spider-Man #96*. Spidey saves a young black kid who mistakenly jumps off a rooftop, as the superhero explains, "The poor guy's stoned right out of his mind." After the rescue, other characters exchange words about drug use and Spider-Man thinks: "My life as Spider-Man is probably as dangerous as any—but I'd rather face a hundred super-villains than toss it away by getting hooked on hard drugs." Peter Parker's African American friend Randy later gets into a heated exchange with Norman Osborn, explaining that blacks hate drugs the most because young people "got no hope," which makes them "easier pickin's for the pushers."

The Amazing Spider-Man #96 (May 1971), published without the Comics Code Authority stamp. © 1939–2022 Marvel Characters, Inc.

Casual readers may have regarded the anti-drug message as yet another nod to realism, but most probably didn't know Stan had received a letter asking for his help from an official at the National Institute of Mental Health, a division of the Department of Health, Education, and Welfare. The executive implored Lee to use Spidey's popularity to fight drug abuse in comic book form. Government officials believed the character's esteem among high school and college students would help them get factual information to this key demographic.

Although Lee realized that mentioning drug use would be a violation of the Comics Code, he decided to fulfill the request. Understanding the broader implications, he explained: "We can't keep our heads in the sand. . . . If this story would help one kid anywhere in the world not to try drugs or to lay off drugs one day earlier, then it's worth it rather than waiting for the code authority to give permission."[13]

Most comic book publishers and editors set internal rules about dealing with the Comics Code. Despite regulations about sex and the depiction of government officials in a bad light, the Code did not include drug abuse. Publishers could not feature werewolves or vampires, but drugs were not explicitly outlawed.

The Amazing Spider-Man #96 did not bear the Comic Code seal of approval. Stan continued the drug plot for the next two issues, revealing that Harry Osborn had a pill addiction. Parker chalks Harry's habit up to him being "so weak." Later, the younger Osborn obtains pills from a dealer (resembling a blond version of Stan Lee), who promises the pills are "just what the doctor ordered." Back at the apartment he shares with Parker, Osborn passes out after taking a handful of pills. When Peter finds him, they are interrupted by the Green Goblin, who wants to kill Spider-Man. After battling the villain above the New York high rises and apartment buildings, Spidey eventually rodeos the Goblin into seeing his hospitalized son. The trauma causes Norman to black out, which ends his villainous ways.

While government officials were happy to have Spider-Man and Lee on their side, not everyone agreed. John Goldwater, the publisher of Archie Comics and founding president of the Comics Magazine Association in 1954, publicly announced disapproval, including declaring topical use of drugs or drug abuse in comic books "still taboo."[14] Yet the far-reaching positive publicity Marvel received handcuffed Goldwater and the CMA. The organization issued no sanctions against Marvel or Lee.

In addition to bringing the Comics Code into modern times, Stan's decision to publish the *Spider-Man* issues put Marvel out ahead of DC, which had been rumored to be working on its own issues based on the same topic. Carmine Infantino, the editorial director at DC, also railed against Marvel, implying that the move should be considered potentially harmful, particularly to children.

Rejecting the code enabled Lee and Marvel to push harder on other social issues and allowed them to take a stab at appealing to more college-aged readers. One method for proving the relevancy of comics focused on introducing nonwhite and ethnically diverse superheroes. In June 1972, Marvel launched *Hero for Hire*, featuring Luke Cage, a black superhero that fought crime in Harlem. Two years later, Cage became *Power Man*, successfully teaming up with white martial arts legend Iron Fist.

Following these pioneering efforts and after the company introduced Black Panther, using the character in a series of titles, Marvel published *Red Wolf* (1972–1973), a Native American superhero. Shortly after, when the television show *Kung Fu* (starring David Carradine) hit the air in 1972, Marvel picked up on the martial arts wave (which included the work of Bruce Lee and others using karate). The company developed *Master of Kung Fu*, featuring Asian superhero Shang-Chi, who first appeared in *Special Marvel Edition #15* (December 1973). By April 1974, the title changed to *The Hands of Shang-Chi: Master of Kung Fu* and began a long, popular run, eventually appearing in crossovers with Marvel's top superheroes.

Lee always harbored ambitions to be more than "just" a comic book writer and editor. When he was a boy, his mother showered him with praise and joked almost daily that Hollywood talent scouts would soon take him from her. He acted out scripts for artists and other writers and enjoyed the constant bustle of hustling from campus to campus as a one-man Marvel marketing machine. Most of these efforts paid dividends in terms of growing fan loyalty or spreading the comic book gospel. Sometimes, however, Lee's willingness to take chances backfired.

In early December 1971, a distinctive ad ran in the hip NYC paper *The Village Voice* announcing "Stan Lee at Carnegie Hall!" in January. For $3.50 in advance or $4.50 at the door, fans could attend the show, which promised "All Live! Music! Magic! and Myth!" The advertisement didn't feature many details, but Thor, Spider-Man, and Hulk were crammed into the image, with Spidey (in characteristically Lee style) promising: "An erudite evening of cataclysmic culture with your friendly neighborhood bullpen gang."[15] Later, the official name of the event changed to "A Marvelous Evening with Stan Lee."

Whether the evening was "marvelous" or not most likely depended on the viewer's feelings about Marvel and its band of superheroes. Most adults, particularly those reviewing the shindig for metropolitan newspapers, found the evening anything but amazing, likening it to an "employer at his own Christmas party" and "a company revue."[16] Lee served as host and ring-leader, which is an apt description, since the night devolved into a chaotic mess. There were second-rate music acts, some vague discussions of comic book arts with Romita and Buscema, and an appearance by new journalism star Tom Wolfe, who completed his white suit ensemble with an Uncle Sam top hat. Other oddities included the world's tallest man, nine-foot-eight-inch Eddie Carmel, reading a poem about the Hulk and Geoff Crozier, an Austra-lian illusionist, performing a strange magic act.[17] The highlight for Lee was reading parts of the poem "God Woke" from the stage with his wife, Joanie, and daughter, J. C. Fans really didn't know what to make of the show and made paper airplanes to lob at the stage in mockery and frustration.

Continually trying to establish Marvel as different, Lee started calling the company the "House of Ideas," which stuck with journalists and became part of the company's cachet. If a downside existed in the surge of Marvel com-ics into the public consciousness, it is that Lee and his bullpen teammates had to balance between entertainment, social issues, and profitability. Stan valued the joy derived from reading comics, but he wanted them to be use-ful: "Hopefully I can make them enjoyable and also beneficial. . . . This is a difficult trick, but I try within the limits of my own talent."[18] Lee wanted to have it both ways—for people to read the books as entertainment but also take them seriously.

At the same time, Marvel had to sell comics, which meant that little kids and young teenagers drove a sizable chunk of the market. In 1970, Lee esti-mated that 60 percent of Marvel's readers were under sixteen years old. The remaining adult readership was enormous given historical numbers but kept Lee focused on the larger demographic. "We're still a business," he told an interviewer. "It doesn't do us any good to put out stuff we like if the books don't sell. . . . I would gain nothing by not doing things to reach the kids, because I would lose my job and we'd go out of business."[19]

The industry moved so quickly that Lee and his creative teams constantly fought to get issues out on time. The number of titles Marvel put out meant that everyone had to be constantly producing. So when Lee was in the office or working from home, he committed to getting content out. Thomas recalls, "Stan and I were editing everything, and the writers were editing what they did, and we had a few assistant editors that didn't really have any authority. . . . That was about it."[20] However, that chaotic atmosphere made it rife for animosities to form or fester. Lee needed content out the door, and Goodman tried to maintain control over cover artwork and other little details that inevitably slowed down the process.

"Stan and Goodman were increasingly on different wavelengths as the time came near the end of their relationship," Thomas explained. "Goodman and his son, Chip, were still making those decisions at that time." According to the editor, "Chip, in that last year or less before Stan took over, was the official publisher as Martin withdrew from the business more. I don't know if Goodman was even in the office then, because I never saw him very much anyway. His office was way at the other end of the hall."[21]

In 1972, Goodman finally made good on his wish to retire, four long years after Cadence took over. He expected that his son Chip would be named the new publisher. Instead, shortly thereafter the new owners showed his son the door—so much for handshake agreements and family ties. Cadence CEO Sheldon Feinberg named Stan Marvel's publisher and president.

The new post meant that Lee would have to step down as editorial director. After some internal wrangling and indecision regarding who would replace him, Lee handed over the duties to Roy Thomas. "Now I'll be able to do things the way I want them," Lee thought, but he was wrong. Instead, he attended a dizzying succession of meetings and strategy sessions to discuss the financial status of all the company's publications, including the men's magazines. "I suddenly realized that I am doing something that millions of people can do better than I can do. The thing I enjoy doing—the creative stuff—I'm not doing anymore." This realization led Lee to give up the president position to concentrate on the publisher's duties.[22]

In the meantime, Goodman didn't stay retired for long. Angered by his son's termination, Goodman retaliated by founding Atlas Comics. He put

Chip in charge and began an aggressive poaching program, even hiring away Lee's younger brother, Larry, to serve as editor. Many other Marvel freelancers and artists also left because Goodman paid more. The desertion grew so prevalent that Lee had to issue a memo reminding staffers and freelancers of Marvel's commitment to them. Although a negative blip for Lee, the industry had changed, so Goodman's maneuverings were outdated. Atlas soon folded.

There were additional growing pains for Lee as publisher and Thomas as editor. Lee had a looser vibe with people but also was a legendary figure. "He sent them off feeling very enthused about doing something new," says writer Mark Evanier, who worked with both Lee and Kirby. "They didn't operate for him out of fear, as they did for some editors."[23] Thomas inherited a staff loyal to Lee, but they still had to churn out some forty titles a month. The production schedule remained king. "I knew I didn't have the power Stan had had as editor-in-chief, because he was right there, and I wasn't looking for that," Thomas recalled. "I wasn't threatened by anybody, and who's going to have a better rapport with Stan than I did? It was very good, most of the time, so I didn't feel that insecure."[24]

Thomas's ascension and Lee's pull toward management did shift the editorial direction, if for no other reason than that Stan wouldn't be writing full time any longer. "It was time to kind of branch out a little bit," Thomas explained. "We wanted to keep some of that Marvel magic, and at the same time, there had to be room for other art styles and other writing styles."[25] The most overt change came when Lee turned in the copy for *The Amazing Spider-Man* #110. The late 1971 issue was the last Lee wrote for the character. Writer Gerry Conway succeeded Lee, and the next books in the series would be cocreated by Conway and star artist John Romita.

While many adults looked down on Lee for writing comic books, especially early in his career, he developed a masterful style that rivals or mirrors those of contemporary novelists. Lee explained:

> Every character I write is really me, in some way or other. Even the villains. Now I'm not implying that I'm in any way a villainous person. Oh, perish forbid! But how can anyone write a believable villain without thinking, "How would I act if he (or she) were me? What would I do if I were trying to conquer the world, or jaywalk across the street? . . . What would I say if I were the one threatening Spider-Man? See what I mean? No other way to do it."[26]

Lee's distinctive voice captured the essence of his chosen medium.

Lee also understood that the meaning of success in contemporary pop culture necessitated that he embrace the burgeoning celebrity culture. If a generation of teen and college-aged readers hoped to shape him into their leader, Lee would gladly accept the mantle, becoming their gonzo king. Fashioning this image in a lecture circuit that took him around the nation, as well as within the pages of Marvel's books, Lee created a persona larger than his publisher or employer. As a result, he transformed the comic book industry.

CHAPTER 10

MARVEL'S MULTITUDE OF MALADIES

Although it might have been difficult to put downbeat words in the mouth of the company's most important promoter, the 1970s were troubling times. Everyone at Marvel—including Lee, the creative teams responsible for putting out the comics, the accountants struggling to make sense of internal spending, and corporate managers determined to rein in the comics division— seemed at war with one another, desperate to counteract sagging sales.

Mirroring the national political and cultural scene, the comic book industry faced years of uncertainty, slippery footing, and ultimately an epic battle for survival. Marvel's per-comic sales plummeted, so the company attempted to offset the decrease by publishing more titles. For example, there were ten comics with "Marvel" in the title (ranging from *Mighty Marvel Western* and *Marvel Triple Action* to *Special Marvel Edition*).[1]

By January 1973, Lee oversaw production of sixty-nine titles, including twenty-eight superhero books, sixteen mystery/monsters, and ten Westerns. Total sales rose, but Marvel published so many comics that it concealed internal weaknesses and industry stagnation. Flooding the market had long been a Goodman trick, enhancing the overall financial picture but simultaneously increasing pressure on the creative teams.

Yet, in front of a microphone or with a reporter nearby, Lee remained positive, trumpeting Marvel's successes. Reading the Stan's Soapbox essays, no one would have guessed at the troubles. After the company replaced DC at the top, Marvel struggled to find its next objective. For some organizations, that drive to the top defines their culture. Marvel had to find a new path.

Amid the chaotic early 1970s, Stan's transition from writer, art director, and editorial lead to publisher proved jarring. In the office, he shifted from creative force to company man, a kind of conduit between the intransigent figures running the corporation at the top of the executive food chain and the chaos of the creative bullpen filled with artists and writers who—like the 1970s as a decade—wanted to buck the system.

Lee struggled to find his place in the unfamiliar corporate system, never fully understanding his fellow "suits" but also constantly worrying about the artists and writers who thumbed their noses at conformity and economic realities. He was the boss, creating an approval process for cover art and copy, while also balancing story lines and juggling workloads.[2] The operation grew too large for one person to manage everything, but the publisher role demanded his attention across business and creative functions.

Unlike his friends and protégés (many younger writers and artists drew inspiration from his work), Lee knew the intricacies of company finances. "What I do mainly is worry about the product we are turning out," Stan explained. "I'm really like an over-all executive editor."[3] Stan worked with Cadence execs on approvals for new magazines and comics, each decision having significant financial consequences since profit margins were so thin.

Even into the 1970s, Lee and other industry insiders expected the superhero craze to eventually fizzle. If Marvel faltered, the best-case scenario for Lee would send him back to his editor's desk, writing multiple books for whatever the next fad might be, again relying on freelance artists to keep the company afloat. Fear drove him to keep a relentless pace. At any given moment, Stan could be overseeing strategic editorial decisions, managing the expectations and meddling of the corporate execs, launching new magazines, or flying from college campus to campus to fulfill his marketing and lecturing roles.

Demographics worked against Marvel. Superhero popularity skyrocketed, yet sales slumped. Readers skewed younger, buying titles like *Archie Comics*, the best-selling comic of 1970 at 515,000 sold per issue versus *The Amazing Spider-Man* at about 373,000.[4] At the end of 1971, the official Audit Bureau of Circulation (ABC) stats revealed that monthly paid circulation had dropped over the preceding three years. Marvel sold about 96 million comic books in 1968, but the figure fell to 91.8 million in 1971, despite more total books on sale.[5] Over the following year and a half, the number would plummet to just over 5.8 million per month or just under 70 million annually for 1972 and 1973. In comparison, DC dipped from about 6.3 million per month in 1968 to just 4.7 million five years later.[6]

Desperate, the comic book division again pushed different fads. Marvel rushed headlong into fantasy and horror, publishing *The Tomb of Dracula*, *The Monster of Frankenstein*, and *Man-Thing*, among others. Stan urged fans to accept the new direction in Soapbox columns, calling the new *Monster Madness* title "the most frantic, far-out, fabulously frenzied monster mag you've ever goose-pimpled over!" He implored readers to obey the first Marvel Commandment in his faux biblical exhortation: "Thou shall not miss it!"[7]

The move into horror came after the Comics Code adapted to shifting cultural norms initiated by Lee's efforts to publish the Spider-Man issue tackling drug use. In 1972, Code regulators officially eliminated restrictions prohibiting horror comics, particularly those featuring werewolves and vampires.

Cadence executives did not really understand the comic book division, so they had difficulty comprehending fluctuating sales numbers or stemming the decline. Historically, comics garnered a high pass-through rate, which meant that for every comic purchased, about three to five additional people read it—a large number of people with no reason to purchase a copy.

Yet no one expected the numbers in 1971 to set a trend. Sales told a different story: Marvel would not reach 1971's monthly circulation (7.4 million copies) threshold again until 1987. Cadence reacted by tightening editorial control but giving Roy Thomas the chance to move in new directions. For example, in 1970 he convinced Stan to support the sword-wielding *Conan the Barbarian* series, and it became a hit.

In late 1972, Lee's role took on a strategic component when he became publisher of Marvel Comics. "I was deciding what books we would publish and what to concentrate on," Stan explained. "I worked with the editor and oversaw most of what we did."[8] With Thomas as new editor-in-chief, they charted a fresh course but had to do so during a period of weak sales. Roy attempted to move comics into new genres less reliant on traditional super-heroes, including Man-books featuring Thing, Ghost Rider, and Dracula. The 1970s seemed a topsy-turvy mix of innovative new characters trying to survive in a down market, while Lee mixed his publisher duties with promo-tions and marketing. Stan's personal celebrity skyrocketed, but decreasing sales rocked Cadence.

Merchandising and licensing had been an afterthought with Goodman. That changed with Cadence but caused schisms between the leadership and the creative staff. Critics of Cadence argued that the company wanted to turn Marvel into a marketing machine, essentially ignoring superheroes and comic books unless they had licensing potential. But licensing did provide some financial relief. In 1973 and 1974, the push resulted in deals with toy companies and publishers, including Columbia Records, Hostess, Mattel, and others.[9] The merchandising deals grew important as circulation waned.

While editor, Lee had been somewhat distanced from licensing, often bemused when he saw a new Spider-Man or Hulk tchotchke. As publisher, though, Lee served as conduit between Marvel and potential advertisers, par-ticularly with young salesmen who grew up reading his comics. Lee's celebrity made him an attraction at trade shows and other venues where Cadence lead-ers hobnobbed with corporate execs. Thus, Lee's importance actually increased as circulation plummeted. Even meager advertising and licensing money meant something when comic books were priced at twenty cents a copy.

Despite the downturn, the public Lee—the face of Marvel—remained as joyful as ever. Legions of fans flocked to see him as he spread the gospel of comic books. In mid-1975, the *Chicago Tribune* dubbed Stan "the creator of a modern mythology" and, more blatantly, "the Homer of pop culture" (a moniker originally used by Princeton students in 1966)[10]—heady stuff for a guy frequently self-conscious about his profession.

Stan increased his lectures, averaging one per week, and went on trips to Europe, Canada, and Latin America. In the first two months of 1975, for

"The creator of a modern mythology . . . the Homer of pop culture." —*Chicago Tribune* describing Stan Lee (Peter Gorner, "Stan Lee's Superheroes")

example, Lee spoke at seven colleges, from Sir George Williams College in Montreal to Augustana College in Rock Island, Illinois. During that stretch, he also did numerous radio shows, interviewed with print journalists, appeared on a Canadian television show, and served as featured speaker at Creation Con in New York City.[11] As Lee's celebrity ballooned, his appearance schedule had to be booked a year in advance.

Attempting to fill Stan's shoes as editor-in-chief turned into a nightmare. As sales bottomed out, Cadence managers increasingly meddled. The friction proved too much for a series of editors that began with Thomas (who left in 1974, contending that he would rather write than worry about climbing corporate ladders and managing staffers) and ended with the promotion of Jim Shooter in 1978.

The revolving door shook up the creative staff and spooked freelancers. For example, when Archie Goodwin took over in 1976, he had broad authority since many people considered him one of the best writers in the business. Yet Goodwin only lasted until late 1977. The strain of Cadence president Jim Galton's cutbacks simply took the joy out of the work.

Yet while both Thomas and Goodwin bristled at the business and strategy aspects of the job, both played an instrumental role in reversing plummeting sales. Before Thomas left, he met with a little-known filmmaker named George Lucas—about to debut a science fiction movie called *Star Wars*. Thomas urged Lee to okay a comic book version, but Stan was lukewarm about the film and denied the request. Thomas, however, continued to pester Lee, finally telling him that Alec Guinness was one of the film's stars. The esteemed actor's role changed Lee's mind. With Stan's approval, Roy worked out a deal with Lucas. The director cut a sweetheart deal with Marvel because he wanted to use the comic book as a lead-in to the film.

When *Star Wars* eventually took the world by storm, Marvel basked in the demand. The six-issue adaptation, written by Thomas (even though Goodwin was then editor), sold more than one million copies per issue—the first comic to hit that figure in decades. When *Star Wars* became a monthly title, Goodwin took over, gladly vacating the editor's chair. Some insiders, particularly Jim Shooter, felt that the *Star Wars* adaptation saved Marvel from certain bankruptcy.

Although Lee relinquished his editorial duties, he never really stopped producing. He couldn't help coming up with new ideas, carrying tiny two-by-three-inch spiral notepads that fit in his front shirt pocket. Stan jotted down thoughts in his scratchy, left-handed scrawl. He also kept a tape recorder bedside for middle-of-the-night inspiration.

As publisher, Stan exerted additional control over publications other than comic books. Whether it was his own feelings of inadequacy or the fear that the superhero craze might end, Lee poured great effort into the magazines. He had always believed working on magazines was a step or two above comic books.

Looking at magazines, it seemed Lee had a difficult time coping with the success and influence of *Mad*. Perhaps he envied publisher William Gaines's ability to get out of comics after the Wertham mess, or maybe it was that he knew and worked with so many of the writers and artists that gave *Mad* its unique voice, such as Al Jaffee, Wally Wood, and others. Stan attempted to duplicate the zany humor and satirical wit in *Crazy* (October 1973), basically using the staff that produced Marvel comics. Although it seemed new, *Crazy* had been one of Goodman's attempts to mimic *Mad* in the early 1950s—a venture that failed.

Crazy featured the "Stan Lee presents" banner. Marv Wolfman, who wrote *The Tomb of Dracula* comic and later created African American vampire hunter Blade, edited the magazine. Thomas served as executive editor. *Crazy* featured a mix of black-and-white illustrations and photographs, the latter captioned with puns and quips. Like *Mad*, the magazine took on popular culture topics, parodying films and fads, like the James Bond thriller *Live and Let Die*, which they changed to *Live and Let Spy*, featuring Agent 07-11 and drawings of scantily clad females. In addition to overseeing the magazine, Lee contributed, often adding one-liners to campy photos, like on the campus streaking craze. A photo of two officers carrying a naked man by the shoulders and feet: "Wait'll they find out I'm the Dean!"[12] The magazine also lampooned current events—taking swipes at race relations, President Richard M. Nixon, and even Marvel, including a recurring feature on the challenges of Teen Hulk.

Growing up, Lee loved newspaper comic strips. His contemporary, *Peanuts* creator Charles Schulz, had inspired a generation of artists to establish their own comic strip franchises. Over the years, Stan created heartwarming strips like *Mrs. Lyon's Cubs* and *Willy Lumpkin*, but they never caught on as he hoped. In October 1976, Lee teamed up with freelance artist Frank Springer to create *The Virtue of Vera Valiant*, a campy strip that satirized TV soap operas. The title character earned her moniker because of her role in an odd love triangle—head over heels for a man whose wife fell asleep on their honeymoon and never woke up.

After time in the Army during World War II and getting an art school education, Springer launched a career in comics but did not start with Marvel until the mid-1960s. Soon, though, like many of Lee's favored free-lancers, the artist worked on several different characters, honing each style under Lee's guidance. Eventually, Springer took over *Spider-Man*, drawing the book from the mid-1970s into the 1980s. When he worked with Lee in the mid-1960s, Springer remembered Stan's unwavering influence: "At that time, Stan Lee was the guy you talked to about whether you did this book or not and how you did it and whether you did the next one."[13]

Vera Valiant featured Lee's madcap sass and dry wit. The strip opened on a macabre note, when Vera's brother Herbert botches a suicide attempt. Vera learns that he is flunking out of correspondence school and is distraught. When she turns to Winthrop, the dashing CPA, for comfort, she exclaims, "What will become of Herbert . . . if he's expelled from correspondence school?" Winthrop deadpans: "We won't let that happen! The world needs podiatrists!" Later, when the accountant confronts the deadbeat sibling, he explains, "She's always dreamed of a podiatrist in the family!" In three panels per day and eight on Sundays, Lee and Springer presented a zany adventure featuring podiatry, space alien real estate agents, and a wife suffering from "sleeping disease" for fourteen years.

Much closer to his heart, Lee debuted a syndicated *Spider-Man* comic strip in 1977. *Spider-Man* sold millions of comic books a year, giving Marvel and Lee a great deal of cachet with newspaper editors. Initially appearing in about one hundred newspapers nationwide, the *Spider-Man* strip—penned by Lee and drawn by John Romita—gave newspapers a shot at attracting a younger readership. By mid-1978, about four hundred newspapers ran the strip, which gave Lee entrée to a new demographic of adult readers.

Stan had some difficulty adjusting to the constraints of a daily strip. How could a writer used to filling page after page boil a plot to three frames? According to Lee, the first box had to recap, the next box moved the story ahead, while the last ended with a cliffhanger. Steadily, he adapted to the minimalist style, growing to love the daily cartoon. The work gave him interaction with readers who wrote detailed letters about plot points, character motivations, and other topics. He enjoyed the interaction: "At least I know someone's out there—someone's really reading the stuff!"[14]

Spider-Man's popularity led the Tribune syndicate to launch a full frontal assault—in response asking DC to create a Justice League of America strip, dubbed *The World's Greatest Superheroes*. Veteran *Superman* writer Martin Pasko served as writer. George Tuska, who had previously been the writer/artist on the *Buck Rogers* strip over its last decade (1959–1967), as well as drawing *Iron Man* and *The Hulk* for Marvel, penciled, and Julius Schwartz edited. Initially the strip centered on the adventures of all the JLA heroes, including Wonder Woman, Batman, and the Flash, but eventually focused primarily on Superman. The competing cartoon strip also found its way into newspapers nationwide.[15]

Discussing his creative process for Spidey, Stan explained: "I first try to come up with a unique human interest angle, or a compelling sub-plot, some problem for Peter that seems virtually unsolvable. And one of the best ways to do that is to say 'What If?'"[16] Lee liked to load in complicated plots and obstacles, creating momentum toward a conclusion: "The formula for the Spidey strip should be to treat it almost like a soap opera."[17] Lee faced an inherent challenge: entice younger readers to daily comic strips, while simultaneously keeping older readers engaged.

Publishing books was in Cadence's wheelhouse. Stan had long hoped to pen a novel and dabbled in self-publishing, so the idea of a series of Marvel books (really more like edited collections with brief new introductory essays) appealed to his vanity and ever-pressing time constraints. The venerable New York publisher Simon and Schuster brought out a series titled Marvel Fireside Books, written or edited by Lee and comprising short essays and reprints of superhero and villain origin stories. Between 1974 and the end of 1979, some eleven Fireside Books were published, ranging from the launch of *Origins of Marvel Comics* (September 1974) to *Marvel's Greatest Superhero Battles* (November 1978).

Readers delighted in the Fireside series, granting them a relatively inexpensive and convenient method for digging into the birth of the Marvel universe (*Origins* cost $11.95 in cloth, while a book on Silver Surfer ran $7.95). Until that time, they had to rely on reprint issues or tracking down old issues. According to a Marvel internal document from May 1978, the series sold well, listing the following sales figures: *Origins* (160,000 sold),

Lee posing with his book *The Origins of Marvel Comics*, 1974. Courtesy of Stan Lee Papers, American Heritage Center, University of Wyoming.

Son of Origins of Marvel Comics (100,000), *Bring on the Bad Guys: Origins of Marvel Comics Villains* (70,000), and 1978's *How to Draw Comics the Marvel Way*, coauthored with artist John Buscema (20,000 hardcover alone).[18] Lee worked on these titles in the evenings, after he finished the *Spider-Man* and *Vera Valiant* newspaper work and other writing commitments.[19]

In 1977, Lee edited one of the titles in the Fireside series, *The Superhero Women*, a book of essays and reprints featuring female heroines and villains, including Wasp, Red Sonja, and Medusa. Lee explained that Marvel never had a policy of creating books for male versus female readers and instead crafted stories "savored by anyone who loves fantasy and adventure."[20] Yet, over the years, Stan had attempted to build readership for female superheroes, scrutinizing subsequent sales figures. His interest seemed to go beyond circulation numbers to a genuine concern for attracting female readers.

Although not considered revolutionary when it came to writing and publishing books for female readers, Lee had great success writing *Millie the Model* and its many offshoots, as well as other titles aimed at girls and young women. He and Kirby had made the Fantastic Four's Susan Storm an interesting character with real power, not just a weak sidekick or stereotypical girlfriend figure (despite some cringe-worthy dialogue in the initial issues). Still, female superheroes were not always progressive. Wasp, for example, spent a great deal of time in early *Avengers* comics gushing over the dreamy Thor and basically flirting with all the male stars, despite her seemingly serious relationship with Henry Pym.

Lee's response to criticisms about Marvel not publishing enough heroines was tied to sales figures. Circulation numbers held final authority. Books that didn't sell could not take up a valuable spot on the limited roster.

The Fireside books were one aspect of the Cadence strategy, but the company also pursued another book lineup designed to entice younger readers, such as *The Mighty Marvel Superheroes Fun Book* (1976) and *Marvel Mazes to Drive You Mad* (1978). Also included were a series of coloring books, activity pads, and even a Marvel cookbook, along with calendars that booksellers could use to entice readers. Marvel even constructed special sales racks designed specifically for its books and collections. The 1977 display featured a three-sided color riser card designed by Lee. The launch of the Spider-Man and Hulk books were timed to the release of the live-action television series featuring the Marvel heroes.[21]

Lee's writing schedule while publisher juggled the Fireside books, approving merchandise and advertising copy, and the comic books themselves. In addition, he wrote a "Publisher's Perspective" column each month for Cadence's *Celebrity* magazine and continued to author Soapbox essays. As outside production companies worked on the live-action adaptations, Lee also contributed as "consulting editor or associate producer," mainly to "read all those scripts and give opinions."[22]

Other projects were outside the Marvel universe. In 1979, *Stan Lee Presents the Best of the Worst* came out. An odd conglomeration of illustrations, pithy facts, and Lee's irreverent humor, *Best of the Worst* drew from Stan's earlier work on Goodman's humor magazines. In *Best of the Worst*, for example, Lee identified Australian William Gold as "The Worst Writer"; Gold wrote fifteen books over eighteen years but only sold one article to a Canberra newspaper, earning a whopping fifty cents. Lee's primary contribution was a sentence after the narrative, joking: "Probably after lengthy negotiations."[23]

Stan spread himself thin, but he enjoyed the freedom. Like other celebrities, he had to maximize his efforts at monetizing fame, explaining: "People feel comic books make millions and millions of dollars, but there are many years when the companies have literally lost money. . . . It's not a case of everybody's pocketing millions and just trampling on the poor artists and writers."[24] Given the freedom to take on additional work outside Marvel, Stan jumped at the chance.

The animation work that had begun in the late 1960s and came together in the early 1970s continued. In 1978, *The New Fantastic Four* appeared. While Lee and Thomas wrote scripts, the show served as the final nail in the coffin of the Lee-Kirby relationship. Although Lee had been able to lure Kirby back to Marvel in 1975, the artist had an uneasy relationship with management and still held a grudge against Stan for numerous slights (some real and many imagined). According to Kirby biographer Mark Evanier, "He was sick of the business" and wanted out.[25]

Perhaps the magic had ended for Stan and Jack or maybe the King couldn't stomach any additional snubs. His final stint at Marvel seemed doomed from the start. He decided against renewing his contract, which would have limited his rights of ownership to past work under copyright and failed to address other issues he had with management. Instead, in 1978, he accepted an offer to be an artist for the *Fantastic Four* series. First with Hanna-Barbera, then with the DePatie-Freleng studio, which ultimately made the FF show, Kirby found deeply respectful colleagues, bosses that cared for him, and enough money to get him out of comics.

Jack and Stan had a notoriously rocky relationship, but their combined successes enabled them to cover over the animosity with a patchwork of excuses. Once the final schism occurred, though, they would never fully mend the break. They ignored the issues that caused the fallout, getting along well enough on the FF animated series that they actually teamed up on *Silver Surfer*, a graphic novel version released in 1978.

Kirby spent his later years blaming Stan for the problems he had with Marvel executives and others, just as he had insinuated that Lee squealed on him and Simon when they were moonlighting for DC in 1941. It is not difficult to imagine Kirby nursing that wound for more than thirty years. Though loving and kind to those around him, his fans, and his family, the King had a long memory when it came to perceived professional slights. The feeling of being a permanent outsider was always front and center—believing his art was underappreciated—even as he was universally acknowledged as the comic book world's greatest artist.

Certainly Kirby could be cantankerous, but he had another side rarely highlighted: quarrels with artistic partners and subsequent feuds or minifeuds. Of course, Jack and Stan had both devotees and critics over their long careers. Some insiders with little or no skin in Kirby's long-term reputation, however, have weighed in on the topic. George Kashdan, a longtime DC writer and editor, explained, "Kirby always had fallouts with friends." He remembered, "Once, we were having lunch together, and he talked about his falling out with Joe Simon."[26] Kirby and Simon were polite in later years but disagreed about Captain America's origin and who deserved more credit. Later, Jack unleashed on Stan, essentially attempting to diminish or eliminate him completely from the creative process. In other instances, Kirby gave himself sole credit for the *entire* Marvel universe.

Kirby's Hollywood efforts seemed rejuvenating. He worked with young, admiring artists and received a salary and benefits commensurate with his status as the industry's titan. Jack later hooked up with Ruby-Spears Productions,

"It was I who brought the ideas to Stan. . . . If I hadn't saved Marvel . . . he would have nothing to work on. He wouldn't be working right now. I don't know what he'd be doing now." —Jack Kirby on the origins of the superheroes, in 1990 (John Morrow, *Kirby and Lee: Stuf' Said!*)

enabling him to work on the animated *Thundarr the Barbarian* (1980–1981). They loved his work and gave him the producer title, which he cherished.

Where Marvel could have used more Lee-Kirby magic was in live-action programming. Reporters salivated in 1975 when Lee announced a *Spider-Man* movie was imminent, though one wire service didn't take comic books or Lee all that seriously, calling him "the man behind Spidey and a horde of other weirdos found in Marvel Comics." Later, the writer dubbed comics "flaky" and filled with "kinky dialogue." Lee, always working to expand the idea that comic books crossed age boundaries, told the reporter: "The books combine humor for college kids with action and adventure for the little ones." Despite the publicity and media response, however, the proposed *Spider-Man* flick never materialized.[27]

In 1977, when *Spider-Man* debuted as a live-action television series, Lee was horrified. "It was so juvenile. Spider-Man had no personality and no humor," Stan explained. "It was one-dimensional." Film technology didn't yet exist to make superheroes larger-than-life. No matter the character, they just seemed like an actor in tights. Lee found the adaptations bland—far less sophisticated than the comics themselves.[28]

Live-action *Spider-Man* worked well, though, in "Spidey Super Stories" on the PBS children's television program *The Electric Company*. Designed to help kids learn to read (dancer Danny Seagren donned the iconic costume), the short skits first aired in the 1974–1975 season, making the program a "must-see" for youngsters who couldn't get enough of the superhero. The writing mimicked Lee's style, but Spider-Man never actually spoke. His speech appeared in word balloons, getting children to practice reading as they watched the text.

Most stories on *The Electric Company* were silly romps. The show's mainstay actors (such as Morgan Freeman and Luis Avalos) played a variety of odd villains and supporting characters and narrated the action. Running about a dozen skits each season for three years, a typical encounter has Spidey battling the Birthday Bandit. The villain speaks in a rhyming, singsong voice ("that foe of fun and festivity"), wearing a playfully colored suit adorned with a cummerbund and top hat, but also steals from children's birthday parties. After a cake-smashing episode and some fisticuffs that gets cake smeared on Spider-Man's costume, the hero fights off the villain, eventually snaring the bandit in a web and thus saving the day. Keeping with the Lee playfulness, the final panel is a drawing of Spidey at a laundromat covered with a blanket while sitting in a chair, waiting for his costume to wash. The skit theme song ends with a brassy horn section. The singer wails: "Nobody knows who you are . . ."

As 1979 drew to a close, Marvel had its internal woes splashed publicly in the pages of the *New York Times*. Utilizing anonymous interviews and insider perspectives, writer N. R. Kleinfield revealed the comic book division as a dysfunctional outfit that pitted editors against writers and artists against management. The days of Lee's Merry Marvel Bullpen and the singsong nicknames seemed like a distant past.

Editor Jim Shooter was the target, labeled "power-thirsty." Shooter, who began his comic book career with DC at the precocious age of thirteen, was either loved or hated by Marvel staffers. His critics accused the imposing writer/editor of having an ego larger than his six-foot-eight-inch frame. A group of Marvel employees were jealous, feeling someone with more seniority should have become editor.

Other unnamed company executives were considered "more interested in coining money from licensing deals than they are in the superheroes." Thomas sided with the creative teams, calling Marvel both "callous" and "inhuman."[29] The article also revealed deep mistrust between the comic book editorial team and management. The creatives wanted to focus on craft, while corporate leaders demanded profits. The age-old battle between inspiration and capitalism roared on.

Lee was lauded in the article but also came under some fire. Kleinfield called Stan a "creative genius" made famous by "inventing heroes" with realistic lives. But an anonymous writer painted a portrait of sour grapes at Marvel HQ, chiding Lee because he "wants to be like Walt Disney" and viewed comic books as "sort of beneath him."[30] The article was a harbinger of general softness in a comic book market squeezed by television and a smaller buying pool. Baby boomers were aging out of the medium. Other longtime fans thought that the comics simply weren't as good as they had been in previous years.

In response, DC Comics and Marvel both cut monthly titles (Marvel from more than forty down to thirty-two). The move made sense from a business perspective, since the companies made more money via licensing deals than comics. But Stan understood the new in-house licensing division ruffled feathers. "It used to be that the only artists in the place were drawing the strips," he explained. "Now we have artists who have to draw box tops."[31] The nightmare scenario for comic book purists had come true—Spider-Man lunchboxes, action figures, and bath towels grew more essential to Marvel than the comic books that ran the superhero stories.

Prior to the cutbacks, the market leaders published dozens of new titles, attempting to grow revenue. In 1979, Marvel's operating income was a measly $1.5 million after sales that exceeded $23 million.[32] Given this tight financial pinch, Lee's Hollywood dealmaking held endless potential but was also an enormous question mark: *if* Marvel could deliver a hit or expand licensing. The traditional notion that comic books drove merchandising was flipped on its head. Clearly, the big two of Marvel and DC were licensing agencies first because that drove revenue.

Depending on one's perspective, the end of the 1970s could be viewed as a complete downer or a new era for Stan. On one hand, as Marvel publisher, he earned over $150,000 a year and created steady additional income from college lectures and television projects. Fans mobbed Stan at comic book conventions. He received thunderous applause from college audiences, students packing tightly around him, just to inch a little closer to the man who created their heroes. In their minds, Lee fundamentally created the central narrative of their young lives. These were heady experiences for a person who had toiled in comics for decades without much adulation or even respect.

Despite his personal success, though, Stan still chafed at the notion he was stuck in comics. He really wanted to make a splash in Hollywood. Lee explained to a reporter: "I would have liked to make movies, to be a director or a screenwriter, to have a job like Norm Lear or Freddie Silverman. I'd like to be doing what I'm doing here, but in a bigger arena."[33] Although a celebrity and out-and-out hero to fans globally, Stan couldn't shake the notion that he could be doing more.

As Lee searched for additional outlets for his superheroes, the effort increasingly brought him to Hollywood, the great American dream factory. As he envisioned the next phase of his career, he looked west to California's golden shores.

CHAPTER 11

THE LURE OF HOLLYWOOD

Whether Lone Ranger's cry of "Hi-Yo, Silver! Away!" or air rushing by as Superman flew through the skies, the early history of television is entwined with superheroes. The *Superman* and *Batman* television shows stirred sales surges in the 1950s and late 1960s. Fans got a thrill seeing their heroes on their living room screens. Marvel hoped to replicate these successes in the 1970s—establishing a foothold in Hollywood, then utilizing TV as a vehicle for launching films. They hoped to drive large profits, thus offsetting the cyclical nature of traditional comic books.

Following the path laid out over the previous century, Stan looked west to the golden shores of California. In his late fifties, he viewed Hollywood as a way to reinvigorate his career. When television networks showed interest in Marvel's superheroes for animated and live-action programming, Marvel president Jim Galton sent Lee to Los Angeles.

Stan's celebrity, combined with the ubiquity of superheroes, opened doors, but he did not call the shots. Hollywood played by different rules. Development took a long time, and many deals died before reaching production. Adding to the challenges, studio executives were skeptical that superheroes would appeal to adults.

Yet the winds of change seemed to be shifting. Marvel's popularity influenced popular culture broadly, particularly science fiction and fantasy films and television. On TV, *The Six Million Dollar Man* (1974–1978) affirmed that audiences would respond to a superhero-like lead. Steve Austin (actor Lee Majors) developed into a phenomenon, spawning comic books (featuring artwork by Lee's friends Howard Chaykin and Neal Adams), albums, and action figures. *The Bionic Woman*, starring Lindsay Wagner as Jaime Sommers (1976–1978), resulted in additional merchandise, ranging from action figures and a board game to lunchboxes (a must-have item for 1970s elementary school children).

Although science fiction and fantasy movies had always been influential, the 1960s paved the way for new narratives. In 1968, *2001: A Space Odyssey* and *Planet of the Apes* generated strong box office sales, while also creating adult-focused storytelling. Later, *Logan's Run* (1976) demonstrated how movies could be enhanced by technology and special effects. In 1977, George Lucas's *Star Wars* launched a new era in film. The Marvel influence was clear. After all, didn't Luke Skywalker seem like a futuristic version of Spider-Man . . . an outsider coping with extraordinary powers? Darth Vader's similarities to Dr. Doom were unmistakable. A year later, the mighty *Superman* (actor Christopher Reeve) flew into theaters, touting the use of special effects to blow the audience's mind. These films proved technology could power plots and characters. It seemed high time for Marvel characters to make the transition.

Lee was increasingly focused on Hollywood. He viewed Los Angeles as "Nirvana," a celestial utopia enabling him to launch a new path without discarding past accomplishments. Any trepidation regarding the move got swept away in excitement and the sheer magnificence of the West Coast— warm breezes blowing off the Pacific Ocean and hidden hillside enclaves deep in thick woods.

The transition from print to television seemed natural in a world increasingly dominated by images and movement. Lee called the Marvel style "a very cinematic approach" marrying dialogue and art.[1] A quick flurry of activity in Los Angeles (deals with several networks and production companies) gave Marvel a lift. However, some of the resulting television shows were weak. Hollywood studio executives underestimated how Lee's style made Marvel superheroes iconic.

Many of Stan's cocreations seemed natural for television, but one of the least likely—the green-skinned, raging behemoth Hulk—actually made it. Former Mr. Universe Lou Ferrigno, a six-foot-five-inch, 285-pound mass of ripping muscles, played Hulk, while veteran actor Bill Bixby was the mild-mannered alter ego, David Banner (changed from Lee's original "Bruce"). Critics weren't that impressed, viewing its popularity as mainly women gawking at Ferrigno, but the drama was aimed at adults. "We've tried to make it an adult show that kids are allowed to watch," producer Ken Johnson explained. Stan appreciated the adaptation, identifying with the cathartic impulses of some viewers: "We'd all like to 'Hulk out' sometimes," he said. "Nobody pushed the Hulk around, and people can identify with that."[2]

CBS later brought Spider-Man, Doctor Strange (changed to "Dr. Strange"), and Captain America to the small screen. *The Amazing Spider-Man* (Nicholas Hammond as Peter Parker) ran off and on for two seasons. *Dr. Strange*, featuring Peter Hooten, debuted as a television film/pilot in September 1978, while *Captain America* also came out as a TV film (starring Reb Brown).

Based on Spidey's pop culture ubiquity, the pilot earned a 30 share, the network's highest rating for 1978. Execs worried, though, that it did not conquer the decisive eighteen- to forty-nine-year-old demographic. They hedged, only ordering five episodes, but the debut scored in the top ten and the series landed in the top twenty for the season. Network officials still deemed it a failure because it didn't attract an older audience.

While young fans (including this author) tuned in, Stan hated it, saying the show "looked silly . . . juvenile, comic-booky." He didn't mince words: "Spider-Man was a TV series for a while, and it was terrible. Just dreadful. It had no personality. No humor. None of the ingredients it should have had."[3] Despite ratings, CBS axed the show. Stan hated the *Spider-Man* series but declared *Captain America* an "abomination."[4] The adaptations had the same challenge—deviating from the overriding concept that Lee and his cocreators established. Stan shuddered at how Hollywood fiddled with the superheroes. From his perspective, Hollywood was shortsighted.

Adding to the challenges, Stan's over-the-top approach didn't translate well in Los Angeles. He habitually announced deals, but the buildup backfired when projects were mired in preproduction or fizzled altogether. "We've been working with other production companies, and I have to go along with what they want to do," Stan explained. "It's just taking forever to come up with a story that everyone agrees on."[5] He and Marvel were stymied. "There is no way of ever predicting which the networks will buy and which they won't," he lamented.[6] "Out here, you get an idea for a movie and years later, you're still trying to get it on the screen." Stan sighed, "Here, it is much more big business. There are contracts and negotiations and turnarounds. I find that a little frustrating, because I like to move fast and write fast."[7] Life in LA seemed a kind of vicious cycle of meetings, negotiations, deals, and waiting. Lee spent more time talking about creativity than producing anything creative.

Despite the aggravations, Stan wanted to relocate permanently with Joan. *Superman*'s popularity gave them a jolt. With influential critic Roger Ebert's thumbs-up providing a boost, the movie earned $300 million. In a letter to eminent French New Wave filmmaker Alain Resnais, Lee told his friend about his "love" for Los Angeles, hoping he might "infiltrate . . . the TV and movie business." He spoke of an imminent deal to make a big-budget Silver Surfer movie with Lee Kramer, the manager/boyfriend of popular singer and actress Olivia Newton-John.[8]

"The fact was that I had fallen in love with L.A. during my many trips," Stan explained.[9] But he hadn't fully convinced Joanie. She warmed to the idea after their apartment in New York was robbed (her jewelry and valuables were stolen). "The most depressing and distressing thing imaginable," Stan remembered. Hollywood would be a fresh start. In line with his jolly persona, Stan put on a brave face, joking to Alain and his wife, Flo: "Lock up your jewelry!"[10]

Stan dabbled in outside projects too. Attempting to employ the Marvel Method, he dictated a plot into a tape machine for *The Night of the Witch*, about a witch that only killed bad guys. Independent filmmaker Lloyd Kaufman (who would later score big with cult classic *The Toxic Avenger*) transcribed the tapes, working the material into a full script. They sold it for a meager $500, but the movie never went into development.[11] Later they worked on *The Man Who Talked to God* for Resnais, but the director did not option the treatment.

Despite his celebrity, Lee was a fledgling scriptwriter. His ideas were at the mercy of people he worked with to craft treatments. In the early 1970s, he had teamed with Resnais to option a couple of scripts, but in the intervening years, none of the projects were completed. The collaborative process fit his frenetic style, but what emerged did not capture Lee's Marvel-like voice.

It seemed as if Stan overcommitted to the Marvel Method. He couldn't find partners to fulfill his vision or who were as talented as Kirby and Ditko.

When Lee got approval from Cadence to move to California, he opened a little shop in the San Fernando Valley in a small, flat building at 4610 Van Nuys Boulevard in Sherman Oaks. Lee described it as a "mini-Pentagon built around a lush garden atrium."[12] Stan laid out aggressive plans, attempting to live up to the "Excelsior" sign hanging on the office door. A lifelong New Yorker, Lee relished the LA sunshine, frequently working in the atrium— quite a difference from cold, gray New York City!

A handful of experienced executives joined Stan. David H. DePatie served as president—an animation veteran who had worked on Dr. Seuss specials and won an Academy Award. "Marvel Productions," according to an announcement, had already initiated several animated and live-action projects, including commercials for Oscar Mayer and Owens-Corning. Stan yearned for a blockbuster film deal, but his main tasks centered on expanding the Marvel universe, including new commercials and licensing agreements. Cadence added the formal title "vice president, creative affairs" to his publisher role.

Time claimed Stan was "chiefly responsible" for turning television into "one big electronic comic book." The magazine joked CBS actually stood for "Comic Book Supplier."[13] In the early 1980s, Marvel Productions scored with several nonsuperhero projects, including *Meatballs and Spaghetti* for CBS's Saturday morning cartoons. The network also aired *Dungeons and Dragons*, based on the popular dice role-playing game.[14]

Stan had greater success in merchandising and licensing, which were essential in amplifying the brand. He spoke at many corporate events, utilizing demographic research to show organizations Cadence's reach. Lee boasted that 92 percent of American youngsters six to seventeen years old read comic books and that six in ten were from middle- and upper-income families. Marvel hired actors to dress up as superheroes to fire up audiences while Stan chatted. The company also rented actors in superhero costumes for mall openings, parades, and state and county fairs.[15]

By the mid- to late 1980s, Lee had distanced himself from comic operations in New York. He barely even read the comics: "Sometimes they stack up so high, I only have a chance to flip through them."[16] Instead, Stan worked on scripts and treatments, watched over animated productions, and shepherded potential deals.

Lee never dropped his role as Marvel spokesman, though he did increase his speaking fee to $3,000 to give colleges *less* incentive to book him.[17] Instead, he spoke at big-ticket events, like comic conventions, and did more interviews. Stan's on-air performance mixed spokesperson, provocateur, pitchman, historian, and actor. He was quick with a sound bite and superhero origin story. In a 1984 interview, Lee boasted that comics were "far bigger than they've ever been," citing Marvel's role in creating "a fan following for comic books, that never existed twenty or thirty years ago."[18]

While this may have been factual, the interview also revealed why some fans were angry with Stan. TV and radio hosts and interviewers took shortcuts—labeling Stan as *the* "creator of such characters as . . ." without attributing *cocreator* status or even mentioning Kirby, Ditko, or others. These media people may not have understood the context, but Stan could have corrected errors. Sometimes he did, but not consistently. These moments seemed like intentional slights, generating animosity. Die-hard fans deduced that Stan sought the full spotlight and credit at the expense of Ditko and Kirby. In his mind, Lee may have sacrificed truth (or the full truth) for the sake of showmanship and the hope of being likable.

In that era, Marvel also hoped to attract more female readers. Stan developed She-Hulk and Dazzler, while planning additional superheroines. The first issue of the *Savage She-Hulk #1* (February 1980) sold 250,000 copies. Lee told a reporter, "We've always wanted to do books about females," but admitted that profits drove editorial decisions: "For years, we were never able to make any of our female characters sell well."[19] Like earlier attempts, readers voted with their dollars; *She-Hulk* lasted only two years.

As he got older, Stan opened up about his writing process. In 1986, he admitted: "I feel that it's as difficult for writers to keep their own personal convictions out of what they write as it is for people in general to keep their personal thoughts . . . out of what they say in conversation." Lee explained that each character "is really me. . . . I'm every single one of them . . . [but] Spider-Man is practically my autobiography." He dedicated three days a week to writing (Saturday, Sunday, and Wednesday), leaving the other days for business meetings and strategy sessions. Just as in New York, he wrote outside, covering his word processor with a cardboard contraption he created. California was a great elixir: "I find myself 'thinking story' almost twenty-four hours a day."[20]

While Stan settled in, another Marvel bomb dropped. In November 1986, Cadence Industries sold Marvel for $46 million to New World Pictures, a production company/distributor. Marvel employees may have loved the deal, but Disney dominated via film and merchandising, not publishing. Becoming "mini-Disney" could be viewed as ominous for comic book staffers.

New World leaders welcomed Stan; members of its board of directors asked for his autograph. Yet there were ominous warning signs too. Reports circulated that new boss Robert Rehme didn't know Marvel from DC. Supposedly, when Rehme realized New World bought Spider-Man, not Superman, he yelled: "Holy sh*t. We gotta stop this. Cannon has the Spider-Man movie."[21]

Still, New World used Spider-Man to extend its brand. They spent $300,000 on a 9,522-cubic-foot balloon for Macy's Thanksgiving Day Parade. Officials estimated that about eighty million TV viewers would see the parade, along with two million in person. In 1987 they brought the character to life, having Spidey marry longtime sweetheart Mary Jane Watson at home plate in Shea Stadium before a sellout crowd of fifty-five thousand on hand to watch the world champion New York Mets. Stan presided over the wedding. The buzz got Lee on *Good Morning America* with popular newscasters Maria Shriver and Forrest Sawyer, and *Entertainment Tonight.*

Despite the public relations successes, New World struggled. The 1987 Black Monday stock market collapse and several flops left the company debt-ridden. Stan's star also dropped—the precarious financial picture rubbed off on him. A New World insider asserted: "Stan's not in the loop, because he's not a player; he's not a partner. He wasn't a vote. But he was like a pit bull. He just didn't want to walk away."[22]

New World had to sell Marvel. Eventually, Ronald O. Perelman, one of the biggest sharks in the capitalist seas, won the bid, offering $82.5 million via an intricate series of shell corporations under his control. Perelman demanded Lee stay aboard.

Celebrating fifty years as a Marvel employee in 1989, Stan once more had a new boss and professional chaos. Yet he responded with his emblematic mix of resolve and enthusiasm. His trump card endured—he symbolized the Marvel universe for generations of fans. To them, Lee was Marvel, no matter what, just as he became the father of superheroes to generations of readers and viewers, regardless of how the characters were actually created.

In 1989, Ronald Reagan appeared on *60 Minutes* shortly before leaving the presidency. Mike Wallace wanted to paint Reagan as a "normal" person, asking him, "You read the comics in the morning?"

Reagan claimed *Spider-Man* was his favorite.[23] Although his critics may have joked that *Spider-Man* was as much as Reagan could handle intellectually, Stan was proud when he heard the news. The leader of the free world began his day with his words!

Reagan's disclosure symbolized how influential the character, Marvel Comics, and Stan had grown. When the world found out that the president was a *Spider-Man* fan, Lee had just turned sixty-six years old, but his exuberance matched a person half his age. His former concerns about living a life bigger than comic books had transformed into an elder statesman role and widespread fame.

However, the presidential stamp of approval stood as a high point in a tumultuous era for Marvel and Lee. The next handful of years would be a roller coaster of highs and lows, rocking the icon and the company he helped immortalize. The challenges, from the public's changing tastes in popular culture to a global financial meltdown, ultimately involved the federal government and an international manhunt. Stan's legacy hung in the balance. He would never give up the battle to bolster his position as the godfather of superheroes.

In the 1980s, Ronald O. Perelman was a mogul with a Midas touch. "It is a mini-Disney in terms of intellectual property," Perelman explained. "We are now in the business of the creation and marketing of characters."[24]

Marvel's sales in 1990 eclipsed $70 million, though profits were just $5.4 million. Still, the profit doubled its total of two years earlier. Some eighty companies licensed Marvel characters (generating $11 million). Perelman's goal was an initial public offering (IPO), which might generate many more millions. In the quest to emulate Disney, the company needed a dominant film division, which led to the creation of Marvel Films.

Bill Bevins, Perelman's top aide and former chief financial officer at Turner Broadcasting, was tapped to run Marvel. He named Lee head of Marvel Films, a kind of retribution after he had been marginalized by the sharks at New World. Stan had viewed Marvel as a Disney-like empire long before his new bosses but wondered if Perelman had the cachet to pull it off.

In 1990, Todd McFarlane launched *Spider-Man #1*, a stylized reboot featuring several colorful covers. McFarlane focused on Spider-Man's visual identity: "to break people of reading a comic book the way they've been used to for the last twenty years."[25] In other words, he launched a new conversation around Spider-Man, just as Stan had done at the dawn of the Marvel universe. Many fans believed Spider-Man had become the most popular character in the world, displacing DC's invincible strongman in the red cape and the scowling guy in the black mask. The issue sold 2.85 million copies, the best-selling comic in history.

Stan frequently trafficked in nostalgia, regularly serving as story consultant for Marvel-related media, like the 1990 NBC movie *The Death of the Incredible Hulk* (again starring Ferrigno and Bixby). Fans saw magic in the Bixby/Ferrigno team, particularly the former's tortured, loner persona.[26]

In 1994, Lee edited *The Ultimate Spider-Man*, a collection of short stories. He provided insight on the character's birth: "No one at Marvel expected Spidey to become a cultural icon. . . . At that time, he was just one of many, many characters that were being continuously hatched, published, abandoned, and forgotten if they didn't catch on." Lee admitted he "cooked up" Spidey after seeing a spider on the window.[27] Still playing with versions of his narrative, Lee alternated between downplaying his efforts as cocreator and a more boisterous tone understood (at least partially) as tongue-in-cheek.

> "No one at Marvel expected Spidey to become a cultural icon. . . . At that time, he was just one of many, many characters that were being continuously hatched, published, abandoned, and forgotten if they didn't catch on." —Stan Lee (John Morrow, *Kirby & Lee: Stuf' Said!*)

The lighthearted banter Stan had with Marvel readers continued the trust he had built over decades. Whether his story about a spider at his desk on the fourteenth floor of the Empire State Building had even a shimmer of truth or was an utter falsehood, readers lapped it up. They believed in "Stan the Man," regardless of criticism from hardcore fanboys or some comic book historians. Fans turned up all over. For example, eminent novelist John Updike prompted a stir, criticizing the *Boston Globe* for cancelling the *Spider-Man* newspaper strip (the paper later rescinded). In response, Lee sent Updike a Spidey sweatshirt for his wife and a framed, autographed copy of the strip—another satisfied fan.[28]

The centerpiece of *The Ultimate Spider-Man* was Lee's novella that revised and expanded the character's origin. Lee's playfulness is on display in the piece—Aunt May whacks a spider while cleaning, exclaiming: "I just can't stand spiders, that's all. Disgusting creatures . . . good and squished." Stan even modified the famous ending phrase: "with great power . . . comes great responsibility."[29]

The Ultimate Spider-Man collection was part of Lee's mythmaking (along with Marvel). The biography section didn't mention Kirby or Ditko, underscoring Stan's role: "Hundreds of legendary characters, such as Spider-Man, the Incredible Hulk, the Fantastic Four, Iron Man, Daredevil, and Dr. Strange, all grew out of his fertile imagination." Certainly, the bio is a type of publicity, but these kinds of winner-take-all statements alienated comic book "true believers" who worshipped at the altar of Ditko and Kirby. From Stan's perspective, he could claim that he didn't write the bio, but as editor, the proverbial buck stopped with him. Still, a careful reader may also notice the book's dedication: "To Steve Ditko, who was there at the beginning."[30] Certainly Ditko would not have found the phrase *was there* satisfying or an accurate picture of his role in Spider-Man's creation.

Perelman took Marvel public with an actor dressed as Spider-Man appearing on the floor of the New York Stock Exchange, waving and shaking hands with traders. Via the IPO, Perelman pulled $82 million from company coffers. He poured $50 million back into his parent companies, essentially guaranteeing himself a 500 percent return on his initial investment and a 60 percent stake in Marvel.

Lee with Spider-Man, 1994. Courtesy of Stan Lee Papers, American Heritage Center, University of Wyoming.

The tantalizing possibility of director James Cameron (after the successes of *The Terminator* and *Aliens*) writing and directing a *Spider-Man* film (thereby launching a friendship with Stan) got Wall Street's interest. The stock price more than doubled, jumping to $35 per share by the end of 1993. Marvel reported revenues of $415 million and earnings at $56 million. On paper, Perelman's stake in Marvel reached $2.7 billion.[31]

Despite what seemed a bright future, there were looming cracks in the foundation. Perelman gambled by purchasing trading card company Fleer in mid-1992 for $286 million. Then Marvel gave toy maker Toy Biz, which specialized in action figures, a royalty-free license in exchange for a 46 percent stake in the New York–based company led by Ike Perlmutter and Avi Arad.

Simultaneously, the comic book industry went into a tailspin. The 1989 *Batman* film (starring Michael Keaton) and the 1992 *Death of Superman* comic book (six million copies sold) reinvigorated sales, but the mania fizzled. In 1995, Marvel reported its first loss under Perelman, losing $48 million, despite sales of $829 million. Debt swelled to about $600 million, essentially cutting off funds for new ventures, like a much-needed Internet division.

Perelman issued junk bonds to continue his acquisition spree. Corporate raider Carl Icahn (even wealthier than Perelman) viewed Marvel as ripe for a hostile takeover, purchasing $40 million in bonds. Eventually, when Marvel had trouble paying its debts, Perelman offered to grant $350 million in exchange for more shares, but Icahn, who then owned 25 percent of the company, refused the deal. Despite the downturn in the comic book market, two of America's richest men launched a financial war with Marvel's future in the balance.

On December 27, 1996, a day prior to Lee's seventy-fourth birthday, Perelman took his final step, plunging Marvel into bankruptcy in a last-ditch effort to thwart Icahn. "The news release was short and not so sweet," said former Marvel executive Shirrel Rhoades. "It sent ripples of fear throughout the comics industry."[32] Ironically, the publishing division held Marvel afloat, while trading cards lost money and advertising and licensing deals evaporated.

In February 1997, the bankruptcy court granted Icahn control. Four months later, he ousted Perelman, but estimates placed Perelman's profit at $200 to $400 million. While Icahn named a management team, diminutive Toy Biz jumped into the negotiations, hoping to protect their licensing agreement. In December, Perlmutter and Arad led an investment group, offering $400 million to purchase Marvel. Over Icahn's objections, the judge approved the counterproposal. Arad had convinced many of the debt hold-ers that Marvel's future as a film company warranted the gamble. His impas-sioned overture would prove prophetic.

Lee played good company soldier during the chaos. "I spend most of my time in the office working on movies, television shows, and animation," he explained. "I stay out of all that business stuff because my area of concern is the creative ends of things." The animated *Spider-Man*, *X-Men*, and *The Incredible Hulk* shows drew large audiences. Stan explained, "That's the most important thing as far as I'm concerned."[33]

Surprisingly, one of Marvel's lesser-known supporting characters—vampire hunter Blade (created by Marv Wolfman and Gene Colan)—was its first breakout film. Released in summer 1998, fans flocked to see star Wesley Snipes, despite mixed reviews from critics. Stan's brief cameo ended up on the cutting-room floor, but *Blade* proved his long-standing belief that Marvel characters would do well on-screen. The movie earned $70 million domesti-cally and $131 million worldwide.

Although past traditional retirement age, Lee focused on innovations, including video games, books on CD-ROM, and the burgeoning Internet. For example, Stan answered fan questions on an AOL home page in the late 1990s. He didn't understand how the web worked but realized its vast potential. Historically, few writers, musicians, artists, or other creative icons remained relevant as they reached Stan's age. Though time seemed against him in the 1990s, he refused to retire, presuming if he stopped, it might sap his will to live. Plus, Stan had a magic elixir—near-constant celebrity buzz. It wasn't that Lee simply didn't want to stop—he genuinely couldn't.

Stan Lee Media! The name had a certain gravitas. Who could have imagined that Stan would launch an Internet company? The marriage of the world's most exciting storytelling channel and the world's most interesting story-teller promised surefire success. Little did reporters and eager fans know that Stan's new venture was doomed from the start!

Lee was smitten with business partner (and Hollywood gadfly) Peter F. Paul, an entrepreneur who had worked with Hollywood legend Jimmy Stewart and orchestrated several high-profile fund-raising campaigns. Paul had successfully boosted heartthrob Fabio's career, displaying a knack for cozying up to the rich and powerful, including President Bill Clinton and wife Hillary. Like a true supervillain, however, Paul disguised a shady past.

The Internet explosion gave Stan an opportunity to prove he could master new media, even at seventy-six years old. "When Peter Paul suggested we start an Internet company, the only thing I really knew about the web was that it was going to be the biggest force for entertainment and communications that the world has ever known. So, naturally, I was excited," Lee explained.[34] Paul estimated that Stan's name alone accounted for $30 million in brand value. He hoped Lee could launch a new superhero universe that they owned outright.

> "I got into comics when they were just starting. I was lucky enough to be able to carve a niche and to make the company I work with the biggest company in the comic book field. Here I have a chance to try and do the same thing again in a new field, which is much bigger, more powerful, and more comprehensive than comics could ever be." —Stan Lee (Jordan Raphael and Tom Spurgeon, *Stan Lee and the Rise and Fall of the American Comic Book*)

Stan liked the idea of competing with Marvel. His long career with them seemed on the ropes. He had felt slighted in recent contract negotiations, chafing at the notion he was simply a figurehead. Lee felt hurt and angry in groveling with new Marvel head Ike Perlmutter on a contract, which cut his previous lifetime contract to a two-year deal at "exactly half what I had been earning." Lee wondered whether the ghost of Martin Goodman might have been guiding the new Marvel leadership team.[35]

Ultimately, Marvel executives grasped Lee's value as the spiritual head of comic books. They couldn't risk a public relations nightmare if Stan joined DC. Attorney Arthur Lieberman negotiated a new agreement—a raise (to more than $800,000 annually for life) and $125,000 each year for the *Spider-Man* newspaper strip. More importantly, the contract included a $500,000 annual pension for Joanie and a 10 percent stake in future Marvel film and TV profits. Stan also had a clause that permitted him to work on outside projects, regardless of publisher or organization.

Stan took several potshots at Marvel, declaring Stan Lee Media—in contrast—would produce online superheroes: "edgy, high-concept, and surprising."[36] He and Paul had visions of partnering with online production firms, creating virtual comic books, launching interactive games, and offering web-based classes with the comic book legend.

Stan Lee Media was headquartered in a nondescript office building twenty miles outside LA on Ventura Boulevard in Encino. The flash came in its gaudy marketing campaign, filled with glossy press kits in bright, brassy colors. The propaganda was a way to attract investors for a potential IPO. Nothing seemed over the top, with media materials exclaiming Stan "exerted more influence over the comicbook industry than anyone in history" and "more than 2 billion of his comicbooks have been published in 75 countries and in 25 languages."[37] The centerpiece was www.stanlee.net, a hub for new characters and products.

On NPR, Stan called web-based comics "really miniature movies. We have actors reading the roles. There are no dialog balloons."[38] The idea of creating a new superhero universe intrigued investors and excited fans. A reporter explained Paul's vision: trading on Lee's past accomplishments, creating "a Stan who could be offered up piecemeal to fans and eager licensing partners from the virtual balcony of a new House of Old Ideas built on the fluid foundation of the Internet."[39]

In August 1999, Paul concocted a reverse merger with Boulder Capital Opportunities, naming the new entity Stan Lee Media (symbol SLEE). As creative lead and chairman, Lee received stock options (six million-plus shares). The options had little initial value but promised to make the holders extraordinarily wealthy (Lee's annual salary was $272,500). In its first year on the top floor of the Encino building (also HQ for Paul's other shadowy businesses), the company grew to 150 employees.

The flagship franchise was *The 7th Portal*, featuring a superhero team battling villains traveling to Earth through a hidden gateway. Stan took a hands-on approach, according to Buzz Dixon, former VP of creative affairs. Initially, Lee focused on six or seven projects, writing outlines and character sketches. "Everything I saw had Stan's creative imprint on it," Dixon said. While Lee and a new bullpen worked on ideas, company officials explained what was really for sale—Stan Lee: "The fact is that Stan is a recognized brand in the global marketplace."[40] No idea seemed too outlandish; Paul and the team considered a Lee clothing line based on his catchphrases and others they might trademark. Interviewers noted that Lee routinely reported to work each morning in his black convertible Mercedes E320 around 9:30 and often stayed until 8 p.m.

On February 29, 2000, *The 7th Portal* debuted at a star-studded gala Paul orchestrated at Raleigh Studios in North Carolina. Television personality Dick Clark hosted the bash, with performances by Jerry Lee Lewis, Ray Charles, and Chaka Khan. Three months later, SLM announced a deal with Paramount Parks to develop a 3-D ride based on the *7th Portal* franchise for its twelve million annual visitors.

Yet Paul kept Lee from decision-making authority. According to insiders, Stan "would sit in business meetings and occasionally say something. But mainly he'd sit there and doodle, or fall asleep."[41] Paul kept the marketing machine operating at full speed, but fewer and fewer deals amounted to any tangible content.

With Stan's involvement as a lure, celebrities also jumped on the bandwagon, including the Backstreet Boys and Mary J. Blige. Pundits saw SLM as the culmination of Lee's career, even positing that under his supervision, SLM might become the Internet era's Disney. It was one thing for the general public to see the "Stan Lee" name attached to an entity and equate it with Marvel's successes, but it was another for the media, stock analysts, and others. The hysteria surrounding the New Economy bubble far outstripped the media's ability to recognize its farcical elements or anticipate the fated consequences.

In early 2000—at the height of the boom—Wall Street valued the company at $31 a share, basically giving SLM the paper wealth ($350 million) to buy Marvel Comics outright. Pop superstar Michael Jackson considered it, personally asking Lee to run Marvel if the deal went through. He agreed, but the acquisition never materialized.

Stan continued to work his strengths, becoming the face of the organization and spokesperson for online comic books. The extraordinary level of hype and willingness to believe in it with little or no validation created the perfect environment for Lee's longing "true believers" to truly believe (and get in on the ground floor of a "Stan the Man" enterprise). He stood among his people—a generation of self-anointed nerds who grew up on superhero stories and loved him.

Although some SLM employees secretly questioned the alleged deals, no one outside Paul and a small group of co-conspirators realized how fast the company burned through funds. Court documents later revealed SLM spent $26 million, while earning just $1 million in revenue.[42] Like other dot-com "bombs," SLM was a house of cards—no substance, just hype and marketing. Even worse, SLM actually engaged in fraud and stock manipulation.[43] The company's 150 workers lost their jobs when the company declared bankruptcy in December 2000, activating SEC and FBI investigations into Paul, Lee, and other executives. While authorities soon cleared Stan, they fixated on Paul. Soon, people around the globe would know his name—the criminal who ensnared Stan Lee in one of the world's most egregious Ponzi schemes.

Two weeks before Stan's seventy-eighth birthday, company staffers (despite ominous news stories about Paul's treachery) bought Stan a seven-foot-tall Spider-Man statue imported from Germany. They hoped in superhero fashion, Lee would save the day. But no superhero could rescue SLM. At a staff meeting, execs fired the entire staff. Stan collapsed. The memories of Goodman repeatedly forcing him to fire staffers and freelancers at Marvel still burned in his heart.[44]

If Paul were a supervillain, one can imagine his slick, tuxedo-wearing exterior masking a transformation into a slimy supersnake or energy mass fueled to superhuman power by money, jewels, or other baubles. He conned celebrities and the business press. The *Los Angeles Business Journal*, for example, had dubbed him "Spider-Man's Business Brain," crediting him for transforming Lee's new characters "into a business empire." Paul called SLM "the Disney of the 21st century."[45]

These over-the-top accolades are classic dot-com exuberance, but officials unraveled a swindle orchestrated by Paul and several henchmen. He had committed other crimes, including reneging on a $250,000 personal loan from Lee and forging Stan's signature on multiple contracts.[46]

On February 16, 2001, SLM filed bankruptcy petitions. Eighteen months later, the Colorado secretary of state dissolved the company. While the legal machinations unfurled, Paul fled. He turned up in Brazil, hoping to avoid prosecutors, but Brazilian agents later arrested the fugitive, imprisoning him for two years before he was extradited in September 2003. Paul attempted to wriggle out of legal troubles, but complaints verified that he bilked various parties out of at least $25 million. In 2005, he pleaded guilty, spending four years under house arrest. In 2009, Paul began a ten-year prison term at a federal institution in Anthony, Texas (paroled in late 2014).[47]

Decades of accumulated goodwill helped Lee dodge the catastrophe. Stan seemed an eccentric grandpa, not a high-tech criminal. However, many of the revelations were unkind, including evidence that Stan had slept through meetings or not paid close attention. Authorities understood Lee did not control the finances or orchestrate the illegalities, but he did recklessly keep his head in the sand, which allowed a company bearing his name to swindle investors.

Perhaps the saving grace for Stan fixed on Paul's astonishing corruption. He duped people more influential than Lee, including the Clintons and Muhammad Ali. Labeled a "sometimes-mysterious figure with searing eyes and grand gestures," Paul became one of the more fantastical, infamous figures of the dot-com age. As if the story weren't screwy enough, Paul later claimed ties to secret government agencies and that the charges were an effort to silence him.[48]

The SLM debacle virtually erased three years of Lee's life and damaged his psyche: "No platitude will ever repair the harm that's been done, to me and countless others," Lee explained. "But one thing's for sure—I'll never be so stupidly trusting again."[49] Most observers deduced the superhero industry's greatest showman would finally call it quits.

From a broader perspective, though, the collapse of the dot-com boom crushed the reputations of many business leaders. The resulting devastation on the global economy made the SLM boondoggle seem like just another dot-com nightmare. As Paul's criminal past and zany claims about working for secret military operations became public, observers realized the conman intentionally targeted Lee.

Stan fought back, not willing to let the debacle dictate his legacy. He returned to his strength—comic books—inking a deal with *Batman* film producer Michael Uslan and DC to reimagine its famous characters in a series called *Just Imagine Stan Lee*. While the series got mixed reviews, the DC deal was a coup. The idea, according to one associate, was to remove the "yoke of worry from Stan's shoulders."[50]

Despite turning seventy-nine years old at the end of 2001, Lee vowed to continue creating superheroes and launching new projects. As usual, Stan tapped into his seemingly endless supply of creativity to fashion a new image—pop culture's elder statesman and the godfather of comic books.

CHAPTER 12

KING OF THE CAMEO

Before *X-Men* hit the big screen in July 2000, Stan met with director Bryan Singer to discuss bringing the characters to life. "There was no template for it," Singer explained. "Comic book movies had died[;] there was no concept of one as anything but camp." Lee's advice took film in a new direction. He encouraged Singer to research the characters himself and scrap earlier scripts.[1]

The strategy worked! After an extensive marketing campaign, *X-Men* set a then-record for comic book films, earning $54.5 million opening weekend. Lee appeared in the movie playing a hot dog vendor. The cameo allowed fans to see "Smilin' Stan," but the box office success ($296 million worldwide) proved superhero films were viable.

Stan's appearance gave him a shot in the arm popularity-wise for a new generation. "It became tradition to see Stan the Man wandering through Marvel productions," he explained.[2] The cameos would continue for more than a generation (even after his 2018 death). The Marvel cinematic universe (MCU) came to dominate contemporary cinema, making Lee one of the most recognized figures in the world.

Yet Stan's astonishing popularity came with controversy. The success of Marvel films dwarfed his failures, but as he aged, Lee got caught up in a string of mediocre productions and lofty announcements of new projects

Film cameos made Stan's face one of the most recognizable in the world. Illustration by Jason Piperberg.

that led nowhere. Fans still viewed Lee as the face of Marvel, but his work outside the cameos was uneven at best. Stan continued to push new ideas, but the concepts simply didn't click. Despite setbacks, Lee responded by playing his most enduring (and endearing) role—himself. Stan amped up his public persona, focusing on nostalgia for the good old days of early comics.

The shifting winds of pop culture helped Lee recalibrate. Just as he and his colleagues had caught the cultural zeitgeist in the early 1960s, Lee did it again in the early 2000s. Something peculiar took place in the fusion of the Internet, cable television, and expanding film—geek culture took over, with superheroes at its epicenter.

Marvel films made superheroes even more hip in the new century than in Lee and Kirby's heyday. Fans lined up for hours just to see Stan or get his signature on their plastic-sealed, cardboard-packaged comics. Time eventually paid Lee back in dividends. People who grew up reading comics (and idolizing Stan) came into power. They paid tribute to their hero.

In November 2001, Lee joined with attorney Arthur Lieberman and producer Gill Champion to form POW! Entertainment (official title: chief creative officer). "I just wanted to show that I can succeed," Lee explained. He emphasized what had been missing at SLM: "working with people who are honorable and competent." The work, however, remained similar to SLM—Stan's ideas for new characters.[3]

Lee's embellishment continued too. An early press release announced a three-film deal with the Sci-Fi Channel, touting Lee as "creator and inventor of the modern superhero," who "revolutionized the comic book industry" via characters that had superpowers but were "none the less plagued by the same doubts and difficulties experienced by ordinary people."[4] These efforts focused on rehabilitating Stan's reputation and underlining his place in comic book history.

POW! negotiated a string of new projects designed to take advantage of Lee's status as pop culture's elder statesman. However, the constant hyperbole and lack of completed products left observers shaking their heads. Inevitably, critics questioned the company's viability since its potential success solely centered on Stan's creativity.

There were successes, though, particularly when the boss utilized the Stan Lee persona. In 2002, mega-popular indie filmmaker Kevin Smith (*Clerks, Dogma*), a lifelong comic book fan (and comic book store owner), released *Stan Lee's Mutants, Monsters and Marvels*, a series of discussions between them, along with additional Lee-centric material, heavy on his glory days and the effects of superheroes on American culture. Smith and Lee had been friends for years, particularly after Stan's extended role in Smith's *Mallrats* (1995). The filmmaker's approval demonstrated how Lee would be placed on a pedestal by his pop culture offspring—a generation of creatives that grew up gazing in wonder at Marvel and "Stan the Man."

Lee published his autobiography, *Excelsior! The Amazing Life of Stan Lee* (ghostwritten by George Mair, 2002), depicting himself as heroic and achieving the American Dream through smarts, hard work, and quick wit. For Lee aficionados, the book was an invaluable portrait, providing many details the icon rarely discussed. But Stan could never fully rip himself from the superheroes he helped birth. He crafted a public persona and narrative that stressed his role as the father of the superheroes.

> "I'm aware that there's got to be a time when I'm not going to be able to do this, but I hope that time is far off, because I'm really enjoying what I'm doing. Somewhere inside of this old body, there's a young guy trapped, trying to get out." —Stan Lee on retirement (Jordan Raphael and Tom Spurgeon, *Stan Lee and the Rise and Fall of the American Comic Book*)

POW! focused on new technology and innovations. In late 2003, Lee served as a consultant for Activision developing superhero video games. He provided input on game design, story ideas, and character development. Many other agreements, projects, and partnerships were in the works, but he was troubled by the slow pace. Sometimes POW! overreached, while other partnerships simply dissolved. These bombs were a black eye for Stan. Some of the deals and business leaders signing them seemed shady, fueling the notion he was selling his name and past successes for a quick buck. Visions of another SLM hung in the air.

Critics lambasted projects that seemed sordid. In 2003, for example, Lee launched *Stripperella*, an animated series with *Playboy* pinup, *Baywatch* actor, and paparazzi provocateur Pamela Anderson. Jumping in bed with Anderson—literally—and other kinds of campy, adult content seemed tacky and mercenary, like Stan was simply selling his name to D-level projects.

Yet there seemed to be no basement in America's desire for garish entertainment. Anderson found him "kooky" and "very eccentric" but loved the idea of an animated series of a stripper turned crime fighter. Part of Spike TV's ("first network for men") animated block of programming, Lee did not write *Stripperella* but served as coproducer, art director, and story editor. He didn't shy away from the cartoon's racy aspects: "It's not what I would call a dirty show. It's kind of funny-sexy, bad taste, as treated tastefully." Stan even compared it to a "late-night version of *The Simpsons*." Although the adult cartoon only lasted one season (thirteen episodes), it was picked up globally, often running uncensored (Spike blurred out topless scenes), including in Australia, the United Kingdom, Germany, Brazil, and Italy.[5]

The success led to a series of deals with MTV and its sister networks. Stan also served as executive producer of MTV's animated *Spider-Man* show.

The network needed content that appealed to a young demographic, and Lee had that pedigree.

In late 2004, Lee began working with *Playboy* founder Hugh Hefner on *Hef's Superbunnies*. Similar to *Charlie's Angels* (the hit ABC show that launched Farrah Fawcett's career), Hefner would send out Playmates to save the world. In overblown style, Stan praised Hefner: "As a fan who bought and cherished the very first copy of *Playboy* in 1953, it is an enormous thrill for me to be partnering with a man who has done so much to shape the culture of the times we live in."[6]

The two had much in common, both born in major American cities in the same decade (Hefner in Chicago on April 9, 1926). Hefner took a more traditional route than Lee: active in high school politics and journalism, he started the school newspaper and created a comic book. Neither saw combat in World War II, and both emerged from the global conflict full of vigor and optimism.

After a brief stint working for *Esquire*, Hefner borrowed $8,000 from dozens of investors to create his magazine. He wanted to name it *Stag Party* but couldn't because Goodman had copyrighted *Stag*. In December 1953, while Lee was editing and writing romance, Western, and cuddly animal comic books, Hefner published the first issue of *Playboy*, featuring a color pinup of Marilyn Monroe. An instant hit—supporters viewed it as a fresh attack on the repressive postwar era. Hefner focused the magazine on urbane, sophisticated readers, showcasing a playful and aspirational lifestyle. Before the decade ended, *Playboy* surpassed *Esquire*, selling one million copies monthly.

Stan admired Hefner's ability to gain credibility in publishing. They became friends, but while each transformed popular culture in their industries, no combined projects materialized. Decades later, Lee's praise for the *Playboy* tycoon went overboard, calling him "one of the great communicators in our society," admitting, "I can't think of anyone I'd rather partner with." The release heaped praise on Lee as well, calling him the "godfather of the modern comic book superhero." Hefner dubbed Stan a "creative genius."[7] Typical for this era in Stan's career, though MTV announced it would run the pilot, the program never aired.

While he hid his true feelings behind his always-smiling, ever-optimistic façade, Stan had something to prove, hoping to finally create franchises that he owned, thereby not having to watch as some new corporate overlord reaped massive profits based on his ideas. He clearly enjoyed signing deals and the resulting media frenzy. What he didn't possess, in contrast to his Marvel years, was a team of creators, artists, and other visionaries that could assist him in transforming ideas into completed projects and products.

The public assumed Stan was rich because he was owner of Marvel and/or its superheroes, but both of these points are incorrect. He did not own the copyright for the characters he created or cocreated. Right or wrong, this is how the comic book industry operated in the early days. The difference between Lee and the others (like Superman creators Jerry Siegel and Joe Shuster) was Stan's self-created position as Marvel's public face. Despite being a self-avowed "company man," he resented that Marvel profited off his ideas, particularly after the movie industry finally caught on to what he had been preaching for decades.

In late October 2002, *60 Minutes II* aired a segment about comic books and the tremendous popularity of superhero films. Much of the piece showcased Stan's impending skirmish with Marvel and whether he might sue his employer. The popular news show painted Marvel as evil—a greedy corporation reaping huge profits off the work of underpaid writers and artists. Lee's contract seemed straightforward, but when it was inked, no one anticipated how superhero films would explode—*X-Men* (2000) earned $300 million worldwide, while *Spider-Man* (2002) became a global phenomenon, drawing some $821 million. Correspondent Bob Simon, employing a bit of spicy language, asked Lee if he felt "screwed" by Marvel. Lee toned down his customary bombast: "I try not to think of it."[8] Most Marvel fans sided with Lee.

Days after the segment aired, Lee filed a lawsuit against Marvel for not honoring the clause that granted him 10 percent of future profits from film and television productions. The grand battle between Marvel and its most famous employee shocked onlookers, sparking headlines around the world. One reporter deduced: "You can't blame the pitchman for standing firm and insisting on his due."[9]

The public nature of the contract and its terms, including a $1 million salary for just fifteen hours of work per week, first-class travel, and large pensions for Joanie and J. C., led some comic book insiders to once again dredge up the argument regarding how negatively comic book artists and cocreators—most notably Jack Kirby—were treated by Marvel (and by extension Lee).[10] The resulting media buzz and idea that Stan was trying to exploit Marvel turned some against him. Critics deduced: Stan got rich, while Jack (and others) didn't. The injustice had been done, and they weren't going to change their opinions, regardless of Lee's contract.

In early 2005, after the courts ruled in Lee's favor, he again appeared on *60 Minutes*. "It was very emotional," Stan said. "I was really hurt. We had always had this great relationship, the company and me. I felt I was a part of it."[11] Marvel attempted to bury the settlement agreement in a quarterly earnings press release, but the news quickly spread, suggesting that it cost $10 million. Of course, the idea that Lee had to sue the company that he spent his life working for and crisscrossing the globe promoting gave journalists the attention-grabbing headline they needed. And while the settlement amount seemed grandiose, it was a pittance from the first *Spider-Man* film alone, which netted Marvel some $150 million in merchandising and licensing fees.

The settlement, however, changed Marvel's trajectory. In a major strategic shift, the company announced that it would produce its own films, rather than license the superheroes as it had been doing since the 1960s. The new approach gave Marvel control not only of the films but the future revenue-generating cable television and video products.

Merrill Lynch extended a $525 million credit line for Marvel to launch the venture (using limited rights to ten Marvel characters as collateral). Paramount signed an eight-year deal to distribute up to ten films, including fronting marketing and advertising costs. Interestingly, the agreement also shed light on the suspect Hollywood accounting practices that film companies use to artificially make it seem as if no single film ever made a profit. For example, the Marvel films collectively raked in $2 billion in revenues between 2000 and 2005, and the cut for licensing equaled about $50 million. Despite his contract, Lee had received no royalties.[12]

Stan realized that in a world driven by pop culture influences and hyperdedicated fans, he could just continue to market himself. He licensed his own image in 2004, founding Stan Lee Collectibles (with personal assistant Max Anderson and entrepreneur Tony Carroll). Fans and collectors could purchase memorabilia signed by Lee and authenticated by the store. For Marvel fans, Lee's image was nearly as recognizable as Spider-Man or Iron Man.

In 2006, in celebration of Lee's sixty-fifth anniversary with Marvel (which would have incorrectly made his start date in 1941), the company released a series of comic books called *Stan Lee Meets . . .* , featuring Lee as a character intermingling with his cocreations. Lee wrote the first adventure with the specific superhero, then others, such as Joss Whedon and Jeph Loeb, penned mini-tributes to him. Comically, most of the heroes and villains Lee meets don't actually like him much or at all.

The episodes Lee wrote were filled with inside jokes and plenty of Lee's corny humor. In the *Spider-Man* issue, for example, the story opens with Lee in the kitchen baking cookies while wearing a Fantastic Four apron. The web-crawler wants to live a "normal" life, approaching Stan for advice, who jokes: "The next time Spidey has a problem—I wish he'd take it to Ditko." In the issue where he meets the Thing, New York City is filled with billboards that make fun of past Marvel artists, such as Gene Colan and the Buscemas, as well as Lee's 1976 commercial for the Personna razor in which he declared himself "Personna Man."

Stan also took his "King of the Cameo" persona into media outside Marvel. On April 28, 2002, Lee guest-starred as an animated version of himself on *The Simpsons* in "I Am Furious (Yellow)." After a comic book craze erupts in Bart's class, the students rush to create superheroes. Lee waltzes into Comic Book Guy's shop, deftly placing an issue of *X-Men* in front of one of *Superman*. Then he criticizes Danger Dude, a comic book Bart creates, but encourages him to keep trying. Lee jokes, "If you fail, you can always open a comic book store." Then, taking a toy Batmobile from a young patron, he attempts to jam a Thing action figure into the car, smashing it into pieces. While the child cries, Stan counters: "Broke, or made it better?" Later, he is portrayed as insane, ripping off his shirt and attempting to transform into Hulk.

Getting in on the reality television craze, Lee hosted the Sci-Fi Channel's *Who Wants to Be a Superhero?*. Season one, which debuted July 27, 2006, featured twelve contestants who created superhero personas. Similar to reality shows like *Big Brother* or *Survivor*, participants engaged in challenges to prove heroism. Lee evaluated them and eliminated the player who was least heroic.

Lee's 1998 contract granted him exclusive rights to his likeness and certain catchphrases, like "Excelsior" and "Stan Lee Presents." POW! used the latter in a series of new animated films released in 2007. *Mosaic* debuted on January 9 and later aired on TV on Cartoon Network. The film starred Anna Paquin (who played Rogue in the X-Men film franchise) as Maggie Nelson, an aspiring actress who gains an array of superhero powers. Returning to the formula he mastered during Marvel's 1960s heyday, Lee created the story lines, but industry veterans completed the scripts. *The Condor*, starring actor Wilmer Valderrama, debuted on Cartoon Network on March 24, 2007, after its direct-to-DVD release several days earlier.

Some fans were disappointed in Lee's POW! work; there seemed to be a fine line between the splashy announcements and marketing hype. To be sure, the company had not produced any memorable characters, much less another blockbuster. Condemning Stan this way might seem disingenuous, though, given the rarity of writers, actors, or artists who continue creating great work at that age. Lee could have retired, living out his remaining years as a cultural icon. Yet he toiled earnestly on new projects, while also fulfilling his Marvel agreements: visiting comic book conventions, appearing in film and television cameos, and various writing projects. Lee's longevity became part of his legend. His tenacity in the early and mid-2000s revealed the depth of his character.

As a modern-day celebrity, Stan fell into the trap of being famous for being famous, which the cameos increased geometrically. Fans asked him about Spider-Man, X-Men, and other superheroes but knew precious little about his career or work. At the same time, the Marvel universe became the dominant box office force globally. Moviegoers who knew little about Lee had a face to place with the famous name. Stan's mug was as recognizable in Beijing and Paris as it was in Chicago or New York.

The cameos upped Lee's cool factor among fans and also with celebrities. Much of the *Iron Man* cast appeared at the 2007 San Diego Comic-Con. When director Jon Favreau announced a special guest, star Robert Downey Jr. glanced to his left, then raised his arms in a victory salute. A huge grin spread across his devilish face. The surprise visitor was Stan, greeted by hugs from Downey, actress Gwyneth Paltrow, and others, while applause thundered.

While fans might never get within a million miles of Downey Jr. or Paltrow, part of Lee's popularity came from accessibility. Fans saw his larger-than-life image on the screen but could meet him at comic book conventions. Stan's approachability set him apart from iconic artists (like Bob Dylan, Mick Jagger, or Bruce Springsteen) who have fans across generations but are essentially walled off.

Stan developed a friendship with Iron Man actor Robert Downey Jr. Illustration by Jason Piperberg.

Lee pressed the flesh and constantly met new generations of crazed fans who just wanted a moment, even if they were too overcome with nerves to pose a question or squeak out "thank you." Few iconic figures of Lee's era (or celebs decades younger) could attract similar crowds. How many celebrities live past ninety, let alone gain millions of followers on Twitter and Facebook?

Stan was the walking, talking, joking, clowning, self-deprecating heritage of the comic book world in the early decades of the twenty-first century. Some honors were serious, though. On November 17, 2008, President George W. Bush honored Lee with the National Medal of Arts and the National Humanities Medal at the White House (the highest award granted by the US government and most prestigious in all the humanities).

Ever the joker, Lee waited behind Academy Award–winning actress Olivia de Havilland. Placing the medal over her head, the president kissed the *Gone With the Wind* actress on the cheek. Lee stepped forward, reaching out his hand, which Bush took in both his. As he smiled, Stan blurted out: "You're not gonna kiss me, are you?" Bush burst into laughter. The next day, media sites around the globe ran photos of Lee and the president sharing a belly laugh.[13]

"You're not gonna kiss me, are you?" —Stan Lee to President George W. Bush (Jordan Raphael and Tom Spurgeon, *Stan Lee and the Rise and Fall of the American Comic Book*)

Most fans did not realize that Stan was not part of Marvel's leadership during the King of the Cameo era. His main work was POW!, slowing down only when his health demanded. Usually, Lee just smiled when continually asked to rehash the Marvel glory days. Sometimes he revealed deeper feelings. In 2009, Lee was asked if Marvel should attempt to acquire Superman when the copyright reverted to the families of Joe Shuster and Jerry Siegel. Lee replied positively but explained, "I'm with Marvel, but I'm not really part of the Marvel decision-making team. . . . I think my title is Chairman Emeritus, but it doesn't really mean much. . . . To prove they haven't forgotten me, I get these cameos in the movies, which is kind of nice."[14]

In 2008, Lee published *Election Daze* under the "Stan Lee Presents" banner, poking fun at political leaders and hearkening back to the 1940s and 1950s when he self-published books of humorous celebrity photos with wiseacre captions. The cover, for example, satirized Bush's mispronunciation of the word "nuclear" and Hillary Clinton's allusion to potential intern challenges. The tongue-in-cheek publication clearly attempted to capitalize on Lee's satire, but the effort lacked much bite in an era when political commentators essentially waged rhetorical warfare twenty-four hours a day on television and the Internet.

Stan's popularity made him a natural for late-night talk shows and popular sitcoms. In March 2010, Lee guest-starred on *The Big Bang Theory*, a show capitalizing on the growing popularity of "geek" culture (later considered one of the most popular TV series of all time). The episode (which attracted sixteen million viewers) has the lead characters attempting to meet the Marvel icon. In a memorable scene, Sheldon (actor Jim Parsons) visits Lee's house (Stan answers the door wearing a navy Fantastic Four robe). When he barges into Lee's home, Sheldon gets arrested. As the show ends, the offbeat scientist gleefully proclaims that he will hang the restraining order next to the one he received from *Star Trek*'s Leonard Nimoy.

In April 2012, Lee launched a YouTube channel (Stan Lee's World of Heroes) with *Fan Wars*. Dedicated to the "hero lifestyle and enthusiast culture," the channel featured scripted and unscripted shows, as well as comic book convention and news coverage. One of the most popular features was "Stan's Rants," a kind of live-action Soapbox column. In each rant, Lee explored a topic that bothered him with a mix of his distinctive wise-guy style and curmudgeonly charm. He delivered the diatribes in vintage, tongue-in-cheek style, exclaiming about a video game version of himself: "Anybody could be Stan Lee! What if a guy isn't worthy? And I'm pretty particular! Never again will I put myself in a position where you, who may not be deserving, can be me!"[15] After a quick start (gaining about half a million subscribers and 163

Stan Lee and Chris Evans, July 2011. © Frederik Hermann.

million views), the Lee YouTube page eventually died on the vine. Similar to other POW! Entertainment initiatives, the YouTube channel launched with a bang and then withered as Lee's attention moved to other projects.

In 2012, Activision turned the comic book creator into an animated superhero in *The Amazing Spider-Man* video game. As Lee, players could swing high above the streets of New York City, shooting webs and confronting villains, just like Lee's iconic character. Voicing the part, Lee begins his electronic adventure by announcing that he is the "king of cameos" and exclaims: "Take that, Hitchcock!"[16]

In late 2013, Lee again appeared alongside the characters in *Lego Marvel Super Heroes*, a role-playing game. In the Marvel version, players can become any of 180 characters (including Lee) and operate in a Lego rendering of New York City. Lee is part of a mission called "Stan Lee in Peril," which places him in dangerous situations. Three years later, there would be another Lego video game, this time based on the Avengers. Players could play as "Iron Stan" (in Iron Man–like armor), but in a humorous nod, the face mask had a built-in moustache.

In January 2014, Lee returned to Springfield, the fictional home of *The Simpsons*, in the episode "Married to the Blob" (twenty-fifth season). Like the 2002 appearance, Lee was teamed with Comic Book Guy. Early in the episode, he urged the shop owner to ask Kumiko, a Japanese manga writer touring America's most tragic cities, out on a date. At the end, he married the couple in the fabled comic book shop.

While these appearances may have seemed like little more than gimmicks, they introduced Stan to a new generation of young people. Just like a fresh legion of fans turned on to classic rockers Aerosmith based on *Guitar Hero*, young video gamers could learn about Stan. YouTube videos posted of people playing the Spider-Man video game as Lee eclipsed three million views (yes, videos of people playing video games!).

In January 2016, *Stan Lee's Lucky Man* debuted on British television's Sky 1, a drama about a troubled police officer who controlled luck (for decades Lee told interviewers this was the superpower he wanted). Drawing about 1.9 million viewers per episode, the series became Sky 1's most successful original drama. It aired for three seasons, with various streaming networks picking it up later.

In mid-2016, *The Hollywood Reporter* presented *Stan Lee's Cosmic Crusaders*, its first branded show. Fabian Nicieza (cocreator of Deadpool) wrote the animated online series, while the magazine and Genius Brands International coproduced it, along with POW! Stan conceived the series, edited the script, and voiced his starring role, where he leads a group of seven aliens who crashed on Earth. They lose their superpowers but, under Lee's tutelage, discover how to employ their powers on this planet. The partnership with *THR* coincided with the magazine's "Stan Lee: 75 Years in the Business" special Comic-Con issue. The series provided another opportunity to expand Lee's brand outside Marvel. *THR* also marketed the series across its platforms, including its website, YouTube channel, Facebook, and Twitter, a combined social media audience of about fifteen million monthly.[17]

At ninety-three years old and arguably never more popular, Stan embarked on a "final appearance" tour, with several cities proclaiming "Stan Lee Day." His status as eminent statesman fueled the tour. "There is an excitement about these comic conventions that nothing can match," Lee explained. "These people are so in love with the pop culture of comic books." Tens of thousands of fans were willing to do anything—and pay any amount—to see Stan and get his autograph. In the Big Apple, Lee explained to the *New York Daily News*: "It's the most incredible thing in the world, because wherever I go, people want my autograph and people say 'thank you for the enjoyment that you brought me.' . . . I must be one of the luckiest guys in the world. . . . It's just great to know that you're wanted and that people actually appreciate the work that you've done."[18]

The challenge for icons as they age is the questions they face (often unspoken) about living up to their past achievements—a tall order, whether Bob Dylan, Robert De Niro, or the Rolling Stones. Stan's challenge was attempting to create a new universe when young people had countless other ways to slip into the heart of popular culture. Why read about a superhero when you can be one in a video game or watch adventures across streaming services? Today, iconic characters are more likely to be created for television or films rather than comics. Marvel's superheroes are popular in part because they are already established in the public's mind. The origin stories are pervasive and thus adaptable for new generations.

As a result, detractors might have pointed at Stan's post-Marvel work and concluded that he coasted on past successes (or the work of Kirby and Ditko) for far too long. But past ninety years old, how many artists even attempt to remain relevant? Stan's legacy was firmly established—one of the great creative icons in American history.

In late 2016 at the Cincinnati Comic Expo, several hundred people stood in line—waiting. They slowly shuffled step-by-step through roped-off areas, attempting to contain excitement and chatting at length in a communal love fest. When their big moment finally took place—meeting Stan face-to-face—nearly to a person they were too dumbstruck to say anything. Some choked out a whispered "thanks."

On paper, the moment might have seemed anticlimactic, but Stan's presence was enough. After getting their Spider-Man poster or Doctor Strange comic book signed, they turned away sporting huge grins, as if it were Christmas morning. They immediately wanted to relive the moment—searching out family, friends, or complete strangers, anybody who would share their joy. A treasured instant in Stan's light—many likened getting his photo or signature as the culmination of a lifetime of fandom, confessing that this was the best time of their lives.

At Stan's Santa Monica office, one may have mistaken the décor for a Stan Lee museum. The bright space burst with shelves of trinkets, including various action figures of Stan and superheroes. An old-school Captain America sat at the front of the desk, daring visitors to lean closer. A stuffed Hulk guarded the computer monitor. Walls were lined with photos—a group shot with the cast of *The Big Bang Theory* and a drawing of Lee drawn as Clark Kent pulling his shirt open to reveal a red Superman "S" emblazoned across his chest. Another showed Lee and Joanie on the red carpet at a Hollywood premiere, and yet another depicted Lee shaking hands with President Reagan. A large Silver Surfer (awash in deep blue and riding a teal-striped surfboard) adorned the wall behind the desk as if jutting directly out at the visitor.

For someone so steeped in comic book and pop culture history as the creator of a new storytelling sensibility, Lee had a keen sense of his past. However, he claimed to have little use for nostalgia. New waves of journalists, interviewers, and fans yearned for his stories of origins and characters, but Stan's outlook was forward—toward the next idea. He scribbled thoughts on tiny two-by-three-inch notepads, tucked away in his front shirt pocket (a lifelong habit). His left-handed scrawl bordered on indecipherable.

Meeting Stan late in his life, one sensed that his public persona grew out of the furtive teenage desire to act, then later morphed into a kind of celebrity identity that enabled him to play up the brash New Yorker stereotype. The caricature, though, fell by the wayside speaking with him one-on-one. In those moments, Lee was thoughtful and reflective, answering questions as if after the many decades, he still couldn't believe his good fortune. Stan's youthful, appreciative outlook offset the exaggerated public displays of braggadocio. In his early nineties, he no longer heard well and his eyesight had worsened. A 2012 heart operation led to a pacemaker that regulated his heartbeat, yet he continued to relish his role as the Marvel universe's spiritual leader.

Asked in 2016 how it felt to inspire generations of fans and artists with his flawed-hero narrative, Lee paused for a moment: "It's an incredibly great feeling, when I think about it. I don't have that much time to think about, but when I do . . ."[19] His voice trailed off, imagining those years flowing outward. The thing about icons is they never really stop creating. Lee's worldview wasn't based on what he did in the 1960s. He believed in the next spark, the new work, always charting a future course.

CHAPTER 13

SAYING GOOD-BYE TO A HERO

"Stan is up there with Walt Disney and George Lucas. . . . He should be ensconced in that pantheon of great American creators whose art has left an indelible mark on not just our culture but the world." —Kevin Smith, filmmaker[1]

In 2018, life turned into a horror film for Stan.

He still grieved Joan's death the previous July 6 at age ninety-five. She had been his bedrock, providing priceless emotional support and keeping a close eye on (and over) his career. Like many creatives, Stan shied away from the intricacies of the business world. Joanie stepped in to oversee those facets and ensured he had the order and creative freedom to continue his hectic schedule of appearances and work. Like many older couples, Joanie's death seemed to accelerate Stan's decline, though no one expected his world to unravel so quickly in his final year.

Over several long months, Lee's support system (including longtime members of his entourage) withered to dust in a flurry of lawsuits, police reports, investigations, accusations, finger pointing, cruelty, and violence. As Stan's closest friends and allies were shut out of his life, they rallied individually and collectively against these forces of evil. In time, as the full picture emerged, a horrific notion took hold: one of the most recognizable names and faces in the world fell victim to elaborate and often violence-filled schemes to rob him of his dignity and fortune. Contemporary society created a new name for this often-misunderstood negligence—elder abuse.

Media reports of the chaos swirling around Lee shocked the comic book world and fans alike. Marvel films were dominating big screens around the world, yet the cocreator of the Marvel universe faced a series of embarrassing and devious plots at the hands of lackeys and hangers-on who wanted a piece of his legacy (and the wealth he would leave behind). After talking with several of Stan's longtime friends and allies who were rushing to his aid, I told *Los Angeles Times* reporter David Ng, "If Stan Lee had a Spidey-sense for con men, the world would be better off and his fortunes would be better off, but he doesn't seem to have that."[2]

One of the primary tenets of elder abuse is that that the wrongdoers scheme to paint a picture to the outside world that counters the internal manipulation actually taking place. Reportedly, 10 percent of the elderly population in America suffers from elder abuse, but the legal system has not caught up, so these crimes are difficult to litigate. For most victims, the crime is hidden behind layers of so-called benefactors who are actually duping the world or counting on no one really paying attention.

Making matters worse, Stan had difficulty advocating for himself. At times it seemed he was exceptionally lucid for a man of ninety-five years old. In other moments, though, he was foggy and unclear. The erratic picture made it difficult to comprehend friend versus foe. Compounding the confusion, the villains largely isolated him. According to *The Hollywood Reporter*, Lee's phone number had been changed and his e-mail commandeered.[3] Stan was basically cut off from his lifetime of friends and supporters. Vultures were circling Lee's Hollywood mansion.

Much of the news that emerged came from police reports and tabloid journalism. One scoundrel after another would claim to be his manager or confidant, accompanying the legend to film premieres or comic conventions, but days or weeks later others would surface, shouting or pointing fingers. There was allegedly a large war chest at the end of the rainbow. No one seemed to know exactly, but some reports pegged Lee's worth at upward of $100 million. With that money on the table, the rats scurried to take their chunk, regardless of the embarrassment, pain, or suffering Stan endured. Attempting to unravel the details, reporter David Hochman explained:

Stan signs a fan's comic books. © Gaviin Nansoong.

The very qualities that industrious people of Lee's generation pride them-selves on—working hard, trusting people, showing respect for authority, raising children to be better off—were traits that did not serve him well as he grew more vulnerable with age. On top of that, Lee didn't like banks and was thought to be stockpiling cash at home, an irresistible temptation for unscrupulous employees.[4]

Sadly, according to Hochman and other investigators, Stan and Joanie's daughter, J. C., was caught up in the misconduct. She probably didn't know it, but she was a conduit, getting involved with unscrupulous people who had targeted her to get closer to her father. But she also had demons. Portrayed by many observers as quick-tempered, prone to violent rages, and supremely entitled by her charmed (and wealthy) life, at times she seemed unhinged, ranting about what she was due and later unleashing a barrage of lawsuits.[5] An influential media outlet called her Stan's "long-troubled dilettante daugh-ter . . . a prodigious shopper with an ill-tempered personality."[6]

One handler connected first to J. C. eventually wormed his way to Stan, illegally purchasing $1 million of real estate in Lee's name by forging his signature and stealing $4.6 million from a bank account. If the money alone weren't enough, the situation turned sick and depraved when reports sur-faced that he even took vials of Stan's blood to mix with ink and later sell in comic books. Another sycophant—Keya Morgan—was in the eye of the storm of alleged Lee abuse. His misdeeds led to his arrest in 2019 on felony charges related to Stan's final months, including false imprisonment and theft. Some media report that Morgan embezzled about $5 million worth of assets from Lee in the final months of his life.[7]

The intensity of the chaos left fans and allies in disbelief (even devolving to groping charges against Lee by a live-in nurse that seemed to be an effort at extortion). Clifford Meth, a longtime friend and writer who had worked with the icon, led an effort by insiders to get the elder abuse case launched, going to the authorities and bringing the abuse to light. "Stan was being picked apart by vultures," Meth explained. "It was disgusting and broke our hearts. Those who knew him were appalled."[8] Others checked in on Stan personally in an attempt to ascertain his well-being, including Spawn creator and art-ist Todd McFarlane and Stan's longtime friend and colleague Roy Thomas. McFarlane told the press that in their last meeting about a month before he died, Stan told his friend that he looked forward to seeing Joanie soon.

"Whatever we think Stan's legacy is today, it's just going to keep going, and there's going to be no end. . . . It still all leads back to the '60s comics that Stan and a handful of artists helped create." —Todd McFarlane, artist/writer ("Stan Lee: A Life of Marvel," *Entertainment Weekly*)

On November 12, 2018, Stan Lee passed away.

Paramedics received an emergency call from Lee's Hollywood Hills home at 8:34 a.m. and took the ailing icon to Cedars-Sinai Medical Center. According to his brother, Larry, Stan had been in ill health over the previous several months, including heart issues and pneumonia. He had breathing problems that were complicated by age and his failing health.

The staggering news triggered a global reaction and outpouring of love and affection.

In China, where they respectfully referred to Stan as "Grandpa," a hashtag honoring him was viewed some 1.21 billion times within twenty-four hours after the news hit. A Chinese site dedicated to sci-fi posted: "Maybe to some people this is just another famous person who passed away, but to us the god of creation has fallen from the sky, a disaster so great that neither the reversal of time nor the assemblance of heroes can correct."[9] This is a tribute that Stan himself might have deemed worthy. Fans could not imagine their hero being gone or what the MCU would look like without a Stan cameo.

On *PBS NewHour*, I spoke with host Judy Woodruff about Stan's unique impact on popular culture, explaining: "Stan's real power was capturing this kind of everyday superhero mentality that people were really attracted to. It wasn't the godlike speaking of a Superman or the stilted language of Batman. It was a language that people could really relate to and understand on a deeply personal level."[10] Tributes from stars of the MCU flooded Twitter and other social media outlets. While billions of fans across the world mourned, a wide range of celebrities joined them, from Paul McCartney and Patrick Stewart to Robert Downey Jr. and Tom Holland. Dozens of other stars from the MCU also chimed in, thanking Stan for his role in creating modern storytelling.

In the years since Lee passed away, November 12 has become a kind of Stan Lee Day around the world. Each year, countless fans flock to social

Fans flocked to see Stan at his countless convention visits. Illustration by Jason Piperberg.

media to rejoice in his life and work. In 2021, Stan's name began trending when fans posted photos posing with him at comic book conventions, while others followed with gifs of his MCU appearances. Given the state of technology, it's no wonder that Stan also made additional posthumous cameos in several Marvel video games for *Spider-Man*, *Miles Morales*, and *Guardians of the Galaxy*. The success of Marvel film and television properties and the billions of dollars bet on its continued popularity ensure that Marvel—and Stan—will remain at the heart of global popular culture.

Is it possible to assess someone like Stan Lee?

Was he simply the superhero invention of Stanley Lieber, the desperately poor Depression-era kid from New York City? Was this new character—like a mask—what the youngster had to create to overcome the odds stacked against him?

If we accept this vantage point, Stan embodies a version of the fabled American Dream—a mainly twentieth-century story of accomplishment following on the back of hard work and tenacity. Others might claim that Lee's success was a combination of talent and lucky timing as the wave of baby boomers came of age and had an overriding influence on American culture.

In some ways, though, we reduce him and the comprehensive range of his experiences if we simply categorize or label him. After all, underneath the celebrity and global fame there was a person—one filled with the complexities of human life. Stan had dreams and aspirations. Although he achieved heights that even his mind probably couldn't have imagined as a young man looking to the future, along the way he also confronted a myriad of personal and professional challenges. As Frank Sinatra sang, "That's life." Every up comes with a down, but character is shaped when a person gets on their feet and "back in the race." Stan's life is about nothing if it isn't about resiliency, created from childhood trauma, willpower, and hard work.

Shifting to pre–Fantastic Four times, Lee carried wounds from the public shaming he felt about working in comics, which included the 1950s national uproar against their alleged "immorality." The humiliation had consequences. After the Marvel explosion that he and others birthed and American culture shifted in their favor, Stan worked the room like a person who had been the lifelong ugly duckling. As a swan, Lee spread his wings, but the self-doubt still festered. So how does a person feel less than and extraordinary simultaneously? The human mind is a complex organ.

When someone like Lee becomes an "overnight sensation" after toiling in a field for decades, the resulting fame has consequences. For every observer who believes that Stan saved comic books and expanded their popularity in the 1960s by becoming the face of the industry, there are others who view him as media-hungry and money-grubbing. Lee wasn't perfect and didn't have an unflawed life, but what he retained was an aura of authenticity, despite an otherworldly level of celebrity that only increased well past the time it falls off for most stars. He was authentic in his passion for life, which resulted in creating characters that people wanted to know better: first talking to children, then teenagers, and eventually adults.

Perhaps even more important, his authenticity rang true with fans. They clamored to meet him and kept him popular for nearly sixty years. His interest in fan engagement could be viewed callously as a way to make money, but autographs and memorabilia have been part of popular culture for decades, if not centuries. Like many people who grew up in the Depression, Stan never trusted that his last paycheck would be followed by another. If he had stopped working at traditional retirement age, it would have been about a decade before the first Marvel film hit theaters. Stan kept working because he saw no other way. The childhood scars never healed.

There is also "inside baseball"-level detail about Lee's role at Marvel during the 1960s heyday that much of the general public knows little about. At the core of this hullabaloo is the fight over who gets the credit (or lion's share of the credit) for creating the Marvel superheroes. There are countless Stan supporters and innumerable others who believe he is some kind of devil based on how one divvies up provenance. For many, this debate represents a line in the sand that cannot be crossed and is at the heart of countless social media arguments.[11]

If you've read this book carefully, you will appreciate a middle ground between Stan and Jack on many fundamental issues—including perspectives they shared about their work and the comic book industry as a whole. Some critics utilize analogies in an attempt to describe their working relationship—from songwriters like John Lennon and Paul McCartney to likening them to filmmakers. None of these comparisons seem to fully capture the connection better than the most frequently used term: cocreators. What emerged from their creative collision is some of the greatest work in American art history. *Their* work.

A key challenge is that, with many of the superheroes, Jack and Stan had no idea that the characters would become iconic or that their stories would be used to drive billions of dollars in the global economy. Success created egos, altered memories, and fueled animosities. The simple fact of the matter is that Stan and Jack both took liberties with the facts over the decades. The full truth about the superhero creation process died with them.[12]

"I believe we never lose our love for those tales of people who are bigger than life."
—Stan Lee ("Stan Lee: A Life of Marvel," *Entertainment Weekly* special edition)

Stan's legacy is that Marvel superheroes are the foundation of modern storytelling. One might ask (semirhetorically) if there is an American author more widely read than Lee or a voice heard more often. Similar to Henry Ford, who did not invent but rather perfected the assembly line, Stan sharpened and defined the antihero character and sold them by the millions to generations of consumers. Unlike Ford's Model T, however, Lee's superheroes adapted as culture changed. That's why today's Fords have little in common with earlier models, but we have had multiple Spider-Mans on the big screen alone. Ford's achievement is the stuff of legend, but Lee's creations have become mythology.

Although Stan was not a baby boomer, he had an undeniable impact on that incredibly large and powerful generation. That generation that would become witty, full of angst and a myriad of dichotomies also showed the country what it was to be human. Heroes *and* human—like a teen with unbelievable superpowers or a self-loathing pilot who becomes a hulking, living, breathing pile of rocks. Lee gave teens and college-aged readers a voice by creating superheroes readers could relate to. Like so much of the boomer era, the influences get messy as locked-down Cold War culture shapeshifted into something different, then transformed again as the 1960s kids became the 1980s Gordon Gekko corporate raiders.

The Fantastic Four transformed the kinds of stories comic books could tell. *Spider-Man*, however, brought the idea home to a global audience. Lee told an interviewer that he had two incredibly instinctive objectives: introduce a "terribly realistic" superhero and one "with whom the reader could relate."[13] While the nerd-to-hero storyline seems like it must have sprung from the earth fully formed, Lee gave audiences a new way of looking at what it meant to be a hero and spun the notion of who might be heroic in a way that spoke to the rapidly expanding number of comic book buyers. Spider-Man's popularity revealed the attraction to the idea of a tainted hero, but the character hit the newsstands at the perfect time; ranging from the growing baby boomer generation to the optimism of John F. Kennedy's Camelot, this confluence of events resulted in a second golden age for comic books.

Just like novelists and filmmakers had always done, it is as if Lee put his hands up into the air and pulled down fistfuls of the national zeitgeist. In this sense, he understood his audience in the same way as Walt Disney or John Updike, who at about the same time was crafting Harry "Rabbit" Angstrom, the American everyman (a character one could certainly imagine reading comic books). Lee as writer did what all iconic creative people do: he improved on or perfected his craft, thus creating an entirely new style that would have broad impact across the rest of the industry and later the world.

Stan shares the same stage that once held Ella Fitzgerald and F. Scott Fitzgerald, as well as Babe Ruth and Norman Mailer. He sits there proudly with Bob Dylan, Toni Morrison, Tom Hanks, Hank Aaron, and Elvis ('cause he just might still be out there somewhere). His legacy is undeniable: Lee transformed storytelling by introducing generations of readers to flawed heroes who also dealt with life's challenges, in addition to the threats that could destroy humankind.

Generations of artists, writers, actors, and other creative types have been inspired, moved, or encouraged by the universe he gave voice to and birthed. Lee did not invent the imperfect hero—one could argue that such heroes had been around since Homer's time and even before—but Lee did deliver it—Johnny Appleseed style, a dime or so a pop—to a generation of readers hungry for something new.

Marvel founded the greatest storytelling universe ever created. Stan did not do it alone. It is impossible to quantify the number of people it has taken to keep Marvel operating and producing since 1939. Artistic collaboration has always been the bedrock of the comic book industry, just like so many other forms of commercial entertainment. Where is the director without the cinematographer or the actor? Where is the writer without the editor and publisher? Heck, those examples are compounded and extended by the hundreds of people it takes to get a creative product into the world. Authors, for example, need the bookseller to physically place thousands of items on a shelf to reach the public.

Looking back at Lee's work can give today's readers new ways of thinking about race and racism, identity issues, culture, and gender. In this way, comic books—then and now—promote two incredibly important skills: critical thinking and contextual analysis. These abilities allow readers to understand themselves and their societies more fully, while simultaneously broadening comprehension of the wider world and its interlocking historical impulses.

Through Lee, Spider-Man famously stated: "With great power there must also come great responsibility." In his writing and editing, as well as the life he led, we learn that great responsibility can include a fundamental commitment to humanity, compassion, and self-respect.

Stan's role as voice of the superheroes cannot be underestimated. He created a narrative foundation that has fueled pop culture for nearly six decades. By establishing the voice of the Marvel universe and shepherding the comic books to life as the head of Marvel, Lee cemented his place in American history.

EPILOGUE

HOW THE MARVEL UNIVERSE CONQUERED THE GLOBE

"There's about 6,000 characters in the Marvel library. . . . If this goes right, we will be telling these stories for many, many, many, many generations to come." —Victoria Alonso, EVP, Marvel[1]

Why is Marvel so different? How did this brand of storytelling conquer the globe?

Since the early 1960s, there has been only one answer: Stan Lee. His unique voice and narrative define the Marvel universe.

At the heart of Marvel's success, Alonso explained, is that "in those stories there's many different characters that you can actually voice." What she identified was the style (and attitude) that Stan permeated throughout the Marvel Age. Need proof? Surf over to Disney+ and listen to Robert Downey Jr. play Iron Man or check out a clip of Tom Holland as Spider-Man on You-Tube. What you hear in their banter is instantly recognizable.[2]

While there are generations of great science fiction films and action movies, the difference between the Marvel cinematic universe (MCU) and the rest is voice. Anyone can make a film packed with action-filled fight scenes, stunning visuals, and out-of-this-world computer-generated imagery, but they can't replicate that style. The Marvel feeling is so ingrained in the heads of fandom that it feels subconscious. It's driven by Lee's voice.

"The dialogue . . . is the most important thing. . . . It's what the person says that matters." —Stan Lee (John Morrow, *Kirby and Lee: Stuf' Said!*)

Here's a quick history lesson: in the early 1960s, after those first couple of superhero comic books became hits (Fantastic Four, Spider-Man, Avengers), Marvel became a part of the cultural zeitgeist, as hip and cool as the latest rock band or film star—in other words, a movement, not merely a comic book publishing company. Riding that wave, Stan stumbled into—then later carefully crafted—a role as the face of comic books. Eager to hit the road, he barnstormed college campuses swollen to the breaking point with baby boomers who wanted to take over the world and had the numbers to bend culture to their wills. Stan turned out to be engaging—nearly mesmerizing—in his belief in the power of comic books, propelling Marvel into the psyche of college-aged readers as if he were some kind of pied piper. Stan also utilized tools to blow up the fourth wall and began talking directly (and frequently!) to readers within the comic book pages (and anyone in the media who would listen). Readers responded, creating Marvel fan clubs by the tens of thousands and buying into the hype.

As a result, Stan either directly trained or inspired a generation of writers in how to compose narrative. That sound people heard in their heads as they read the comics became the house style for a generation and a half of people who were forming their cultural worldviews. Then, when they began their own careers, those writers and creators went out into the entertainment world, each success spreading Lee's attitude.

What happened over the course of a decade or so couldn't possibly be duplicated, so formulaic in retrospect that it seems impossible that it happened. Baby boomers grew up with Stan's voice in their heads. For Gen Xers, though, Marvel's style is entrenched. As each generation aged out of traditional comic book reading age, Lee's voice became commensurate with nostalgia. Immersed in a heavily capitalistic entertainment-driven culture, embedded stories are ones that get retold, and Marvel superheroes became a balm for a cultural explosion driven by cable television, global box office calculations, and the Internet. In what seems like the blink of an eye, the Marvel voice became *the* voice of modern storytelling.

Stan flying through the streets of New York City! Illustration by Jason Piperberg.

Yet the term *voice* is difficult to comprehend. Jerome Charyn, one of the most important writers in American literary history, describes it instead as "music." Charyn's concept, although focused on books, can be applied to Lee's comic book writing: "Writing . . . is about the music, it's about the voice. This is what predominates. The music is all, the music is total, it's absolute." Stan's dialogue provided Marvel with a kind of music that readers could hear and that matched their internal rhythms, resulting in an experience that transformed them. "It's music alive with extreme sympathy," Charyn explained. "There is no space between you and the text."[3] As a result, readers could feel the Marvel style, while simultaneously Lee's patter paralleled the cultural explosion booming across society. We hear this in the Beatles' *Sgt. Pepper's Lonely Hearts Club Band*, Stanley Kubrick's *Dr. Strangelove* and *2001: A Space Odyssey*, and J. D. Salinger's short stories.

For this revolution to unfold, the spark needed an accelerant, like Bob Dylan, the Beatles, James Brown, or *Star Wars*. In terms of sheer numbers, one could argue that, based on Stan's voice and attitude, Marvel has a wider reach around the world than any other entertainment vehicle or entertainer. The past success of Marvel film and television properties and the billions of dollars bet on its continued popularity ensure that Marvel will remain at the heart of global popular culture.

Let's not merely rest our argument for Marvel's conquest of the globe on opinion or anecdote. Researchers have attempted to pin down the reasoning behind why the MCU has been so dominant and pervasive. An academic study in *Harvard Business Review* by Spencer Harrison, Arne Carlsen, and Miha Škerlavaj gets at the primary reasons: "The secret seems to be finding the right balance between creating innovative films and retaining enough continuity to make them all recognizably part of a coherent family."[4]

> "You made so many believe in the good, the heroic, the villainous, the exciting, most of all you were giving and gracious to us all." —Samuel L. Jackson, as Nick Fury in the MCU ("Paying Their Respects: Stan Lee: A Life of Marvel," *Entertainment Weekly*)

Next, the team looked at individual aspects of the MCU. They studied scripts, film crews, directors, and critical reaction, leading to several additional points emerging: the movies "showcase differing emotional tones" and are "visually different," and the most critically acclaimed films "are the very ones that are viewed as violating the superhero genre."[5] In other words, *Iron Man* is funny, but *Thor* is often sad (though frequently hilarious). *Guardians of the Galaxy* is a space opera zipping across galaxies, while *Spider-Man* is set in Queens and Manhattan. *Black Panther* is filled with social commentary, as is *Captain Marvel*. Again, the through point is voice.

Form the entire MCU into a ball, but don't expect the contraption to roll straight—purposely. Moviegoers recognize (and have been taught) that each film will be different in tone, look, and outcome. They know the origin stories (and, with Spider-Man, have seen them several times on film). Yet fans also know that each new film or television series is going to seem fresh and new—an *experience*, not just a piece of entertainment.

For contemporary audiences, that experience is also inclusive, another point Alonso identified: "You cannot have a global audience and not somehow start to represent it." The success of Black Panther, for example, went against unofficial Hollywood rules that a film wouldn't open if it had "a completely Black cast." According to Alonso, 51 percent of the Marvel audience is female and 28 percent Hispanic: "If we don't represent the people that watch what we make, eventually they'll go elsewhere because somebody else will figure it out." Disney isn't alone in this strategic thinking, but the results confirm the point.[6]

And let's not forget how important the consistent use of Easter eggs has been, not only within the films but as the credits roll. The anticipation alone gets the fan community revved up for future installments (as did Stan's cameo appearances, which most fans still yearn for, even years after his passing).

An even more elemental facet of Marvel's success is its commitment to a shared set of core values via storytelling. According to best-selling author and comics writer Brad Meltzer, Stan "gave an entire generation creeds to live by . . . vital cornerstones of their belief systems." The power of his stories was in how people assimilated them. "Stan Lee gave them real-world applications for all those values. And unlike politicians, corporations, advertising, or anything else, those lessons were *good*. For the sake of good."[7] The idea is not that Marvel entertainment must live up to these principles at every moment, but overall the ideals Stan punctuated established a tone and framework that could support a universe.

The superheroes that Lee and his cocreators brought to life in Marvel comic books remain at the heart of contemporary storytelling. Lee created a narrative foundation that has fueled pop culture across all media for nearly six decades. By establishing the voice of Marvel superheroes and shepherding the comic books to life as the creative head of Marvel, Lee cemented his place in American history. According to veteran industry analyst Paul Dergarabedian, the results have been breathtaking: "The profound impact of Stan Lee's creations and the influence that his singular vision has had on our culture and the world of cinema is almost immeasurable and virtually unparalleled by any other modern day artist."[8]

From my perspective, this viewpoint does not diminish the role Jack Kirby played in cocreating the superheroes or the thousands of additional hands it took to create the comic books, animated series, TV shows, or films

Lee leads the crowd in a cheer of "Excelsior!" (2015). © Gage Skidmore.

over parts of the last ten decades. Every successful idea, person, organization, or entity is built by many, but again, what was the accelerant?

How did the Marvel universe come to dominate global popular culture? Largely based on Stan Lee supplying a voice to a mythology. Certainly, the creation of the Marvel universe was a team effort, like all forms of entertainment; nothing is created in a vacuum. There are unheralded people in the process and those who deserve as much credit as Lee for their roles. Yet it was the unmistakable "music" that Lee conceived that launched a cultural revolution.

At the height of the Great Depression, a desperately poor recent high school graduate entered a nondescript office building with little knowledge of what took place inside its towering concrete walls. He emerged with a full-time job paying $8 a week. Even someone with Stan Lee's imagination could not have conjured up what would unfold in his marvelous life or its consequences on modern storytelling.

Yet he did give us a hint of what was in store, mischievously scribbling, "Stan Lee is God" on that high school ceiling.

Lee at an appearance in Cincinnati (2016). Courtesy of Suzette Percival.

ACKNOWLEDGMENTS

Is it possible to calculate all that goes into writing a book? *Stan Lee: The Man behind Marvel* is the culmination of a lifetime of reading, research, and enjoying comic books within the long through line of studying popular culture. I taught myself to read so that I could unlock the joys of *Spider-Man* and the *Avengers*. Later I grew obsessed with the reality-bending *What If . . .?* series. I do not remember a time without Stan Lee, and the "Stan Lee Presents" banner is ever-present in my mind's eye.

I was lucky enough to spend some time with Stan in late 2016. When I asked him how it felt to inspire generations of fans and artists with his flawed hero narrative, he paused for a moment. Looking wistfully off into the distance, he explained: "It's an incredibly great feeling, when I think about it. I don't have that much time to think about, but when I do . . ." His voice trailed off. With a brief grin and eyes almost sparkling behind his semidark glasses, my wife, Suzette, and I could see his pride and hear it in his voice. Thinking back on that time now, my hands still tremble a bit. How often does one get to stand in the shadow of greatness?

As you have read in the preceding pages, Lee's career and impact on popular culture has not been without controversy. Given the billions of dollars at stake in the Marvel universe across films, comics, merchandise, and everything else related to the company across the globe, the hullabaloo will likely never end. As you've also now learned, I think *both* Stan Lee and Jack Kirby deserve equal credit for their creations, as does Steve Ditko for his cocreation of Spider-Man. Equal. My advice to those so quick to argue for or against these creators is to dig in and come to your own conclusions.

My attempt to tell Stan's story centered on multi-archival research and using that material, plus interviews, newspaper articles, essays, blogs, and all other information I could get my hands on to create my own interpretation. That's all history is, in the end. History is not what *actually* happened, rather a snippet and an elucidation. As such, the ideas and analysis are mine, as are any errors of judgment. I would like to extend my deepest appreciation to the amazing team at the American Heritage Center (AHC) at the University of Wyoming. How Lee's papers got to Laramie, Wyoming, is itself a great story. The archivists and librarians I worked with were so professional and provided access to material that few had previously seen.

I would also like to thank the team at the Billy Ireland Cartoon Library and Museum at the Ohio State University. Additional resources, including rare books and Marvel materials, were hunted down at the Cincinnati and Hamilton County Public Library, Stow-Munroe Falls Public Library, and Lane Public Library in Oxford, Ohio. Newspapers.com is an invaluable source, as are the many digital databases that help the historian find and utilize materials. I read deeply in the Marvel back catalog via the Marvel Unlimited subscription service.

Thanks to the many editors and staffers I have had the great pleasure to work with at Rowman & Littlefield! Christen Karniski has been a wonderful editor and guide as we took another headlong dive into Stan's epic life. Her steady and thoughtful work made this a much better book. I would also like to thank everyone who had a hand in this book at R&L over the years, including the design team, copyeditors, marketing team, and the production staff—first-rate one and all. A huge thanks to illustrator, comic artist, and storyteller Jason Piperberg for his Marvel comic book–inspired cover design. His work on this book brings Stan alive for a new generation of readers.

I would like to thank several friends and scholars who helped me along the way, including Arthur Asa Berger, who is simply one of the nation's great creative minds. His friendship with Stan gave me another point of reference, and I greatly appreciate his advice and support. Thanks too go to Carl Rollyson—in my mind the dean of American biography—who always says, "The answer to one biography is another biography." His work is inspirational, and I used his thinking as a guide as I wrote this book! Thanks as well to my mentor and friend Phillip Sipiora and to the memory of the great historian Lawrence S. Kaplan. I am constantly inspired to be a stronger writer and thinker by Jerome Charyn. He has had a profound impact on me. Thank you, too, to Jerome's wife, Lenore Riegel, for continued friendship and support.

A big shout-out to several friends who have offered unwavering support on the journey, including Brian Jay Jones, one of America's best biographers, and Kyle Sarofeen, the publisher of Hamilcar Publications and a guy I'm happy to call friend! I would also like to thank Jim Thompson, Alex Grand, and the Comic Book Historians group they run on Facebook. I have learned so much as a member. I have also learned so much at Comics' Silver Age, run by the eminent Clifford Meth.

Josh Schwartz is a trusted friend, advisor, and confidante. Thanks, buddy, for all you've done for me and Stan's story! My thinking about history, life, and friendship has been shaped and formed by Thomas Heinrich. He is more than a friend—a brother for life.

This book is dedicated to our two daughters, Kassie and Sophia. Thank you to you both for all the love in the world and being the wonderful young women you are! An additional thanks to Kassie for being my young adult advisor on the manuscript, images, and cover. She and her friends provided great help from a teen perspective. I would also like to extend my thanks to Michel Valois, Carole and Laurent van Huffel, Matthew van Huffel and Trang, Benjamin van Huffel, and Nicholas van Huffel.

Finally, nothing is possible without the love and support from my wife, Suzette. She is also my research partner, cowriter, best friend, and north star. Thank you, my love, for everything. Excelsior!

NOTES

CHAPTER 1

1. Stan Lee and George Mair, *Excelsior! The Amazing Life of Stan Lee* (New York: Simon and Schuster, 2002), 26.

2. "The Marvelous Life of Stan Lee," *CBS News*, January 17, 2016, https://www.cbsnews.com/news/the-marvelous-life-of-stan-lee/.

3. Lee and Mair, *Excelsior!*, 26; Stan Lee, Peter David, and Colleen Doran, *Amazing Fantastic Incredible: A Marvelous Memoir* (New York: Touchstone, 2015), n.p.

4. Lee and Mair, *Excelsior!*, 26.

5. Stan Lee, "1975 San Diego Comic-Con Convention," YouTube, https://youtu.be/MhJuBqDTM9Q.

CHAPTER 2

1. The astronomical sum equates to about $2,730, based on calculating "Real Wealth." Samuel H. Williamson, "Seven Ways to Compute the Relative Value of a U.S. Dollar Amount, 1790 to present," MeasuringWorth.com, 2021. "Real Wealth measures the purchasing power of an income or wealth by its relative ability to buy a (fixed over time) bundle of goods and services such as food, shelter, clothing, etc. This bundle does (in theory) not change over time."

2. Gur Alroey, *Bread to Eat and Clothes to Wear: Letters from Jewish Migrants in the Early Twentieth Century* (Detroit, MI: Wayne State University Press, 2011), 10; Dana Mihailescu, "Images of Romania and America in Early Twentieth-Century Romanian-Jewish Immigrant Life Stories in the United States," *East European Jewish Affairs* 42, no. 1 (2012): 28.

3. Mihailescu, "Images of Romania and America," 32.

4. Stan Lee, interview by Mark Lacter, "Stan Lee Marvel Comics Always Searching for a New Story," *Inc.*, November 2009, 96.

5. Stan Lee and George Mair, *Excelsior! The Amazing Life of Stan Lee* (New York: Simon and Schuster, 2002), 7.

6. Ibid., 11.

7. Quoted in Jordan Raphael and Tom Spurgeon, *Stan Lee and the Rise and Fall of the American Comic Book* (Chicago: Chicago Review Press, 2003), 4.

8. Lee and Mair, *Excelsior!*, 12, 9.

9. Stan Lee, "Excelsior!" (Autobiography) Outline, July 30, 1978, Box 96, Stan Lee Papers.

10. Lee and Mair, *Excelsior!*, 10.

11. Stan Lee, "Comic Relief: Comic Books Aren't Just for Entertainment," *Edutopia*, August 11, 2005.

12. Lee and Mair, *Excelsior!*, 13.

13. Lee, "Excelsor!" (Autobiography) Outline.

14. Quoted in Stan Lee, interview by Mike Bourne, "Stan Lee, The Marvel Bard," *Alter Ego* 3, no. 74 (2007): 26.

15. Quoted in *With Great Power: The Stan Lee Story*, directed by Terry Douglas, Nikki Frakes, and William Lawrence Hess (Los Angeles: MPI Home Video, 2012).

16. Stan Lee, "History of Marvel (Chapters 1, 2, 3)," Unpublished, Marvel Comics—History (Draft of "History of Marvel Comics"), 1990, Box 5, Folder 7, Stan Lee Papers, 2. Notice the alliterative names?

17. Quoted in Raphael and Spurgeon, *Stan Lee*, 8.

18. Ibid.

19. Lee and Mair, *Excelsior!*, 15.

20. Raphael and Spurgeon, *Stan Lee*, 7.

21. Lee and Mair, *Excelsior!*, 6.

22. Stan Lee, interview by David Hochman, "Playboy Interview: Stan Lee," *Playboy*, April 11, 2014.

23. Mark Alexander, "Lee and Kirby: The Wonder Years," *The Jack Kirby Collector* 18, no. 58 (Winter 2011): 5.

CHAPTER 3

1. Blake Bell and Michael J. Vassallo, *The Secret History of Marvel Comics: Jack Kirby and the Moonlighting Artists at Martin Goodman's Empire* (Seattle: Fantagraphics, 2013), 98.

2. Stan Lee interview, "Interview with Stan Lee (Part 1 of 5)," *IGN*, June 26, 2000, https://www.ign.com/articles/2000/06/26/interview-with-stan-lee-part-1-of-5.

3. Gerard Jones, *Men of Tomorrow: Geeks, Gangsters, and the Birth of the Comic Book* (New York: Basic, 2004), 108.

4. Ibid., 158.

5. Ibid., 159.

6. Sean Howe, *Marvel Comics: The Untold Story* (New York: Harper, 2012), 14.

7. Quoted in Mark Evanier, *Kirby: King of Comics* (New York: Abrams, 2008), 45.

8. Howe, *Marvel Comics*, 20.

9. Joe Simon, *My Life in Comics* (London: Titan Books, 2011), 114.

10. Quoted in ibid., 113.

11. Ibid., 114.

12. Quoted in Stan Lee, Peter David, and Colleen Doran, *Amazing Fantastic Incredible: A Marvelous Memoir* (New York: Touchstone, 2015), n.p.

13. Stan Lee and George Mair, *Excelsior! The Amazing Life of Stan Lee* (New York: Simon and Schuster, 2002), 30.

14. Stan Lee, "History of Marvel (Chapters 1, 2, 3)," Marvel Comics—History (Draft of "History of Marvel Comics"), 1990, Box 5, Folder 7, Stan Lee Papers, 9.

15. Quoted in Shirrel Rhoades, *A Complete History of American Comic Books* (New York: Peter Lang, 2008), 36.

16. Stan Goldberg, interview by Jim Amash, "The Goldberg Variations," *Alter Ego* 3, no. 18 (October 2002): 6.

17. Arie Kaplan, *Masters of the Comic Book Universe Revealed!* (Chicago: Chicago Review Press, 2006), 49.

18. Quoted in Rhoades, *A Complete History*, 36.

19. Lee and Mair, *Excelsior!*, 30.

CHAPTER 4

1. Rebecca Robbins Raines, *Getting the Message Through: A Branch History of the U.S. Army Signal Corps* (Washington, DC: Center of Military History, US Army, 1996), 256.

2. Mike Benton, *The Comic Book in America: An Illustrated History* (Dallas, TX: Taylor, 1989), 35–41.

3. Quoted in Sean Howe, *Marvel Comics: The Untold Story* (New York: Harper, 2012), 24.

4. Quoted in ibid., 25.

5. Stan Lee, interview by Steven Mackenzie, "Stan Lee Interview: 'The World Always Needs Heroes,'" *The Big Issue*, January 18, 2016, http://www.bigissue.com/features/interviews/6153/stan-lee-interview-the-world-always-needs-heroes.

6. Stan Lee, "Excelsior!" (Autobiography) Outline, July 30, 1978, Box 96, Stan Lee Papers.

7. Quoted in Stan Lee and George Mair, *Excelsior! The Amazing Life of Stan Lee* (New York: Simon and Schuster, 2002), 37.

8. Stan Lee, "Comic Relief: Comic Books Aren't Just for Entertainment," *Edutopia*, August 11, 2005, http://www.edutopia.org/comic-relief.

9. Lee and Mair, *Excelsior!*, 44.

10. Ibid., 45.

11. Blake Bell and Michael J. Vassallo, *The Secret History of Marvel Comics: Jack Kirby and the Moonlighting Artists at Martin Goodman's Empire* (Seattle: Fantagraphics, 2013), 158.

12. Stan Lee, "Only the Blind Can See," *Joker* 1, no. 4 (1943–1944): 39; reprinted in Bell and Vassallo, *Secret History*, 159.

13. Lee and Mair, *Excelsior!*, 43–44.

14. Lee, "Excelsior!" (Autobiography) Outline.

15. Lee and Mair, *Excelsior!*, 56.

16. Timely script editor Al Sulman claims he created the character after Lee asked him to come up with a Wonder Woman–like heroine.

17. Joe Simon, *My Life in Comics* (London: Titan Books, 2011), 166–67.

18. Lee and Mair, *Excelsior!*, 64.

19. Stan Lee, *Secrets Behind the Comics* (New York: Famous Enterprises, 1947), 6, 22.

20. Stan Lee, interview by David Anthony Kraft, "The FOOM Interview: Stan Lee," 1977, in *Stan Lee Conversations*, ed. Jeff McLaughlin (Jackson: University Press of Mississippi, 2007), 68.

21. Lee, "Excelsior!" (Autobiography) Outline.

22. Ibid.

23. Stan Lee, "Where I Span a Hero's Yarn," *Sunday Times*, May 12, 2002, F3.

24. Lee, "Hero's Yarn."

25. Lee, "Excelsior!" (Autobiography) Outline.

26. "Urges Comic Book Ban," *New York Times*, September 4, 1948, 16.

27. Quoted in Thomas F. O'Connor, "The National Organization for Decent Literature: A Phase in American Catholic Censorship," *Library Quarterly: Information, Community, Policy* 65, no. 4 (1995): 390.

28. Lee and Mair, *Excelsior!*, 92, 93.

29. Quoted in David Hajdu, *The Ten-Cent Plague: The Great Comic-Book Scare and How It Changed America* (New York: Farrar, Straus and Giroux, 2008), 264.

30. Ron Goulart, *Great American Comic Books* (Lincolnwood, IL: Publications International, 2001), 217.

31. Lee and Mair, *Excelsior!*, 93.

32. Ibid., 94.

33. Stan Goldberg, interview by Jim Amash, "The Goldberg Variations," *Alter Ego* 3, no. 18 (October 2002): 9.

34. Richard Harrington, "Stan Lee: Caught in Spidey's Web," *Washington Post*, February 4, 1992, D1.

35. Lee and Mair, *Excelsior!*, 99.

36. Quoted in Howe, *Marvel Comics*, 32.

37. Lee and Mair, *Excelsior!*, 87, 88.

38. Quoted in Howe, *Marvel Comics*, 35.

CHAPTER 5

1. John Romita, "Face Front, True Believers! The Comics Industry Sounds Off on Stan Lee," *Comics Journal* 181 (October 1995): 83.

2. Julius Schwartz, interview by Roy Thomas, "All-Schwartz Comics: A Conversation with Editorial Legend Julius Schwartz," *Alter Ego* 3, no. 7 (2001), http://www.twomorrows.com/alterego/articles/07schwartz.html; Shirrel Rhoades, *A Complete History of American Comic Books* (New York: Peter Lang, 2008), 70–71.

3. Rhoades, *Complete History*, 72–73.

4. Blake Bell and Michael J. Vassallo, *The Secret History of Marvel Comics: Jack Kirby and the Moonlighting Artists at Martin Goodman's Empire* (Seattle: Fantagraphics, 2013), 75.

5. Quoted in Bell and Vassallo, *Secret History*, 45.

6. Stan Lee and George Mair, *Excelsior! The Amazing Life of Stan Lee* (New York: Simon and Schuster, 2002), 112.

7. Stan Lee, *Origins of Marvel Comics*, rev. ed. (New York: Marvel, 1997), 10.

8. Craig Tomashoff, "Move Over Batman . . ." *Los Angeles Reader*, January 26, 1990.

9. *Stan Lee's Mutants, Monsters, and Marvels*, directed by Scott Zakarin (Burbank, CA: Sony Pictures, 2002), DVD.

10. Roy Thomas, "A Fantastic First," in *The Stan Lee Universe*, ed. Danny Fingeroth and Roy Thomas (Raleigh, NC: TwoMorrows, 2011), 17.

11. Stan Lee and Jack Kirby, *Marvel Masterworks: Fantastic Four, Nos. 1–10* (New York: Marvel, 2003), n.p.

12. *Stan Lee's Mutants*.

13. Stan Lee, Peter David, and Colleen Doran, *Amazing Fantastic Incredible: A Marvelous Memoir* (New York: Touchstone, 2015), n.p.

14. Quoted in Les Daniels, *Marvel: Five Fabulous Decades of the World's Greatest Comics* (New York: Harry N. Abrams, 1995), 87.

15. "*Fantastic Four #1* Synopsis," reprinted in Thomas, "Fantastic First," 16.

16. Stan Lee interview, *Stan Lee Universe*, 11.

17. Lee and Mair, *Excelsior!*, 124.

18. Stan Lee and Jack Kirby, *Marvel Masterworks: Fantastic Four, Nos. 11–20* (New York: Marvel, 2003), n.p.

19. Quoted in Daniels, *Marvel*, 85, 87.

20. Stan Lee, *Bring on the Bad Guys*, rev. ed. (New York: Marvel, 1998), n.p.

21. Ibid.

22. Lee and Kirby, *Marvel Masterworks: FF, Nos. 11–20*, n.p.

CHAPTER 6

1. Mark Lacter, "Stan Lee, Marvel Comics Always Searching for a New Story," *Inc.*, November 2009, 96.

2. Don Thrasher, "Stan Lee's Secret to Success: A Marvel-ous Imagination," *Dayton Daily News*, January 21, 2006, sec. E.

3. Lacter, "Stan Lee, Marvel Comics Always Searching," 96.

4. Quoted in ibid.

5. Stan Lee and George Mair, *Excelsior! The Amazing Life of Stan Lee* (New York: Simon and Schuster, 2002), 126–27.

6. Ibid., 126.

7. Roy Thomas, "Stan the Man and Roy the Boy: A Conversation between Stan Lee and Roy Thomas," in *Stan Lee Conversations*, ed. Jeff McLaughlin (Jackson: University Press of Mississippi, 2007), 141.

8. Ibid.

9. Lee and Mair, *Excelsior!*, 127.

10. Thomas, "Stan the Man," 141.

11. Lee and Mair, *Excelsior!*, 127.

12. Ibid., 128.

13. Leonard Pitts Jr., "An Interview with Stan Lee," in *Stan Lee Conversations*, ed. Jeff McLaughlin (Jackson: University Press of Mississippi, 2007), 96.

14. Quoted in Lee and Mair, *Excelsior!*, 128.

15. Stan Lee, Peter David, and Colleen Doran, *Amazing Fantastic Incredible: A Marvelous Memoir* (New York: Touchstone, 2015), n.p.

16. Lee and Mair, *Excelsior!*, 135–36.

17. Stan Lee, "That's My Spidey," *New York Times*, May 3, 2002, http://www.nytimes.com/2002/05/03/opinion/that-s-my-spidey.html.

CHAPTER 7

1. Stan Lee and George Mair, *Excelsior! The Amazing Life of Stan Lee* (New York: Simon and Schuster, 2002), 120.

2. Stan Lee, *Son of Origins of Marvel Comics*, revised edition (New York: Marvel, 1997), 69.

3. Pierre Comtois, *Marvel Comics in the 1960s: An Issue by Issue Field Guide to a Pop Culture Phenomenon* (Raleigh, NC: TwoMorrows, 2009), 20.

4. Stan Lee, *Origins of Marvel Comics*, revised edition (New York: Marvel, 1997), 165.

5. Larry Lieber, interviewed by Danny Fingeroth, *WriteNow!* 18 (Summer 2008): 5.

6. Quoted in Will Murray, "Stan Lee Looks Back: The Comics Legend Recalls Life with Jack Kirby, Steve Ditko, and Heroes," in *Stan Lee Conversations*, ed. Jeff McLaughlin (Jackson: University Press of Mississippi, 2007), 182.

7. Lee and Mair, *Excelsior!*, 160.

8. Quoted in Les Daniels, *Marvel: Five Fabulous Decades of the World's Greatest Comics* (New York: Harry N. Abrams, 1995), 99.

9. Lee, *Origins of Marvel Comics*, 215.

10. Lee, *Son of Origins*, 110.

11. Ibid., 10.

12. Stan Lee, interviewed by Dick Cavett, "The Dick Cavett Show: An Interview with Stan Lee," in *Stan Lee Conversations*, ed. Jeff McLaughlin (Jackson: University Press of Mississippi, 2007), 15.

13. Quoted in Dewey Cassell, ed., *The Art of George Tuska* (Raleigh, NC: TwoMorrows, 2005), 57.

14. Ibid., 58.

15. Gene Colan, interviewed by Tom Field, "The Colan Mystique," *Comic Book Artist* 13 (May 2001), http://twomorrows.com/comicbookartist/articles/13thomas.html.

16. Dennis O'Neil, interviewed by Danny Fingeroth, *The Stan Lee Universe*, ed. Danny Fingeroth and Roy Thomas (Raleigh, NC: TwoMorrows, 2011), 53.

17. Ibid.

18. *Stan Lee's Mutants, Monsters, and Marvels*, directed by Scott Zakarin (Burbank, CA: Sony Pictures, 2002), DVD.

19. Ibid.

20. Quoted in Chris Gavaler, "Kirby vs. Steranko! Silver Age Layout Wars," *The Hooded Utilitarian*, July 12, 2016, http://www.hoodedutilitarian.com/2016/07/kirby-vs-steranko-silver-age-layout-wars/.

21. Ibid.

22. Lee, *Origins of Marvel Comics*, 164.

CHAPTER 8

1. *Stan Lee's Mutants, Monsters, and Marvels*, directed by Scott Zakarin (Burbank, CA: Sony Pictures, 2002), DVD.

2. Quoted in Paul Lopes, *Demanding Respect: The Evolution of the American Comic Book* (Philadelphia: Temple University Press, 2009), 65.

3. Craig Tomashoff, "Move Over Batman . . . " *Los Angeles Reader*, January 26, 1990.

4. David Kasakove, "Finding Marvel's Voice: An Appreciation of Stan Lee's Bullpen Bulletins and Soapboxes, *Write Now* 18 (Summer 2008): 57.

5. Mark Alexander, "Lee & Kirby: The Wonder Years," in *Jack Kirby Collector* 18, no. 58 (Winter 2011): 8.

6. Ibid.

7. Quoted in Danny Fingeroth, *The Stan Lee Universe*, ed. Danny Fingeroth and Roy Thomas (Raleigh, NC: TwoMorrows, 2011), 52.

8. Ibid.

9. Stan Lee, interview by Dan Hagan, "Stan Lee," *Comics Interview*, July 1983, 55.

10. Leonard Sloane, "Advertising: Comics Go Up, Up and Away," *New York Times*, July 20, 1967.

11. Ibid.

12. Quoted in ibid.

13. Lopes, *Demanding Respect*, 66.

14. Mike Benton, *The Comic Book in America: An Illustrated History* (Dallas, TX: Taylor, 1989), 71.

15. Stan Lee, "Excelsior!" (Autobiography) Outline, July 30, 1978, Box 96, Stan Lee Papers, American Heritage Center, University of Wyoming.

16. Stan Lee and George Mair, *Excelsior! The Amazing Life of Stan Lee* (New York: Simon and Schuster, 2002), 142.

17. Quoted in Dick Cavett, "The Dick Cavett Show: An Interview with Stan Lee," in *Stan Lee Conversations*, ed. Jeff McLaughlin (Jackson: University Press of Mississippi, 2007), 16.

18. Ibid.

19. M. Thomas Inge, "From the Publisher's Perspective: Comments by Stan Lee and Jenette Kahn," in *Stan Lee Conversations*, ed. Jeff McLaughlin (Jackson: University Press of Mississippi, 2007), 105.

20. Stan Lee, Peter David, and Colleen Doran, *Amazing Fantastic Incredible: A Marvelous Memoir* (New York: Touchstone, 2015).

21. Lee and Mair, *Excelsior!*, 179.

22. Quoted in Sean Howe, *Marvel Comics: The Untold Story* (New York: Harper, 2012), 92.

23. Quoted in ibid., 104.

24. Quoted in Cavett, "The Dick Cavett Show," 18.

CHAPTER 9

1. Norman Mark, "The New Super-Hero (Is a Pretty Kinky Guy)," *Alter Ego* 3, no. 74 (2007): 20.

2. Michael Goldman, "Stan Lee: Comic Guru," *Animation World Magazine*, July 1997, 8.

3. Quoted in Mark, "The New Super-Hero," 20.

4. Ibid.

5. Quoted in ibid., 21.

6. Quoted in Brian Cunningham, ed., *Stan's Soapbox: The Collection* (New York: Marvel, 2009), 16.

7. Quoted in Stan Lee, interview by Mike Bourne, "Stan Lee, The Marvel Bard," *Alter Ego* 3, no. 74 (2007): 30.

8. Cunningham, *Stan's Soapbox*, 31.

9. Mark Evanier, *Kirby: King of Comics* (New York: Abrams, 2008), 157.

10. Joe Simon, *Joe Simon: My Life in Comics* (London: Titan, 2011), n.p.

11. Ibid.

12. Lawrence Van Gelder, "A Comics Magazine Defies Code Ban on Drug Stories," *New York Times*, February 4, 1971, 37.

13. Quoted in ibid., 38.

14. Ibid.

15. "Stan Lee," Billy Ireland Cartoon Library and Museum Biographical Files, Ohio State University Billy Ireland Cartoon Library and Museum.

16. "Comics Come to Carnegie," *New York Post*, January 6, 1972, 44.

17. Ibid.

18. Quoted in Van Gelder, "A Comics Magazine," 28.

19. Ibid., 33.

20. Roy Thomas, interview by Jon B. Cooke, "Son of Stan: Roy's Years of Horrors," *Comic Book Artist* 13 (May 2001), http://twomorrows.com/comicbookartist/articles/13thomas.html.

21. Ibid.

22. *Stan Lee's Mutants, Monsters, and Marvels*, directed by Scott Zakarin (Burbank, CA: Sony Pictures, 2002), DVD.

23. Quoted in Thomas J. McLean, "Unique Collaborations Set Marvel Apart," *Variety*, July 19–25, 2004, B12.

24. Thomas, "Son of Stan."

25. Ibid.

26. Stan Lee, *The Best of Spider-Man* (New York: Ballantine, 1986), 10.

CHAPTER 10

1. Memo, "Marvel Comics, Classification and Frequency of Titles," January 16, 1973, Memoranda 1969–1976, Box 7, Folder 1, Stan Lee Papers, American Heritage Center, University of Wyoming.

2. Stan Lee, Memo, "Approval of Covers, Etc.," n.d., Memoranda 1969–1976, Box 7, Folder 1, Stan Lee Papers, American Heritage Center, University of Wyoming.

3. Stan Lee, interview by David Anthony Kraft, in *Stan Lee Conversations*, ed. Jeff McLaughlin (Jackson: University Press of Mississippi, 2007), 65.

4. Mike Benton, *The Comic Book in America: An Illustrated History* (Dallas, TX: Taylor, 1989), 74.

5. "ABC Audit Report-Magazine: Marvel Comic Group," Memoranda 1969–1976, Box 7, Folder 1, Stan Lee Papers, American Heritage Center, University of Wyoming.

6. Jonathan Hoyle, "Comic Sales (Monthly Average in Millions) for Marvel and DC, 1950 to 1987," The Fantastic Four 1961–1989 was the Great American Novel, http://zak-site.com /Great-American-Novel/comic_sales.html.

7. Quoted in Brian Cunningham, ed., *Stan's Soapbox: The Collection* (New York: Marvel, 2009), 59.

8. Quoted in Les Daniels, *Marvel: Five Fabulous Decades of the World's Greatest Comics* (New York: Harry N. Abrams, 1995), 156.

9. Memo, "We Must Be Doing Something Right!" Memoranda 1969–1976, Box 7, Folder 1, Stan Lee Papers, American Heritage Center, University of Wyoming.

10. Peter Gorner, "Stan Lee's Superheroes," *Chicago Tribune*, July 17, 1975, B1.

11. Sherry Romeo, "Inter-Office Memo," December 17, 1974, Memoranda 1969–1976, Box 7, Folder 1, Stan Lee Papers, American Heritage Center, University of Wyoming.

12. Stan Lee, "Streaking," *Crazy*, July 1973, 16. San Francisco Academy of Comic Art Collection, Ohio State University Billy Ireland Cartoon Library and Museum.

13. Quoted in David Hench, "Maine Artist Recalls Spider-Man Work," *Portland Press Herald* (Maine), May 5, 2007, A1.

14. Stan Lee, *Best of Spider-Man* (New York: Ballantine, 1986), 6.

15. Dewey Cassell, ed., *The Art of George Tuska* (Raleigh, NC: TwoMorrows, 2005), 105.

16. Lee, *Best*, 8.

17. Stan Lee, interviewed by Dan Hagen, *Comics Interview*, July 1983, 57.

18. Memo, "S&S Sales," Marvel Comics Group—Facts and Figures 1976–1978, Box 6, Folder 4, Stan Lee Papers.

19. Lee interview by Kraft, 67.

20. Stan Lee, *The Superhero Women* (New York: Simon and Schuster, 1977), 8.

21. "Fireside Paperbacks Marketing Flyer," Articles—1977, Box 32, Folder 2, Stan Lee Papers.

22. Lee interview by Kraft, 67.

23. Stan Lee, *The Best of the Worst* (New York: Harper & Row, 1979), 10.

24. Stan Lee, interview by Mike Gold, in *Stan Lee Conversations*, ed. Jeff McLaughlin (Jackson: University Press of Mississippi, 2007), 43.

25. Mark Evanier, *Kirby: King of Comics* (New York: Abrams, 2008), 189.

26. George Kashdan, interview by Jim Amash, "Sales Don't Tell You Everything," *Alter Ego* 3, no. 94 (June 2010): 49.

27. "'Spider-Man' to be Featured in Action Film," *New Castle (PA) News*, April 16, 1975, 8.

28. Lee Stewart, "Spinner Takes All," *The Sunday Times* (London), May 12, 2002, Newspaper Source, EBSCOhost (accessed February 21, 2015).

29. N. R. Kleinfield, "Superheroes' Creators Wrangle," *New York Times*, October 13, 1979, 25.

30. Ibid.

31. Quoted in ibid., 26.

32. Paul Lopes, *Demanding Respect: The Evolution of the American Comic Book* (Philadelphia, PA: Temple University Press, 2009), 71.

33. Quoted in Sean Howe, *Marvel Comics: The Untold Story* (New York: Harper, 2012), 215.

CHAPTER 11

1. "Marvels of the Mind: The Comics Go Hollywood," *Time*, February 5, 1979.

2. Quoted in Paul Weingarten, "The Hulk," *Chronicle-Telegram* (Elyria, OH), October 30, 1978, B-9.

3. Craig Tomashoff, "Move Over Batman . . . " *Los Angeles Reader*, January 26, 1990.

4. Stan Lee, interview by Pat Jankiewicz, in *Stan Lee Conversations*, ed. Jeff McLaughlin (Jackson: University Press of Mississippi, 2007), 108.

5. Tomashoff, "Move Over Batman."

6. Stan Lee, interview by Jim Salicrup and David Anthony Kraft, "Stan Lee," *Comics Interview*, July 1983, 48.

7. Tomashoff, "Move Over Batman."

8. Letter, Stan Lee to Alain Resnais, May 23, 1979, Correspondence 1977–1980 (Folder 1 of 2), Box 14, Folder 1, Stan Lee Papers, American Heritage Center, University of Wyoming.

9. Stan Lee, Peter David, and Colleen Doran, *Amazing Fantastic Incredible: A Marvelous Memoir* (New York: Touchstone, 2015), n.p.

10. Letter, Stan Lee to Alain Resnais, Stan Lee Papers.

11. Letter, Michael Herz to Sam Arkoff, July 5, 1979, Correspondence 1977–1980 (Folder 1 of 2), Box 14, Folder 1, Stan Lee Papers, American Heritage Center, University of Wyoming.

12. "Marvel Entertainment Group Forms Marvel Productions Ltd.," Marvel Update, Summer 1980, 6, Scrapbook Feb. 1980–Nov. 12, 1984, Box 129, Stan Lee Papers, American Heritage Center, University of Wyoming.

13. "Marvels of the Mind."

14. Lee, interview by Salicrup and Kraft, "Stan Lee," 48.

15. "Comic Characters Put a Zing in Product Promotion," *The Sales Executive*, April 1, 1980, 4.

16. Terry Young, "Spider-Man's About to Get Real, Says His Creator," *Toronto Star* (Canada), July 6, 1986.

17. Stan Lee to Francelia Butler, November 21, 1980, Correspondence, Box 14, File 4, Stan Lee Papers, American Heritage Center, University of Wyoming. The fee would be between $10,000 and $20,000 in 2020 (Samuel H. Williamson, "Seven Ways to Compute the Relative Value of a U.S. Dollar Amount, 1790 to present," MeasuringWorth.com, 2021).

18. Stan Lee, interview by Margaret Jones and John R. Gambling, "Good Afternoon New York," WOR/Radio, June 22, 1984. Interviews with Stan Lee 1970–1989, Box 3, Folder 10–11, Stan Lee Papers, American Heritage Center, University of Wyoming.

19. Quoted in Judy Klemesrud, "Savage She-Hulk New Comic Heroine," *New York Times*, January 20, 1980.

20. Stan Lee, *Best of Spider-Man* (New York: Ballantine, 1986), 9, 10, 12–16.

21. Quoted in Sean Howe, *Marvel Comics: The Untold Story* (New York: Harper, 2012), 295.

22. Quoted in ibid., 311–12.

23. Mike Wallace, "Ronald Reagan Remembered," *60 Minutes*, June 6, 2004, http://www.cbsnews.com/news/ronald-reagan-remembered.

24. Quoted in Dan Raviv, *Comic Wars: How Two Tycoons Battled over the Marvel Comics Empire—And Both Lost* (New York: Broadway, 2002), 12.

25. Quoted in Les Daniels, *Marvel: Five Fabulous Decades of the World's Greatest Comics* (New York: Harry N. Abrams, 1995), 225.

26. Michael E. Hill, "Where Does The Hulk Buy Clothes?: Anywhere He Wants, Of Course," *Washington Post*, February 18, 1990, O8.

27. Stan Lee, ed., *The Ultimate Spider-Man* (New York: Berkeley, 1994), 10, 11, 13.

28. John Updike, "Cut the Unfunny Comics, Not 'Spiderman,'" *Boston Globe*, October 27, 1994. July 1994 to November 1994, Coll 8302, Box 137, Stan Lee Papers, American Heritage Center, University of Wyoming.

29. Lee, *Ultimate*, 22, 110.

30. Ibid., 342, 7.

31. Adam Bryant, "Pow! The Punches that Left Marvel Reeling," *New York Times*, May 24, 1998, http://www.nytimes.com/1998/05/24/business/pow-the-punches-that-left-marvel-reeling.html.

32. Shirrel Rhoades, *A Complete History of American Comic Books* (New York: Peter Lang, 2008), 155.

33. Michael Goldman, "Stan Lee: Comic Guru," *Animation World Magazine*, July 1997, 8.

34. Quoted in Gary Dretzka, "At 77, 'X-Men' Creator Stan Lee is as Busy as Ever," Knight Ridder/Tribune News Service, July 22, 2000.

35. Stan Lee and George Mair, *Excelsior! The Amazing Life of Stan Lee* (New York: Simon and Schuster, 2002), 223.

36. Quoted in Dretzka, "At 77."

37. Stan Lee Media Press Kit, 1999, Stan Lee Media Publicity Folder 1999, Box 127, Stan Lee Papers, American Heritage Center, University of Wyoming.

38. Quoted in Madeleine Brand, "Growing Trend of Online Comics," *Morning Edition*, NPR, January 20, 2000.

39. Michael Dean, "If This Be My Destiny," *Comics Journal* 232 (April 2001): 8.

40. Ibid., 8, 10.

41. Quoted in Howe, *Marvel Comics*, 408.

42. Anthony D'Allessandro, "Lee Bounces Back into Business with POW!" *Variety*, July 19–25, 2004, B14.

43. "Co-Founder of Comic Company Pleads Guilty," *Los Angeles Times*, March 10, 2005.

44. Howe, *Marvel Comics*, 408–9.

45. Shelly Garcia, "Spider-Man's Business Brain," *Los Angeles Business Journal*, August 21, 2000, 29.

46. Jon Swartz, "Stan Lee Rises from Dot-Com Rubble," *USA Today*, May 12, 2004.

47. *Stan Lee, Plaintiff, -against- Marvel Enterprises, Inc. and Marvel Characters, Inc., Defendants.* 02 Civ. 8945 United States District Court for the Southern District of New York 765 F. Supp. 2d 440; 2011 U.S. Dist. LEXIS 11297 February 4, 2011, Decided February 4, 2011, Filed; *United States of America, Appellee, -v.- Peter Paul, Defendant-Appellant, Stephen M. Gordon, Jeffrey Pittsburg, Charles Kusche, Jonathan Gordon, Defendants.* Docket Nos. 09-3191-cr (L), 09-4147-cr (con) United States Court of Appeals for the Second Circuit, 634 F.3d 668; 2011 U.S. App. LEXIS 4473, February 17, 2011, Argued. March 7, 2011, Decided.

48. Swartz, "Stan Lee Rises."

49. Lee and Mair, *Excelsior!*, 233.

50. Larry Schultz, e-mail message to Stan Lee, January 12, 2001, Correspondence, 1995–2010, Box 106 (2016-09-22 142037), Stan Lee Papers, American Heritage Center, University of Wyoming.

CHAPTER 12

1. Bryan Singer, interview by Adam Chitwood, "The Epic Bryan Singer Interview: 'X-Men Apocalypse,' the Superhero Genre, Timelines, and More," *Collider*, April 21, 2016.

2. Stan Lee, Peter David, and Colleen Doran, *Amazing Fantastic Incredible: A Marvelous Memoir* (New York: Touchstone, 2015), n.p.

3. Anthony D'Alessandro, "Lee Bounces Back into Business with POW!" *Variety*, July 19–25, 2004.

4. "POW! Entertainment Partners in the Production of Three Live Action Flicks," *PR Newswire*, October 6, 2004.

5. Quoted in Virginia Rohan, "Stan Lee's Project with Pam Anderson Looks Like a Bust," *The Record* (Bergen County, NJ), June 26, 2003.

6. "Alta Loma Entertainment & POW! Entertainment to Develop Animated Series Hef's Superbunnies," *PR Newswire*, July 18, 2003.

7. Ibid.

8. Quoted in Michael Dean, "Stan Lee's Hour of Glory," *Comics Journal* 267 (April/May 2005): 23.

9. Brent Staples, "Marveling at Marvel: You Say Spider-Man, but I Say the Thing," *New York Times*, March 25, 2005.

10. "Who Deserves the Credit (and Cash) for Dreaming Up Those Superheroes?" *New York Times*, January 31, 2005.

11. Quoted in David Kohn, "Superhero Creator Fights Back," *60 Minutes*, October 30, 2002.

12. "Marvel Settles Suit with Lee," *Los Angeles Times*, April 29, 2005.

13. Joel Garreau, "Stan Lee and Olivia de Havilland Among National Medal of Arts Winners," *Washington Post*, November 18, 2008; Lee, David, and Doran, *Amazing Fantastic Incredible*, n.p.

14. Stan Lee, "Stan Lee Talks about Time Jumper at San Diego Comic-Con 2009," bigfanboy, July 30, 2009, YouTube video, https://www.youtube.com/watch?v=hixwR_c_R_4.

15. Stan Lee, "Stan Lee is Spider-Man," Stan Lee's World of Heroes, June 21, 2012, YouTube video, https://youtu.be/I-lL8LD8SJQ?list=PL027ADE83FF495FA3.

16. Matt Clark, "Amazing Spider-Man Game Features Playable Stan Lee," MTV.com, May 9, 2012.

17. "Stan Lee's POW! Entertainment Teams with Hollywood Reporter on New Series 'Cosmic Crusaders,'" *The Hollywood Reporter*, June 21, 2016.

18. Stan Lee, interview by Ethan Sacks, "Stan Lee Muses on His Final New York Comic Con," *New York Daily News*, October 10, 2016.

19. Stan Lee in discussion with the author, Cincinnati Comic Expo, September 24, 2016.

CHAPTER 13

1. Quoted in "Stan Lee: A Life of Marvel," *Entertainment Weekly* special issue, November 30, 2018, 40.

2. David Ng, "As Marvel Movies Soar," *Los Angeles Times*, June 29, 2018.

3. Gary Baum, "Stan Lee Needs a Hero," *The Hollywood Reporter*, April 10, 2018, https://www.hollywoodreporter.com/movies/movie-features/stan-lee-needs-a-hero-elder-abuse-claims-a-battle-aging-marvel-creator-1101229/.

4. David Hochman, "The Last Days of Stan Lee," *AARP Magazine*, October/November 2020.

5. See Eriq Gardner, "Stan Lee's Daughter Sanctioned," *The Hollywood Reporter*, June 26, 2020, as well as the many other stories about her frivolous lawsuits since Stan's death.

6. Baum, "Stan Lee Needs."

7. Bernie Zilio, "Marvel Legend Stan Lee Was a Victim in His Final Days, Reveals REELZ Documentary," *Radar*, June 25, 2021, https://radaronline.com/p/marvel-stan-lee-victim-final-days-death-autopsy-reelz-documentary/.

8. Peter Sblendorio and Nancy Dillon, "Stan Lee," *New York Daily News*, November 12, 2018.

9. Jake Newby, "China Reacts," *Radii*, November 13, 2018.

10. "How Stan Lee Helped 'Revolutionize' Comic Books," *PBS NewsHour*, November 12, 2018.

11. Abraham Reiser in *True Believer: The Rise and Fall of Stan Lee* (New York: Crown, 2021) portrays Lee negatively at just about every turn. Roy Thomas called it good "95 percent of the time" but said the remaining 5 percent ruin it: "The author often insists, visibly and intrusively, on putting his verbal thumb on the scales, in a dispute he seems ill-equipped to judge." Roy Thomas, "Roy Thomas, Former Marvel Editor, Pushes Back on New Stan Lee Biography," *The Hollywood Reporter*, February 23, 2021, https://www.hollywoodreporter.com/movies/movie-news/roy-thomas-former-marvel-editor-pushes-back-on-new-stan-lee-biography-guest-column-4136571/.

12. For an interesting blow-by-blow account, see John Morrow's valuable *Kirby and Lee: Stuf' Said!*, expanded second edition (Raleigh, NC: TwoMorrows, 2019).

13. *Stan Lee Conversations*, ed. Jeff McLaughlin (Jackson: University Press of Mississippi, 2007), 77.

EPILOGUE

1. Quoted in Nancy Tartaglione, "Marvel's Victoria Alonso," *Deadline*, June 14, 2021.

2. Ibid.

3. Sophie Vallas, ed., *Conversations with Jerome Charyn* (Jackson: University of Mississippi Press, 2014), 157, 60.

4. Spencer Harrison, Arne Carlsen, and Miha Škerlavaj, "Marvel's Blockbuster Machine," *Harvard Business Review*, July–August 2019, https://hbr.org/2019/07/marvels-blockbuster-machine.

5. Ibid. The Harrison et al. article is brilliant! Please go find it online and read it.
6. Tartaglione, "Marvel's Victoria Alonso."
7. Brad Meltzer, "Stan Lee," *Entertainment Weekly*, December 14/21, 2018, 90–91.
8. Frank Pallotta, "Marvel Heroes," CNN, November 12, 2018.

INDEX

ABOUT THE AUTHOR

Bob Batchelor is an award-winning cultural historian and biographer who has published books on Bob Dylan, *The Great Gatsby*, *Mad Men*, and John Updike, among other topics. *Rookwood: The Rediscovery and Revival of an American Icon: An Illustrated History* won the 2021 Independent Publishers Book Award for fine art. *The Bourbon King: The Life and Crimes of George Remus, Prohibition's Evil Genius* won the 2020 Independent Publishers Book Award for historical biography. *Stan Lee: The Man behind Marvel* was a finalist for the 2018 Ohioana Book Award for nonfiction.

Bob's books have been translated into a dozen languages, and his work has appeared or been featured in the *New York Times*, *Cincinnati Enquirer*, *Los Angeles Times*, and *Time*. Bob is also the creator and host of the podcast *John Updike: American Writer, American Life*. He has appeared as an on-air commentator for the National Geographic Channel, *PBS NewsHour*, PBS, and NPR. Bob hosted "TriState True Crime" on WCPO's *Cincy Lifestyle* television show.

Bob earned his doctorate in American literature from the University of South Florida. He has taught at universities in Florida, Ohio, and Pennsylvania, as well as Vienna, Austria. Bob and his wife, Suzette, live in North Carolina and have two teenage daughters.

Like many others, Bob thinks Spider-Man is the most important comic book creation of all time. His all-time favorite Marvel comic book series is *What If . . .?*, and his favorite MCU film is *Avengers: Endgame*.